MEDIA MANAGEMENT AND ECONOMICS RESEARCH IN A TRANSMEDIA ENVIRONMENT

ELECTRONIC MEDIA RESEARCH SERIES
Sponsored by the Broadcast Education Association

SPORTS MEDIA: TRANSFORMATION,
INTEGRATION, CONSUMPTION
Edited by Andrew C. Billings

MEDIA AND THE MORAL MIND
Edited by Ron Tamborini

MEDIA MANAGEMENT AND ECONOMICS RESEARCH IN A TRANSMEDIA ENVIRONMENT

Papers from the 2012 Broadcast Education Association Research Symposium

Symposium Chair/Editor
Alan B. Albarran
The University of North Texas

NEW YORK AND LONDON

First published 2013
by Routledge
711 Third Avenue, New York, NY 10017

Simultaneously published in the UK
by Routledge
2 Park Square, Milton Park, Abingdon, Oxfordshire OX14 4RN

First issued in paperback 2015

Routledge is an imprint of the Taylor & Francis Group, an informa business

© 2013 Taylor & Francis

The right of Alan B. Albarran to be identified as the author of the editorial material, and of the authors for their individual chapters, has been asserted in accordance with sections 77 and 78 of the Copyright, Designs and Patents Act 1988.

All rights reserved. No part of this book may be reprinted or reproduced or utilized in any form or by any electronic, mechanical, or other means, now known or hereafter invented, including photocopying and recording, or in any information storage or retrieval system, without permission in writing from the publishers.

Trademark notice: Product or corporate names may be trademarks or registered trademarks, and are used only for identification and explanation without intent to infringe.

Library of Congress Cataloging in Publication Data
Media management and economics research in a transmedia environment / edited by Alan B. Albarran.
 pages cm. – (Electronic media research series)
"Consists of papers presented at the 2012 Research Symposium held in conjunction with the annual convention of the Broadcast Education Association"– Introduction.
 1. Mass media–Management–Congresses. 2. Mass media–Economic aspects–Congresses. 3. Convergence (Telecommunication)–Congresses. I. Albarran, Alan B., editor of compilation. II. Broadcast Education Association (U.S.)
 P96.M34M385 2013
 302.23–dc23
 2012042130

ISBN 13: 978-1-138-92558-8 (pbk)
ISBN 13: 978-0-415-81815-5 (hbk)

Typeset in Sabon
by Out of House Publishing

CONTENTS

List of Figures   viii
List of Tables   ix
Notes on Contributors   xi
Series Editor's Foreword   xv
DR. DONALD G. GODFREY, CHAIR, BEA RESEARCH COMMITTEE, ARIZONA STATE UNIVERSITY

Introduction   1
ALAN B. ALBARRAN, THE UNIVERSITY OF NORTH TEXAS

SECTION I
Media Management and Economics Research from Senior Scholars   3

1   Media Management and Economics Research: The First 75 Years   5
ALAN B. ALBARRAN

2   Future Prospects for Cable Telecommunications in an Over-the-Top World   18
MICHAEL O. WIRTH AND RON RIZZUTO

3   Innovation Failure: A Case Study Analysis of Eastman Kodak and Blockbuster Inc.   46
RICHARD A. GERSHON

CONTENTS

SECTION II
MME Research from Junior Scholars   69

4 Application of the Long Tail Economy to the Online
News Market in Taiwan: Civic Participation Matters   71
J. SONIA HUANG AND WEI-CHING WANG

5 Order of Market Entry: Examining First Mover
Advantages among Social Networking Sites   94
JIYOUNG CHA

6 An Argument for News Media Managers to Direct
and Use Audience Research   121
RACHEL DAVIS MERSEY

7 Responding to Systematic Reform, Market Change, and
Technological Innovation: China's Book Publishing
Industry in Rapid Transformation   133
GUOSONG SHAO, YINGPING WEI, JINGAN
YUAN, AND CHUNHUA ZHANG

SECTION III
Latin American and Hispanic MME Research   145

8 Convergence in the Mexican Media Industry 2011   147
MARÍA ELENA GUTIÉRREZ-RENTERÍA AND
JOSEFINA SANTANA VILLEGAS

9 A Case Study on Media Diversification: Caracol
and RCN TV Channels—Beyond the Traditional
Business Model   160
GERMÁN ARANGO-FORERO

10 Twitter Use among English and Spanish Language
Television Stations: A Traffic and Content Analysis
of Dallas-Fort Worth Local Television Twitter Accounts   174
JULIAN RODRIGUEZ

11 The State of Spanish Language Media 2012   196
GABE OTTESON, JESSICA A. PERRILLIAT,
AND ALAN B. ALBARRAN

CONTENTS

SECTION IV
Media Management Issues for New Media/Transmedia   217

12 Television Industry's Adoption of the Internet:
    Diffusion of an Inefficient Innovation   219
    HARSH TANEJA AND HEATHER YOUNG

13 The Transmedia Experience in Local TV News:
    Examining Parasocial Interaction in Viral Viewership
    and the Online Social Distribution of News   242
    JOY CHAVEZ MAPAYE

14 Managing and Financing Small-Budget Transmedia
    Production: The Case of Norwegian Recycling   261
    CRAIG A. STARK

Index   273

FIGURES

1.1	Examples of Interdependent Factors Influencing Management and Economics	8
4.1	Analytical Framework of the Long Tail Economy for Online News	78
5.1	Framework for Performance of Social Networking Sites	99
8.1	Total Percentage of Characteristics that Define Traditional Media in Mexico on the Web, 2011	156
10.1	NBC5 and CBS11 Twitter Traffic Scatter Plot (All Active Weekdays) ($n = 175$)	183
10.2	FOX4 Twitter Traffic Frequency Distribution	185
10.3	DFW Television Stations Online Networks	192

TABLES

1.1	The Three Schools of Management	6
1.2	Theoretical Domains in Media Economics Research	7
1.3	Important Media Management Books	10
1.4	Representative Media Economics Books	12
1.5	Key Events Impacting MME Research	14
2.1	Subscribership and Market Shares of Multichannel Video Program Distribution Providers	19
2.2	Cable MVPD Competitive Advantages/Disadvantages	21
2.3	DBS MVPD Competitive Advantages/Disadvantages	22
2.4	Telco MVPD Competitive Advantages/Disadvantages	23
2.5	OTT Penetration and Market Potential in 2011	24
2.6	Over-the-Top (OTT) Video Competitive Advantages/Disadvantages	25
2.7	Predictions Regarding Cable's Future	40
3.1	Successful Innovation: Feature Elements	47
4.1	Online Advertising Revenue in Taiwan	74
4.2	Top 20 Most Popular News Sites in Taiwan	80
4.3	Inter-coder Reliability of the Long Tail Indices among Taiwan's News Sites	83
4.4	The Extent of Long Tail Tools Adopted by Taiwan's News Sites	85
4.5	The Most Frequent Long Tail Tools Adopted by Taiwan's News Sites	87
4.6	Correlations between the Long Tail Tools and Traffic Performance among Taiwan's News Sites	89
4.1A	The Extent of Long Tail Tools Adopted by News Sites in the United States (N=204)	90
5.1	Social Networking Sites Operated in the US (1995–present: February 2012)	101
5.2	Social Networking Sites' Alliances/Partnerships (1995–2012)	105
5.3	Early Followers' Acquisitions (1995–2012)	109

LIST OF TABLES

5.4	Social Networking Sites' Strategic Decisions (1995–present: February 2012)	112
6.1	Sample of Descriptions of Experiential Brands	127
6.2	Motivators and Inhibitors of Magazine Readership	129
8.1	Principal Strategic Alliances of Mexican Companies in the Telecommunications Sector (2011)	151
8.2	Principal Mexican Radio Companies	152
8.3	Largest Mexican Chain Companies Ranked by Number of Newspapers	153
9.1	Colombia: Media Advertising Share, 2000–2010	162
9.2	Colombia: Television Audience Share, 2007–2010	166
9.3	Gap between Audience Share and Advertising Investment Share in Pay TV in Latin America	166
10.1	DFW TV Stations' Twitter Traffic Pearson Correlations for All Active Days ($n = 245$)	181
10.2	DFW TV Stations' Twitter Traffic Pearson Correlations for All Active Weekdays ($n = 175$)	182
10.3	DFW TV Stations' Twitter Traffic Frequency Distribution	184
10.4	DFW TV Stations' Tweet Thematic Content	187
10.5	DFW TV Stations' Twitter Syntax Use (October 9–22, 2011)	188
12.1	Phase One: "Tata TV Portals"	226
12.2	Phase Two: "Now Streaming"	228
12.3	Phase Three: "The Genie Is Out of the Bottle"	230

CONTRIBUTORS

Alan B. Albarran is Professor and Chair of the Department of Radio, Television, and Film at The University of North Texas. His teaching and research interests revolve around the management and economics of the communication industries.

Jiyoung Cha is Assistant Professor of Film and Video Studies at George Mason University. She received her Ph.D. in Mass Communication with a minor in Marketing from the University of Florida and her Master's degree in Television, Radio, and Film at the S.I. Newhouse School of Communications at Syracuse University. Her research focuses on adoption of new media, business models of new media, and interrelationships between new technologies and traditional media from management and marketing perspectives.

Zhang Chunhua earned a Ph.D. in the School of Journalism at Fudan University, China. Dr. Chunhua's research interests include media systems and policy, and cultural industries studies.

Germán Arango-Forero is Associate Professor in the Faculty of Communication at Universidad de La Sabana-Colombia. He is current general secretary of LAMMA (Latin American Media Management Association) and a doctoral candidate in Communication Science from Universidad Austral, Buenos Aires. His main research focus is audience fragmentation, audience measurement, media economics, and media industries in developing economies.

Richard A. Gershon is Professor and Co-Director in Telecommunications and Information Management at Western Michigan University. He teaches courses in media management and telecommunications. He is the author of *Media, Telecommunications and Business Strategy* (2nd edition) (2013) and *The Transnational Media Corporation: Global Messages and Free Market Competition*, selected winner of the 1998 book of the year by the US Cable Center. Dr. Gershon is a Fulbright scholar having held visiting appointments at the University of Navarra, Spain and Nihon University, Japan.

María Elena Gutiérrez-Rentería is Full Professor at the School of Business and Economics and the School of Communications at Universidad Panamericana, Mexico. She was Director of the School of Communications and Academic Director of the Economics and Business School at Universidad Panamericana, Guadalajara. She holds a Ph.D. in Public Communications from Universidad de Navarra, Spain, and studies in Media Management and Entertainment from IME & IESE Business School in New York. She is a member of Mexican National System of Researchers. Her research and articles are devoted to the media and telecommunications industries in Mexico.

J. Sonia Huang is Assistant Professor in the Department of Communication and Technology at National Chiao Tung University, Taiwan. Her research focuses on media economics and strategic management. She has five years of work experience in broadcast television industry; holds an M.A. in Journalism and Mass Communication from the University of Wisconsin at Madison and a Ph.D. from The University of Texas at Austin School of Journalism.

Joy Chavez Mapaye is Assistant Professor in the Department of Journalism and Public Communications at the University of Alaska Anchorage. She received her doctoral degree from the University of Oregon. Dr. Mapaye's dissertation was honored with the Broadcast Education Association's Kenneth Harwood Outstanding Dissertation Award in 2011. Her research interests include television, new media/digital culture, marketing communication, and health communication.

Rachel Davis Mersey obtained her Ph.D. from the University of North Carolina at Chapel Hill. Dr. Mersey is Associate Professor at the Medill School of Journalism, Media, Integrated Marketing Communications at Northwestern University. She is the Senior Director of Research at Northwestern University's Media Management Center and a fellow at the Institute for Policy Research. Her first book, *Can Journalism Be Saved? Rediscovering America's Appetite for News*, was published in 2010.

Gabe Otteson is a Graduate Research Assistant at the Center for Spanish Language Media at The University of North Texas. He earned a Bachelor's degree in Electronic Media and Film from Northern Arizona University. He is currently in his second year of an industry studies Master's program.

Jessica A. Perrilliat a former Graduate Research Assistant at the Center for Spanish Language Media at The University of North Texas.

She graduated in 2012 with a Master's degree in Media Industry Studies.

Ron Rizzuto is Professor at the Reiman School of Finance at the University of Denver. He is the author of one book and numerous articles and is an internationally known expert in the big picture of acquisitions and finance, specializing in corporate mergers, strategic partnerships, and acquisitions with particular focus on the cable telecommunications, energy, transportation, and banking industries.

Julian Rodriguez is a Lecturer in the Department of Communication at The University of Texas at Arlington, where he earned his M.A. in Communication. His research interests include Hispanic media, multimedia production, and broadcast news. He currently serves as the Vice President of Texas Association of Broadcast Educators (TABE).

Guosong Shao obtained his Ph.D at The University of Alabama. He is Professor and Dean of the Journalism School at Nanjing University of Finance and Economics, China. He has published more than ten articles in the area of media management and economics. He is also the author of *Internet Law in China* (2012), the first book that systematically explores the legal doctrines and principles that apply to the Internet and related activities in China.

Craig A. Stark earned his Ph.D. at The Pennsylvania State University. He is an Associate Professor in the Department of Communications at Susquehanna University. His research interests include radio history, access and localism issues regarding public radio and digital broadcasting technologies, emerging media technologies, audio production, and the development of small-scale transmedia production.

Harsh Taneja is a Ph.D. candidate in the Media, Technology, and Society Program at Northwestern University. His program of research investigates the impact of audience fragmentation on media industries. He is interested in how and why audiences consume media as they are free to choose between multiple platforms and content options. In addition, he is interested in the measures and methods that media industries are employing to measure audiences across platforms.

Josefina Santana Villegas is a Full-time Professor at Universidad Panamericana, Mexico, where she teaches Media Research at the School of Communications. She holds a Ph.D. in Education from ITESO University.

Wei-Ching Wang is Assistant Professor at the Graduate Institute of Mass Communication, National Taiwan Normal University. She holds a Ph.D. from the Department of Radio–TV–Film from The University of

Texas at Austin. She specializes in information societies and information communication. Her research interests include ICT policy and economic issues in an information society.

Yingping Wei obtained his M.A. at the Renmin University of China. He is pursuing a Ph.D. in Media Economics. He currently specializes in digital content licensing systems.

Michael O. Wirth is Professor and Dean at the College of Communication and Information, University of Tennessee, Knoxville. He is the author of two books and numerous articles and book chapters and is an internationally known expert in the field of cable telecommunication and broadcast economics, law, and management.

Heather Young conducts behavioral research as a User Experience Specialist at User Centric, Inc. She earned her M.A. in the Media, Technology, and Society program at the School of Communication at Northwestern University, where she studied the impact of new communication technologies on television viewing practices.

Jingan Yuan earned a Ph.D. from the University of Alabama. Dr. Yuan is Associate Professor of Economics at Southwestern University of Finance and Economics, China. Her major research areas focus on International Finance and Time-Series Econometrics.

SERIES EDITOR'S FOREWORD

In 2008, the Broadcast Education Association (BEA) initiated a new program promoting original research. The result was the creation of the BEA Research Symposium and publications. The annual symposium forum, chaired by national scholars, includes organized presentations, papers, and discussion of leading-edge research within the BEA Annual Conference.

The purpose of the BEA Symposium is as a catalyst for future research. It honors leading scholars of the discipline and features their work along with new and upcoming scholarship. The Symposium was launched in 2008, with Jenning Bryant's focus on Media Effects. Linda Kaid followed in 2009, with TechnoPolitics.

New to the BEA Symposium in 2010 was a partnership with Taylor & Francis to publish symposium research through the newly established Electronic Media Research Series, created for this purpose. Along with the BEA Research Symposium Series, this publication provides a keystone research text for those researching within the discipline. It will bring the reader up to date with the topics and it reflects the current work within the field as well as providing a comprehensive bibliography and index, facilitating further research. In 2011, Andrew C. Billings published *Sports Media: Transformation, Integration, Consumption* (Routledge). In 2011, Ron Tamborini published *Morality and the Media* (Routledge).

Alan B. Albarran's *Media Management and Economics Research in a Transmedia Environment* becomes the third published work of the Symposium and Taylor & Francis. This landmark work centers on economy and media management within a diverse, international, historical, and constantly changing interdependent environment.

Dr. Donald G. Godfrey
BEA Research Committee Chair, 2007–2012
Symposium Series, Executive Editor

INTRODUCTION

This edited volume, entitled *Media Management and Economics Research in a Transmedia Environment*, consists of papers presented at the 2012 Research Symposium held in conjunction with the annual convention of the Broadcast Education Association. On behalf of the 22 authors contributing to this work, we are very pleased to share this collection of research with you following its presentation at BEA 2012.

In October 2010, I was invited to serve as the Chair of the 2012 Research Symposium by Dr. Donald Godfrey, then the Chair of the Research Committee and a long time member and officer in the BEA, as well as a professional colleague and friend. I was honored to receive Don's invitation, in part due to my own years of service to the BEA as an officer and former President, and as a recipient of the 2009 Distinguished Scholar Award. I was also humbled to join a list of distinguished scholars before me who had undertaken this task for the BEA.

In organizing the symposium, we followed a model that had been successful with other BEA Research Symposia in that we used a mix of papers from senior scholars, junior scholars, and graduate students as well as papers that were invited and also drawn from an open call. The papers collected here represent the wide diversity that make up the media management and economics area, with some papers focused on transmedia and other papers addressing contemporary issues from both a domestic and global perspective. Scholars from the United States were joined in the symposium by researchers from Mexico, Colombia, Taiwan, China, India, and South Korea.

In organizing the symposium, I am grateful for the assistance from Don Godfrey who answered many questions over email and the telephone and for the support from the BEA National Office via Executive Director Heather Birks, and Office Manager Traci Bailey. At The University of North Texas, Christine Paswan helped with hours of proofreading and additional editing. I also appreciate the support of my wife and best friend, Beverly Albarran.

We hope you find the discussion on media management and economics research in a transmedia environment compelling and intriguing. We also

INTRODUCTION

hope it generates more questions, ideas, and topics for future studies in an area of the field that is dynamic and exciting to work in.

Dr. Alan B. Albarran
The University of North Texas

Section I

MEDIA MANAGEMENT AND ECONOMICS RESEARCH FROM SENIOR SCHOLARS

1

MEDIA MANAGEMENT AND ECONOMICS RESEARCH

The First 75 Years

Alan B. Albarran

Research centered on the managerial and economic aspects of the media industries has a rich, diverse, and interdependent history. It is hard to say exactly when the earliest investigations began by scholars, as the earliest published work that can be identified appeared in the 1940s. However, there were many governmental investigations and Congressional hearings that were concerned with the development of the media industries in the United States, particularly if they focused on economic practices and efforts to curb power and control.

By 2015, the media management and economics (MME) field will be approximately 75 years old. While we are 3 years from that date, it is helpful to consider where the field has grown and what lies ahead as it reaches this pivotal benchmark. To that end, this chapter will explore several topics in considering the first 75 years of MME research and scholarship. First, how do we define media management and media economics? Second, what are the important historical milestones in the development of MME research? Third, where is media management and economics research at in the twenty-first century as it nears 75 years of existence? Fourth, what are the important research propositions the field needs to consider as it moves forward?

Defining Media Management and Media Economics

Despite a long heritage as an area of study, there is little consensus among scholars as to what constitutes a working definition of media management or media economics. Albarran (2008), summarizing his tenure as Editor of the *International Journal on Media Management*, could "not claim to have any answers as to how to *define* the field of media management" (p. 184, italics added). Picard (2006), one of the founding scholars

Table 1.1 The Three Schools of Management

Name	Philosophy	Key Theories
Classical School	Increase productivity and efficiency	Scientific Management, Administrative Management, Bureaucratic Management
Behavioral School	Consider the goals of the employees to help improve organizational productivity	Hawthorne effect, Motivation, Theory X and Y, Theory Z
Modern Approaches	Considers both micro- and macro-forces impacting the organization in order to improve productivity	Management by Objective, Total Quality Management, Systems Theory, Leadership, Resource Dependence, Strategic Management

Source: Adapted by the author from various sources.

in the field of media economics, posited a similar view by writing "in a technical sense, there is no such thing as media economics" (p. 23). Both of these views were not stated to be pessimistic, as much as it is difficult to offer definitions for such a complex and evolving area(s) of study.

Albarran and Picard and many other scholars agree that the study of media management and the study of media economics historically involved the *application* of managerial and economic concepts and theories to the media industries. In their nascent stages of development, the first scholars/researchers looked to existing theories in the domains of business and management, along with theories in general economics that would help in conducting the early research on the media industries.

In the area of media management, this meant drawing from the generally-agreed upon schools of management: the classical school, the behavioral school, and the modern school of management thought. Albarran (1997) and others authoring texts on media management have used this framework in several editions. The three schools are compared in Table 1.1.

In considering media economics, Picard (2006) posits that the field was organized among three domains (theoretical, applied, and critical) operating at different levels of analysis. This framework is presented in Table 1.2.

These frameworks have helped in the development of the fields of media management and economics, but they have not necessarily clarified exactly how the fields should be defined. This has become even more

Table 1.2 Theoretical Domains in Media Economics Research

Domains	Theoretical Foundations	Level of Analysis	Topics Examined
Theoretical	Neoclassical Economics	Consumer, Firm, Market, Industry	Supply, demand, price, production, elasticity, concentration, diversity
Applied	Industry-based Also influenced by Neoclassical Economics	Consumer, Firm, Market, Industry	Structure, conduct, performance, spending, diversification, strategy
Critical	Marxist Studies British Cultural Studies Political Economy	Nation-State Global	Ownership, power, policy decisions, social and cultural effects of media, globalization, welfare

Source: Albarran (2010a); Picard (2006).

challenging given the tumultuous changes that have occurred over the past few decades as a result of technological, regulatory, economic, globalization, and social forces (Albarran, 2010b; Downes, 2009).

The defining of these fields becomes even more muddled from a defining standpoint when we consider all the possible permutations involved in each area. For example, in considering media management research, there are many possible levels of focus. One might focus on management activities at the corporate or ownership level, studying those actions or responses to external forces that corporate officers and CEOs encounter. One might focus on management at the level of an organization, such as a television station, newspaper, or digital enterprise. Even there, "management" occurs at different levels of the organization, so there is a need to further define and differentiate among these levels. Even self-employed individuals in media management, whether engaged in consulting, marketing, research or other activities, have to "manage" their own business and make decisions. These examples just point to the challenges of how to define media management.

The situation is no different with the study of media economics. Economic activities occur at many different levels. Albarran (2010a) argues for four different levels of analysis (individual, household, nation/state, global) when considering what he calls "the media economy." There are also many different types of economic transactions that occur from business to consumer, business to business, and consumer to consumer, that could constitute a part of media economics. The entire area

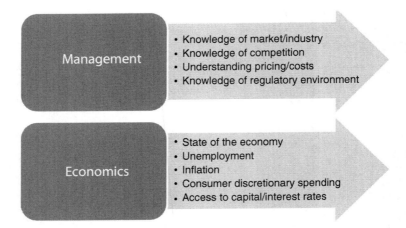

Figure 1.1 Examples of Interdependent Factors Influencing Management and Economics

Source: Author's rendition.

of critical scholarship, which is concerned with concepts like hegemony, power, technological determinism and others (just to name a few), also claims part of the field, yet is vastly different when considering micro and macroeconomic forces.

Despite the challenges in trying to define what media management and media economics is, we do know that the two areas are in fact related and interdependent with one another. That is the focus of the next section of this paper.

The Interdependent Nature of Media Management and Economics

Perhaps some of the challenges in trying to define both media management and media economics are due in part to their interdependent nature. Management is responsible for the economics of an entity, usually with a goal to earn profits for owners and shareholders. Yet, management's ability to earn profits is dependent on many factors, such as the number of competitors in a market, the state of the economy, unemployment, inflation, and in the case of the media industries, consumer discretionary spending (see Figure 1.1).

All types of businesses combine managerial and economic responsibilities. While there may be particular roles or titles that specialize in one area or the other, the higher up the organization one is more likely to encounter managers who spend a good amount of their time monitoring and analyzing the financial/economic condition of their enterprise. For example, in a typical electronic media facility a comptroller will prepare financial statements that are reviewed by the General Manager. Down one level, department heads will typically have authority over a budget in addition to their day-to-day managerial responsibilities. The department heads, usually considered middle managers, may not deal with economics on a daily basis—but are mindful of the economics of their part of the enterprise and the need to control expenses.

This interdependent nature between management and economics has of course evolved over time with the media industries. Contemporary media managers must now be concerned with a number of digital platforms that have their individual revenue/expense ratios to consider. These new platforms—ranging from smart phones and tablet devices to name just two—continue growing in popularity and further fragmenting the traditional audience/media relationship. Many digital platforms have to date failed to produce the kind of revenues generated by their analog or "traditional" holdings. Former NBC Executive Jeff Zuker once quipped about "trading analog dollars for digital pennies" which was later amended to "digital dimes" (Verna, 2010). Efforts to continue to monetize current and emerging digital platforms remain a huge management challenge.

The ideas presented in this section are of course done so considering a capitalistic orientation, under which the majority of the world's markets operate. In authoritarian systems, the nation/state controls the market system, and markets are typically non-competitive.

Media Management: Milestones and Development

In assessing the development of the fields of media management (and later media economics), a simple framework will be used to provide organization. We will consider the leading books that have been published that have influenced the field, and the predominant theories that have guided the field during its first 75 years of existence. We will then consider some of the key milestones that have made up the MME field in a decade by decade look at the evolution of media management and economics research.

Published Books in Media Management

A number of books have been published over the years in the area of media management. Some would be described today as industry-based books, others as textbooks, and others as research investigations. Table 1.3 presents the author's selection of representative books published in the field of media management over the past 75 years. A brief caveat—Table 1.3 only reflects works published in English in the United States. There have been many books on media management written by international

Table 1.3 Important Media Management Books (full citations in references)

Author(s), Title, Date of Publication	Brief Synopsis
Reinsch. *Radio Station Management* (1948)	First book devoted to radio management; designed for industry practitioners/use
Thayer. *Newspaper Business Management* (1954)	One of the earliest books focused on the newspapers; industry-oriented
Quall & Martin. *Broadcast Management* (1968)	First textbook with a focus on management, concentrating on broadcasting
Giles. *Newsroom Management* (1987)	Integrates both theory and practical application in explaining state of newspaper management
Sherman. *Telecommunications Management* (1987)	Widely adopted text on media management; three editions published before author's death
Lavine & Wackman. *Managing Media Organizations* (1988)	Theory-based book designed as a teaching or research text. Broad-based approach to media
Albarran. *Management of Electronic Media* (1997)	Now in fifth edition; focuses on electronic and digital media industries
Gershon. *The Transnational Media Corporation* (1997)	Centers on the role of transnational media corporations with case studies on key companies
Chan-Olmsted. *Competitive Strategy for Media Firms* (2005)	Application of strategic management to the media industries
Albarran, Chan-Olmsted, & Wirth. *Handbook of Media Management and Economics* (2006)	Compilation of both fields with several chapters devoted to managerial topics and agenda for future research

Source: Compiled by Author.

scholars, and most of these tend to be country-specific works and not well known to English language readers.

Important Theories used in Media Management Research

In assessing media management research, Mierzjewska and Hollifield (2006) found that "most theory is drawn from the larger field of organizational studies" (p. 39), but recognized that media management is unique because of the nature of its information products and economic characteristics. The authors reviewed 15 years of published research (1988–2003) in the *Journal of Media Economics* and the *International Journal on Media Management*, and found that there were six common approaches clustered into six categories: Strategic management theories (54); Technology, innovation, and creativity (21); Audience/consumer theories (12); Contingency/ efficiency theories (9); Political economy and normative approaches (5); and Organizational/professional cultural theories (5).

Aside from published research in *IJMM*, a review of the last 70+ years of research devoted to media management topics will find studies that utilize a number of common theories developed in other areas of communication research, broadly defined. These include diffusion of innovations, uses and gratifications, economic theory, and leadership.

Absent are theories that are unique to the area of media management, and have been refined and tested over time. It is not surprising in one sense given the "young" nature of the field of study, and a smaller base of researchers who are interested in the topic in comparison to the larger area of communication research. But the lack of unique theory building is also one of the pitfalls affecting media management research, and something the field of study needs to address in order to encourage future development.

Media Economics: History and Development

Published Books in Media Economics

Published books in media economics came much later than that of media management. While one can find chapters in edited volumes and anthologies and scholarly journals that consider media economic topics, texts devoted solely to the field of media economics did not appear until the late 1980s, then a large number of books were published in the 1990s and 2000s.

As the case with media management books, one can find media economics books whose topics are industry focused; works that would be considered research compilations; textbooks; and books that present critical perspectives. Table 1.4 presents the author's view of some of the representative books published in the field of media economics, with a brief synopsis of the content.

Important Theories used in Media Economics Research

Like media management research, theories guiding research have tended to be drawn from the larger field of economics and applied to the media industries. In examining the body of published research in media economics, one finds a dominance of studies using the established Industrial Organizational model drawn from neoclassical economics. The IO model

Table 1.4 Representative Media Economics Books (full citations in references)

Author(s), Title, Date of Publication	Brief Synopsis
Toussaint Desmoulins. *Le'economie de medias* (1978)	First known book devoted to media economics; only published in French
Vogel. *Entertainment Industry Economics* (1986)	Widely cited, data-rich industry-based book covering all of the entertainment industries
Picard. *Media Economics* (1989)	First book devoted solely to media economics
Owen & Wildman. *Video Economics* (1992)	Edited volume detailing economic structures of "new" video markets/industries
Albarran. *Media Economics: Understanding Markets, Industries and Concepts* (1996)	First media economics book designed as a university text. Second edition published in 2005
Albarran & Chan-Olmsted. *Global Media Economics* (1998)	Edited volume examining media industries by key countries
Alexander, Owers, & Carveth. *Media Economics, Theory and Practice* (1998)	Edited volume organized by industry; three editions published
Croteau & Hoynes. *The Business of Media* (2002)	Research work blending critical and industry perspectives on role of media and society
Picard. *The Economics and Financing of Media Firms* (2002)	Application of economic and financial concepts to the media industries
Albarran, Chan-Olmsted, & Wirth. *Handbook of Media Management and Economics* (2006)	Compilation of both fields with several chapters devoted to media economics topics and agenda for future research

Source: Compiled by Author.

is also known in the literature as the Structure–Conduct–Performance model (SCP), as it considers the market structure, conduct of the major players in the market, and the performance of the market.

An offshoot of the IO/SCP framework is the resource-based view (RBV) that considers that each firm in a market offers a set of unique resources that it uses to achieve a competitive advantage or position in a market. RBV has often been studied in conjunction with strategic management topics, another example of the interdependent nature between the areas of media management and media economics (e.g., Chan-Olmsted, 2005)

The principle of relative constancy developed by McCombs (1972), and niche theory developed by Dimmick (2003) are two areas of theory widely used across the field that have spawned a number of studies.

Relative constancy is concerned with consumer spending on the media, while niche theory looks at competition and coexistence among firms seeking similar resources.

New areas of theory are starting to emerge and show promise. One of the more interesting areas of theory development is that of attention economics (Davenport & Beck, 2001). Attention economics is particularly relevant given the wide degree of fragmentation we are witnessing as a result of more and more choices and platforms for consumption. Attention economics considers concepts like allocation, but also psychological attributes used by consumers in how they devote attention and how strongly they attend to media content products.

Important Events in Media Management and Economics Research

Table 1.5 presents a summary of important events that have influenced media management and economic research.

Media Management and Economics in the Twenty-first Century

This review and discussion results in a paradox as one tries to determine exactly where media management and economics research is at in the second decade of the twenty-first century. One can argue that the field is rich and diverse, drawing on multiple perspectives from scholars around the globe, investigating new technologies, delivery systems, and digital platforms. Conversely, one can argue MME research still suffers from a lack of identity and its ability to define itself, and from a lack of theoretical and methodological development which should be realized in a field of study approaching 75 years.

What makes this so interesting is that we are at a point in time where media management and economics—however defined—has more areas than ever available for research and investigation. The opportunities to conduct interesting research on many different types of media activities is unique.

This paradox over the state of the field will not be solved in this review; therefore, let us consider what we do know regarding where MME stands at this particular point in its history by considering some research propositions that would help in further development of the field.

Propositions and Needs for Future Research

In assessing the first 75 years of media management and economics research, the following propositions are provided as a way to summarize

Table 1.5 Key Events Impacting MME Research

Decade	Milestone
1940s	Earliest books appear on topics related to media management; postwar development of media around the globe lays foundation for future growth
1950s	Television emerges as a mass medium; research on newspaper management appears
1960s	Satellites facilitate global communication; television becomes dominant medium and research follows shift
1970s	Development of cable/satellite television results in shifts in research as scholars follow suit; newspapers begin secular decline in circulation; technology adoption accelerates with debut of video recording devices
1980s	Internet becomes a mass medium with email primary application; network dominance by television ends; first journals devoted solely to media management and media economics debut; universities begin to offer concentrations in media management
1990s	New technologies and delivery systems lead to fragmentation of audiences; research delves into new media; first World Media Economics Conference held and starting in 1998 begins biennial meetings in even-numbered years
2000s	*Journal of Media Economics* and *International Journal on Media Management* editorial boards show composition of scholars exhibits strong diversity and encompasses the globe with Africa the only missing continent; *Handbook of Media Management and Economics* published in 2006; social media emerges as a new consumer-driven platform
2010s	Explosion of social media adds to a very fragmented and diverse media landscape; many university programs modify curriculum and direction to account for shifts in new media; research related to new media technologies occurs more frequently than research devoted to "traditional" media

Source: Compiled by Author.

the state of the field as we "look back" and plan for the future. The propositions are the author's views; hopefully this will spur some discussion among scholars in the field as they consider adding their own propositions and further refining these ideas.

- There is a growing body of MME literature that offers many practical and theoretical contributions. Yet, overall, the field has struggled for its own sense of notoriety and standing, and the ability to clarify the contributions it makes to the larger area of communication science.
- We do not have consensus on how to define media management and economics research despite 75 years of investigation. The field needs

to recognize that management and economics occur on different levels of an organization and are interdependent concepts.
- The field can use greater theoretical development. One can argue there are no unique theories found in media management and economics research; instead, there are applications of theories developed in other fields or adapted for analysis in an MME context.
- Likewise, the MME field can benefit from new methodological tools to help understand data and their meaning. This is especially true in media economics research where we lack new tools to assess such important areas as concentration across industries and the importance of intellectual property.
- There is more interest in the MME field than at any time in its history, and more opportunities for study given the plethora of distribution platforms and new ways to connect information goods with consumers.

Given these propositions, how should our attention as a field now focus in regards to a future research agenda? What follows are a few general directions for future research in the MME area from where we stand at this point in time.

- Media management and economics research has tended to take place at a single level of analysis, yet we know that management occurs *across* levels and that economic activities function the same way. Research should be based on these multiple levels and consider how the various levels impact one another.
- In the same sense as the previous point, we have few studies that are conducted across time, such as longitudinal studies or time-series analysis. Much of the research is conducted at single points in time, which is unable to observe longer term trends and patterns that may exist and affect business practices.
- More theoretical development is needed, especially in the area of media management where there are no theories unique to the field. Media economics would also benefit from greater theory development, especially as new platforms and mediums enter the markets.
- Methodological tools are at best outdated and in need of refinement, especially in the area of media economics. An example is in the study of concentration, where the field still relies on measures developed decades ago that only take into account unrelated and unique markets.
- MME is truly a global phenomenon. Yet the majority of research is limited to management or economic practices in a single nation. Integrating a global perspective could provide new ways to evaluate

and assess managerial and economic performance across countries/regions of the globe.

These are just a few ideas that will help to strengthen the research in the MME field. With the rapid pace of evolution from technology and other forces impacting the media industries, we know there will be ongoing change and modification as to how we approach media management and economics. We can look to the past for the work that has provided a good foundation on which to build new directions and new opportunities for study and inquiry.

References

Albarran, A. B. (1996) *Media economics: Understanding markets, industries and concepts*. Ames: Iowa State University Press.
Albarran, A. B. (1997). *Management of electronic media*. Belmont, CA: Wadsworth.
Albarran, A. B. (2008). Defining media management. *The International Journal on Media Management* 10 (4), 184–186.
Albarran, A. B. (2010a). *The media economy*. New York: Taylor & Francis.
Albarran, A. B. (2010b). *The transformation of the media and communication industries*. Pamplona, Spain: EUSNA.
Albarran, A. B. & Chan-Olmsted, S. (1998). *Global media economics: Commercialization, concentration and integration of world media markets*. Ames: Iowa State University Press.
Albarran, A. B., Chan-Olmsted, S. M., & Wirth, M. O. (2006). *Handbook of media management and economics*. Mahwah, NJ: Lawrence Erlbaum Associates.
Alexander, A., Owers, J., & Carveth, R. (1998). *Media economics: Theory and practice*. Mahwah, NJ: Lawrence Erlbaum Associates.
Chan-Olmsted, S. M. (2005). *Competitive strategy for media firms*. New York: Taylor & Francis.
Croteau, D. & Hoynes, W. (2002). *The business of media: Corporate media and the public interest*. Thousand Oaks, CA: Pine Forge.
Davenport, T. H. & Beck, J. C. (2001). *The attention economy: Understanding the new currency of business*. Boston: Harvard University Press.
Dimmick, J. (2003). *Media competition and coexistence: The theory of the niche*. London: Lawrence Erlbaum Associates.
Downes, L. (2009). *The laws of disruption: Harnessing the new forces that govern life and business in the digital age*. New York: Basic Books.
Gershon, R. A. (1997). *The transnational media corporation: Global messages and free market competition*. Mahwah, NJ: Lawrence Erlbaum Associates.
Giles, R. H. (1987). *Newsroom management: A guide to theory and practice*. Indianapolis: R. J. Berg.
Lavine, J. M. & Wackman, D. B. (1988). *Managing media organizations*. New York: Longman.
McCombs, M. (1972). Mass media in the marketplace. *Journalism Monographs* 24.

Mierzjewska, B. I. & Hollifield, C. A. (2006). Theoretical approaches in media management research. In Albarran, A. B., Chan-Olmsted, S. M., & Wirth, M. O. (Eds.). *Handbook of media management and economics* (pp. 37–66). Mahwah, NJ: Lawrence Erlbaum Associates.

Owen, B.M. & Wildman, S.S. (1992) *Video economics*. Boston: Harvard University Press.

Picard, R. G. (1989). *Media economics*. Thousand Oaks, CA: Sage.

Picard, R. G. (2002). *The economics and financing of media firms*. New York: Fordham University Press.

Picard, R. G. (2006). Historical trends and patterns in media economics. In Albarran, A. B., Chan-Olmsted, S. M., & Wirth, M. O. (Eds.). *Handbook of media management and economics* (pp. 23–36). Mahwah, NJ: Lawrence Erlbaum Associates.

Quall, W. L. & Martin, L. A. (1968). *Broadcast management: Radio, television*. New York: Hastings House.

Reinsch, J. L. (1948). *Radio station management*. New York: Harper & Brothers.

Sherman, B. (1987). *Telecommunications management*. New York: McGraw-Hill, Inc.

Thayer, F. (1954). *Newspaper business management*. New York: Prentice-Hall.

Toussaint Desmoulins, N. (1978). *Le'economie de medias* [The economy of media]. Paris: Press Universitaires de France.

Verna, P. (2010, October 7). *How much longer can old-guard media slow the shift of dollars to digital video?* Retrieved March 22, 2012 from: http://www.emarketer.com/blog/index.php/buy-mansion-digital-dimes/

Vogel, H. (1986). *Entertainment industry economics*. New York: Cambridge University Press.

2

FUTURE PROSPECTS FOR CABLE TELECOMMUNICATIONS IN AN OVER-THE-TOP WORLD

Michael O. Wirth, Ph.D. and Ron Rizzuto, Ph.D.

Introduction

The world of what's possible with respect to video distribution has changed dramatically over the past 15 years (see for example Owen, 1999; Tedesco, 1999; Wirtz, 2011). Technological innovation has: expanded broadband speeds and capacity; increased the ability to digitally compress video signals; and improved consumers' ability to watch video programming when and where they want it on a variety of large and small video display devices (Grant & Meadows, 2010). This means that existing multichannel video program distributors (MVPD) face a potential sea shift in how consumers wish to receive their video programming (Moffett, Deo, Possavino, & Chan, 2010, November 30). Today's "broadband over-the-top world" has the potential to unleash the capitalistic winds of "creative destruction" (Cox & Alm, 2008; Schumpeter, 1942) that could dramatically impact the business prospects of mature MVPDs such as cable and direct broadcast satellites (DBS) (Hawley, 2010; Olgeirson & Myers, 2011).

This chapter analyzes the potential impact of over-the-top video distribution on cable multiple system operators (MSOs) by focusing on the following research question: How will the increased potential for disintermediation or bypass of cable's core video product via over-the-top media impact the future viability of the cable telecommunications industry? An answer to this question is developed: (1) by providing an overview of the current market situation with respect to video distribution via cable, DBS, telephone companies, and over-the-top video; (2) by identifying the regulatory, competitive, consumer demand and technological threats faced by cable MSOs with respect to maintaining their video distribution market position; (3) by identifying the regulatory, competitive, consumer demand and technological opportunities possessed by cable MSOs to

Table 2.1 Subscribership and Market Shares of Multichannel Video Program Distribution Providers

MVPD Providers	MVPD Number of Subscribers (M) (Market Share in %)[1]
Cable	59.8 (58.8)
DBS	33.36 (32.8)
Telcos	6.51 (6.4)
Other (BSPs, PCOs, BRS)	2.03 (2.0)
TOTAL	101.7 (100.0)

[1] MVPD number of subscribers and market shares are as of December 2010 as assembled from various sources: *Broadcasting & Cable, Mult channel News, NCTA*, and *SNL Kagan*.

help them maintain their video distribution market position; and (4) by providing a brief discussion of the future viability of the cable telecommunications industry to close the paper.

Current MVPD and OTT Video Delivery Market Situation

Multichannel Video Program Distribution Market Overview

Cable

As of December 2011, the $98 billion cable telecommunications industry has come a long way from its humble beginnings as a business built around the retransmission of over-the-air television signals for which cable operators did not pay copyright fees (Parsons, 2008; Southwick, 1998). Thanks to continuous technological innovation, aggressive capital investment, evolving consumer demand for video/telecommunication products, and the removal of many regulatory impediments, the contemporary cable telecommunications industry is the largest and best positioned distributor of US multichannel video programming (59 percent share—see Table 2.1) and broadband high speed data service (60 percent share—Moffett, Possavino, & Deo, 2010, October 18). It also generates strong incremental revenue from VoIP telephone service, which constitutes the third part of its "triple play" offering, with a 25 percent share of the US wired residential voice market (Moffett, Deo, Possavino, & Chan, 2010, December). The largest MSOs (Comcast and Time Warner Cable) derive approximately 50 percent of their revenues from their broadband and telephone services, up from 35 percent in 2006 (Moffett, Deo, Possavino & Chan, 2010, December). The other

50 percent of the cable industry's revenue comes from its core video product.

Cable is the clear MVPD market leader for a number of reasons (see Table 2.2). In particular, cable's market incumbency/first mover market advantages in two of its three "triple play" products (multichannel video and high speed data) give it a significant leg up on its multichannel competitors (Ammori, 2010; Bortz Media & Sports Group, 2010). In addition, spending $180.1 billion on capital expenditures, since the passage of the *Telecommunications Act of 1996* (SNL Kagan, various years, as retrieved from NCTA.com), to build a broadly available, high capacity, hybrid fiber coax (HFC) network, has allowed cable MSOs to reinvent themselves as telecommunication companies offering a variety of new services and products and providing them with an advantaged market position relative to their MVPD competitors (Moffett, Deo, Possavino, & Weisgall, 2010, February 16).

DBS

DirecTV became the first provider of high powered DBS service in June 1994 followed by DISH Network, which was launched by EchoStar in March 1996 (Grant & Meadows, 2006). DBS has many advantages as a one way multichannel video distribution platform (see Table 2.3). When DBS service first launched, it was able to offer its subscribers higher quality audio and video signals than cable could provide along with a larger number of channels (due to the fact that DBS was 100 percent digital from day one). Today's broadband digital HFC cable systems have greatly reduced or eliminated DBS's quality advantages while also allowing cable MSOs to deliver a variety of products that DBS cannot deliver (e.g., interactive video services like video on demand (VOD) along with data and voice services) (Moffett, Deo, Possavino, & Weisgall, 2010, June 8). DBS is still a very profitable business. However, given the disadvantages noted in Table 2.3, it has a very uncertain future (Moffett, Deo, Possavino, & Chan, 2010, December).

Telcos

Incumbent local exchange carriers (ILECs), Verizon (FiOS) and AT&T (U-verse), have only recently (Verizon in 2005 and AT&T in 2008) become meaningful competitors with respect to multichannel video distribution (AT&T U-verse, 2012; Verizon FiOS, 2012). Verizon has invested approximately $25 billion to build a fiber to the home (FTTH) broadband digital network (called FiOS) that passes approximately 16 million premises or (70 percent of the homes in Verizon's ILEC areas of operation). AT&T has invested approximately $25 billion to build

Table 2.2 Cable MVPD Competitive Advantages/Disadvantages

Cable Advantages	Cable Disadvantages
1) Marketplace incumbency/first mover with respect to multichannel video and broadband/high speed data	1) Market leader position exposes cable to increased levels of regulatory scrutiny that retards cable's ability to respond to competitors
2) Superior ability to deliver interactive services (e.g., video on demand)	2) Investor profitability expectations may reduce cable's ability to make capital investments in response to competitive threats (Moffett, Deo, Possavino, & Chan, 2010, December)
3) Superior ability to "manufacture" additional bandwidth at a relatively low marginal cost	3) Consumer unhappiness with cable service quality
4) Clear market leader with respect to two of three products in its "multiproduct bundle" (multichannel video and broadband/high speed data services)	4) Much higher capital intensity than DBS
5) Well positioned to deal with cord cutting thanks to best, most widely available, high capacity broadband network into the home (Moffett, Deo, Possavino, & Chan, 2010, December)	5) Service upgrade rollouts are much slower than DBS due to local nature of cable distribution
6) Revenue gains from broadband and voice have been far greater than losses in video (Moffett, Deo, Possavino, & Chan, 2010, December)	6) Local nature of cable business, makes national brand development much more difficult for cable MSOs

Source: Authors' Compilation.

a fiber to the node (FTTN) broadband digital network (called U-verse) that passes 30 million premises (or 55 percent of the homes in AT&T's ILEC areas of operation) (Moffett, Deo, Possavino, & Chan, 2010, December).

The biggest advantage of telco MVPD competitors is consumer unhappiness with cable (see Table 2.4; Spangler, 2011, October 17). Likewise, in those market areas where FiOS and U-verse are available, Verizon and AT&T are offering multichannel video, data, and voice packages that are highly competitive with incumbent cable operator "triple play" offerings (see FiOS package offerings at http://www.verizon.com and

Table 2.3 DBS MVPD Competitive Advantages/Disadvantages

DBS Advantages	DBS Disadvantages
1) Consumer unhappiness with cable	1) Inability to cost-effectively deliver interactive services like video on demand
2) Regulation guarantees access to most popular cable program services and provides some protection from cable and telco MVPD providers	2) Inability to cost-effectively provide broadband/high speed data service
3) National service provides upgrades immediately to all subscribers	3) Must partner with other providers (primarily telcos) to deliver a "multi-product bundle" of telecommunication services
4) Digital video/audio of the highest quality	4) Especially vulnerable to consumer "cord cutting" impact due to lack of cost-effective broadband service (Moffett, Deo, Possavino, & Weisgall, 2010, June 8)
5) Significantly lower capital intensity than wire based MVPD providers	5) Significantly higher subscriber acquisition costs (SAC) than other MVPDs
6) Highest MVPD return on invested capital (ROIC) (Moffett, Deo, Possavino, & Chan, 2010, December)	6) Standalone MVPD business is mature and facing increased competition from cable, telcos, and OTT video providers

Source: Authors' Compilation.

U-verse package offerings at http://www.att.com). However, telco MVPD overbuilders face a number of significant challenges/disadvantages (see Table 2.4). Most importantly, telcos' core wireline business continues to decline, having lost 50 percent of their access lines since 2000 (Moffett, Deo, Possavino, & Chan, 2010, December). Likewise, except for those market areas covered by FiOS and U-verse, telco broadband service consists of traditional, twisted pair (i.e., not fiber) DSL service (digital subscriber line), which is an inadequate long term broadband competitor for cable's increasingly high speed broadband service offering (Moffett, Deo, Possavino, & Chan, 2010, December). In spite of the deep pockets possessed by ILECs (Verizon and AT&T but not CenturyLink [formerly Qwest]), telcos' inferior distribution network (except for FiOS and to some extent U-verse) relative to cable's, coupled with the problems ILECs face with respect to their core wireline and DSL products, suggests that telcos face a challenging future (Moffett, Deo, Possavino, & Chan, 2010, December).

Table 2.4 Telco MVPD Competitive Advantages/Disadvantages

Telco Advantages	Telco Disadvantages
1) Consumer unhappiness with cable	1) Core wireline business has lost nearly 50% of its access lines since 2000 (Moffett, Deo, Possavino, & Chan, 2010, December)
2) Regulation guarantees access to most popular cable program services	2) Decision of Verizon (FiOS) and AT&T (U-verse) to overbuild themselves has led to significant cannibalization of existing telco data and voice revenues (Moffett, Deo, Possavino, & Chan, 2010, December)
3) Marketplace incumbency/first mover with respect to wireline telephone services	3) Overbuilding incumbent cable operators already offering triple play services (video, voice, and data) with highly capital intensive FiOS and U-verse services is very difficult from an economic perspective (Moffett, Deo, Possavino, & Chan, 2010, December)
4) Excellent to average ability to deliver interactive services (FiOS and U-verse vs. legacy DSL service)	4) Telco MVPD business proposition is made more difficult as a result of competition from DBS
5) All multichannel video business revenues are incremental	5) Revenue gains from video business and high speed data service are not enough to offset core wireline and traditional DSL service losses
6) Well positioned to deal with cord cutting in FiOS and U-verse network homes	6) Lowest MVPD return on invested capital (ROIC) (Moffett, Deo, Possavino, & Chan, 2010, December)
7) Deep pockets associated with ILEC status	7) In long run, legacy telco plant is inadequate multichannel video and high speed data competitor for cable's high capacity broadband delivery system

Source: Authors' Compilation.

Over-the-Top (OTT) Video Market Overview

The broadest definition of OTT video is "the delivery of video and audio, via the internet, directly to user(s) connected devices" (Moyler & Hooper, 2009). This definition would include the potential delivery of video content to 105.7 million smart phones, 61.6 million games consoles, 20+

Table 2.5 OTT Penetration and Market Potential in 2011

Market Metrics	Number (M)[1]
TV Households	115.9
Multichannel Households	101.7
High Speed Data Subscribers	79.8
Households with OTT Devices	26.3*
Total Multichannel Substitutes (OTT HHs)	4.5 (4.0%)

[1] Number of Households and Subscribers.

Source: Olgeirson & Myers, 2011.*Internet connected video game consoles, standalone set-top boxes, internet connected TVs and Blu-Ray Players, PCs/Home Media Servers.

million tablets, and 6 million over-the-top boxes such as Roku or Apple TV (Winslow, 2012b, January, p. 10).

Such a broad definition of OTT video is problematic because it is difficult to make direct comparisons to cable, DBS, and telcos given the lack of comparability of "screen size" and length of programming (short vs. long form video). As a consequence, the analysis that follows uses a narrower definition of OTT video: it is the delivery of video content over the unmanaged internet to PCs, game consoles, and TVs via a broadband connection. In other words, OTT video is the internet delivery of television and movies as a substitution for multichannel video services provided by cable, DBS, or telcos (Hawley, 2010; Olgeirson & Myers, 2011).

SNL Kagan estimates (see Table 2.5) that there were 4.5 million OTT video households in the US at year-end 2011. This is a penetration rate of approximately 4 percent of all TV households. It is interesting that Kagan's estimates of OTT video households are similar to those of Magna Global, which estimated that OTT video households totaled 3 million in 2011 (Viewer watch, 2012).

SNL Kagan's data underscore the substantial potential for OTT video given that there are 79.8 million high speed subscribers and 26.3 million households that have such OTT video devices as: internet connected video game consoles; standalone set-top boxes (Apple TV, Roku, Boxee, and Vudu hardware designed to provide access to internet delivered content to the TV); internet connected TVs and Blu-Ray Players; and PCs/Home Media Servers (see Interactive Television Institute, 2012, for a profile of the different OTT video players and devices).

The primary motivations for consumers to choose OTT video instead of cable, DBS, or telco delivered multichannel video are choice and control (see Table 2.6). Consumers can select what they want to watch from the professionally packaged content available on the internet (including

Table 2.6 Over-the-Top (OTT) Video Competitive Advantages/Disadvantages

OTT Advantages	OTT Disadvantages
1) Consumer choice—consumers have the ability to select and pay for only what they want to watch	1) Not all video programming is available for OTT consumption. In particular, live events and sports are two key areas where the programming is limited 2) There are numerous programmers who limit or withhold content from OTT video subscribers (Pye & Acker, 2011; Spangler, 2011, September 1)
2) Consumers have greater ability to select the package(s) of programming that they can afford (Moffett, Deo, & Chan, 2011, September 13)	3) Consumers have to settle for lower quality programming—"good enough" instead of great TV (Moffett, Deo, & Chan, 2011, September 13). In addition, purchasing a TV series for $0.99 per episode from iTunes video store may turn out to be more expensive than other MVPD alternatives
3) Consumers can personalize their TV viewing	4) OTT video consumers have to spend more time in making their video program choices, and they will have more than one bill
4) Consumers have access to a greater array of programming. Consumers can select from programming provided by cable and broadcast networks as well as user generated programming on the internet	5) It is challenging for OTT video consumers to navigate through millions of video programs and content clips (Moyler & Hooper, 2009)
5) There are continual improvements in the quality of OTT video. These include: increasingly fast high speed connections and greater availability of internet connections to TV sets	6) OTT video has substantial room for improvement. The success of OTT video is likely to invite usage based pricing for high speed connectivity

Source: Authors' Compilation.

programming from cable and broadcast networks) or from user generated content, and they can watch it whenever they wish to do so. In addition, consumers only want to pay for what they actually watch. In one sense, OTT provides an "a la carte" video choice that is unavailable from MVPDs. Another key benefit of OTT video is that it allows consumers to "create" more affordable video packages compared to those offered by MVPDs (even though the quality of the package will be lower).

> No one would argue that the entertainment choices offered by Netflix are *better* than what's available from cable—and neither are those offered by Hulu, nor YouTube. But when faced with a choice of pay TV or a third meal, will *some* customers choose to make do with a back catalog of off-the-run TV shows and movies? Of course they will.
>
> (Moffett, Deo, & Chan, 2011, September 13, p. 10, original emphasis)

The key disadvantage of OTT video is the lack of adequate business models for content owners. As a consequence, a substantial amount of video content is not available to OTT consumers. The current business models for content owners rely on the collection of subscription fees from consumers by MVPD operators and/or the generation of advertising revenues based on the number of viewers watching the advertising. Both of these revenue streams for content owners are intimately tied to the business models of the MVPD content aggregators. Before content owners will embrace a "direct-to-consumer" OTT business model, the new model will have to produce sufficient revenue to offset the revenue lost as a result of moving away from the MVPD "content aggregator" model (Moffett, Kirjner, Deo, Findlay, Parameswaran, & Chan, 2012, January 27). One related impediment to migrating to an OTT "direct-to-consumer" model is the need to change consumer expectations that programming content is "free" (Berman, 2011).

Threats

Regulatory Threats

Overview

The history of cable regulation by the FCC and Congress makes it clear that significant changes (perceived or actual) in video/information/telecommunication market structure, conduct, and performance are likely to result in modifications in how cable is regulated. When regulations are increased, cable's economic fortunes are negatively impacted (Parsons, 2008). When regulations are decreased, cable is positively impacted (Parsons, 2008). As with all industries, cable entrepreneurs prefer "deregulation" or "steady state regulation" to "reregulation." As a result, the cable industry engages in a variety of strategies to convince regulators to reduce and/or maintain regulation of the industry. Strategies include lobbying the FCC and Congress, engaging in industry self-regulation, minimizing the use of actual or perceived "predatory" business practices, hiring experts to conduct "independent" studies focused on key issues related to industry competition and regulation, working to improve the industry's customer service ratings, and "supporting" regulations that facilitate the establishment/maintenance of a "competitive" marketplace.

Regulatory Limitations on Competitive Responses

If the cable industry's advantaged position with respect to its broadband delivery network results in an increase in the industry's actual or perceived market power, the FCC and/or Congress could decide to promulgate new regulations/pass new legislation to limit cable's ability to respond to competitive threats from its rivals including "over-the-top" video competitors (Economides, 2011). The *Cable Television Consumer Protection and Competition Act of 1992* provides an example of the type of action Congress can take if it becomes unhappy enough with the market conduct of incumbent cable MSOs so that it feels the need to step in to protect less well positioned market rivals from cable's market power. The US Department of Justice could also take action against the cable industry for any anticompetitive behavior that is considered to violate the US antitrust laws through its Antitrust Division (Ammori, 2010; Eckert, 2011).

Usage Based Price Discrimination and Regulation

If cable implements an "effective" usage based price discrimination scheme with respect to distribution by over-the-top video providers via cable's high speed broadband network, cable MSOs could maintain their overall profit margins by increasing the price OTT competitors must pay for over-the-top internet video distribution while decreasing the cost consumers pay for cable's video service (Moffett, Deo, Possavino, & Pan, 2009, June 11). However, if cable is too aggressive, the FCC and/or Congress is likely to limit cable's ability to engage in this form of market conduct (Moffett, Deo, Possavino, & Weisgall, 2010, May 10). Usage based pricing is closely related to the concept of network neutrality, which means that consumers are allowed "to access any content over the internet, without restrictions of speed, receiving device, service platform or content" (Hawley, 2010, p. 35). The FCC's recently promulgated network neutrality rules (see "FCC acts to preserve internet freedom and openness," 2010) provide the framework within which usage based pricing schemes can take place (see "The difference engine: Politics and the web," 2010).

A Compulsory License for OTT Video

Establishment of a compulsory licensing approach with respect to internet "retransmission" of some of the video programming carried over-the-air (OTA) and via multichannel video distribution systems would increase the amount of potentially sustainable "high quality" video distributed via the internet and could increase consumer cord cutting (Wirth & Collette, 2001). Video copyright holders adamantly oppose establishment of a compulsory license for over-the-top video providers. However, in spite of the arguments against doing so (see Wirth & Collette, 2001), Congress could decide to lower the cost of MVPD market entry for over-the-top video providers by establishing something similar to what was established for the cable industry in the *Copyright Revision Act of* 1976.

Common Carrier Status for Cable

The ultimate regulatory threat to cable's ability to compete as a multichannel video program distributor would be to change its legal status to that of a common carrier. Communication common carriers are required to hold themselves out to the public on a first come, first serve, non-discriminatory basis and they are not allowed to affect the content of what they carry (i.e., they are not allowed to originate content). Given the regulatory history of cable (especially the *Cable Communications Act of 1984*), it seems very unlikely that Congress would reverse course and impose common carrier status. However, if the market power of incumbent cable operators becomes great enough and if the industry exerts its market power through sufficiently inappropriate market conduct, Congress could change its mind and decide to make cable a common carrier. The threat of common carrier status is much greater for cable's broadband/high speed data service than for its core multichannel video service.

Competitive Threats

OTT Consumer Devices and Content Providers

Many new TV-capable devices and content providers have entered the video marketplace in the past decade with the hope of delivering video to consumers "over-the-top." TV-capable content devices include PCs, game consoles, mobile phones, tablets, standalone set-top boxes, and Blu-Ray players. OTT content providers include hybrid TV/internet content providers (e.g., Google), individual TV networks and movie studios, independent programmers (Irish TV), pure internet content providers (Netflix, YouTube, Amazon, Hulu, etc.), and consumer generated content (Hawley, 2010). As the number of OTT market participants increases, more innovation will take place and competitive threats that could lead to increased cord cutting will emerge at a faster pace.

Possible Out-of-Market MVPD OTT Video Strategy

A cable MSO or telco TV provider could utilize the internet to deliver traditionally packaged cable video content "over-the-top" to subscribers outside of their facilities based markets of operation. An example of this approach would be if an MSO like Comcast decided to offer a premium cable networks package online to consumers outside of the markets in which it offers cable service. Subscribers to other MSOs (e.g., Time Warner Cable) could then drop their cable based video service in favor of Comcast's by connecting to Comcast's OTT video service via Time Warner Cable's broadband/high speed data service. The authors are not aware of any traditional MVPDs mounting an OTT video service offering of this type. However, they would certainly be well positioned to do so if they thought it made sense from a business perspective, and it would likely lead to increased cord cutting.

Business Model Sustainability

Development of a sustainable business model for internet video distribution will increase consumer "cord cutting." One of the key factors limiting the penetration of OTT is the lack of video content. As noted above, many content providers are unwilling to make their content available to OTT when there is very little revenue upside but substantial revenue downside if they alienate their core MVPD affiliates. For example, when Starz announced its streaming deal with Netflix in 2008, cable, DBS, and telcos were unhappy with the deal (Spangler, 2011, September 1). If content providers find a business model that allows them to generate incremental revenue from OTT providers while maintaining their core revenue base, OTT will receive a substantial boost.

Intellectual Property Rights Enforcement

If video copyright holders do an inadequate job of enforcing their intellectual property rights, greater amounts of illegal and/or undesirable OTT video distribution will occur resulting in increased consumer cord cutting. The music industry provides an example of what can happen to an industry when it fails to adequately protect its intellectual property rights.

OTT vs. Content Aggregator Profitability

If major video content owners begin to believe that distributing programs directly to consumers via the internet is more profitable than distributing video programs through MVPD content aggregators (i.e., cable, DBS and telcos), the quality and quantity of OTT video content will increase as will consumer cord cutting.

New OTT Video Content

Development of economically viable internet-only audio/visual content, not currently distributed by cable or other MVPDs, would increase the quantity and quality of OTT video programming and will lead to increased consumer cord cutting. A very likely example of this would be a "niche" programming genre that does not have a large enough customer base to justify the launch of a linear channel or even a VOD service by cable, but which gains traction as an internet-only service. If the quality of the "niche" programming is excellent and the customer base is passionate, this would be a positive development for OTT. A critical mass of such "niche" video content would provide OTT video providers with a significant competitive boost.

Consumer Demand Threats

Consumer Demand for TV Everywhere

Consumer demand for mobile access to everything, including video, poses a significant threat to a wired medium like cable (Bothun, 2009; Hawley, 2010; Viewer watch, 2012). If cable's "TV Everywhere" initiative is unsuccessful at fending off the threat posed by mobile devices such as tablets, smart phones, over-the-top boxes (e.g., Roku and Apple TV), and video streaming enabled game consoles, OTT video providers will have an area of natural advantage in which to market to consumers and cord cutting will increase (Winslow, 2012b, p. 10).

Consumer Free Internet Content Expectations

Consumer expectations that video content on the internet should be free will lead to increased cord cutting if consumers blame cable for keeping desired video content off of the internet (Bothun & Lieberman, 2010, 2011; Hawley, 2010). Millennials (i.e., younger consumers) are especially likely to engage in increased cord cutting activity (or simply never subscribe) because "they are growing up with the expectation that content is generated and consumed on their terms, not ... those of the programmer or the operator" (Hawley, 2010, p. 18).

Declining Real Income Impacts

A decrease in real income for the average consumer (i.e., the decline of the middle class) will lead to increased cord cutting.

> After food, shelter, and transportation each month, the bottom 40% of US households had just $100 of disposable [income] left for *everything* else ... [So] they have nothing left for cable TV ... wireless phone service ... clothing ... debt service or retirement.
> (Moffett, Possavino, & Deo, 2010, October 22, p. 1)

Consumer Demand for Long Tail Content

Increased consumer demand for "long tail" video content, for which distribution via the internet is the most economically feasible means of distribution, could lead to increased cord cutting ("Accessibility driving demand for content according to Deloitte's 'state of the media democracy' survey," 2012; Anderson, 2008). Unless cable operators can identify economically feasible ways to monetize video's long tail, they will not be able to reduce this type of cord cutting (Harris, 2012; "The 'long tail' of video is about to get longer—What role will cable play?," 2005; "Wagging the video long tail," 2012).

Technological Threats

Bandwidth Investment Requirements

In 2008, Alcatel-Lucent estimated the bandwidth required to meet consumer needs in the home as 140–230 Mbps downstream and 37–56 Mbps upstream (Hawley, 2010, pp. 26–27). As Hawley observed, "it is realistic to say that 100 Mbps will become insufficient sooner rather than later." Such bandwidth needs will require ongoing investment by cable operators to upgrade their networks. If these investments lead cable MSOs to increase the price they charge consumers for video services, consumer cord cutting is likely to increase.

Network Capacity Investment Recovery Time

As noted above in the discussion of regulatory threats, the FCC's Net Neutrality rules make it possible for network operators to engage in usage based pricing to fairly allocate the cost of their networks. In spite of the potential to match bandwidth usage with cost via a usage based pricing scheme, this area of public policy remains quite controversial.

In all likelihood, there will be a significant lag between network usage and cost allocation. In the interim, cable operators will have to expand network capacity without assurances that they will be fairly compensated. For example, traffic measurements from Sandvine, as reported by Bernstein Research (Kirjner, Parameswaran, & Chan, 2012) indicate that in spring 2011, Netflix, YouTube, and BitTorrent accounted for 29.7 percent, 11.0 percent, and 10.4 percent, respectively, of Peak-Hour Downstream Internet Traffic. In all likelihood, these users did not pay their pro rata share of network costs. Over time, usage based pricing should help remedy this situation. However, in the short run, cable operators are subsidizing OTT video distributors, which lowers the cost of OTT video distribution and increases the potential for consumer cord cutting.

Technological Obsolescence and Increased Capital and Operating Costs

As consumers migrate to additional devices to receive their video content, cable operators need to invest in customer premises equipment (CPE), software, and head end equipment in order to accommodate new consumer devices. In addition, cable operators need to invest in new customer experience management personnel and processes to better serve their customers. Making such investments and improvements will be required just to stay competitive. The "table stakes" for operators will continue to increase, which will have a negative impact on overall cable profit margins. Likewise, cable MSO efforts to improve the customer experience will become more challenging due to the increased complexity of the video environment.

Smart Phones and Wireless Network Capacity

Development of better, faster smart phones and of higher speed wireless networks will expand the quality and quantity of video programming available to wireless subscribers. This will lead to an increase in consumer cord cutting.

Tablets

As tablets become cheaper and faster, they will begin to displace computers and television sets. As consumers begin to use 4G wireless connections instead of a cable modem for broadband connectivity, OTT video usage will increase. In this scenario, consumer cord cutting will cause cable operators to lose both video and broadband customers and revenues (JSI Capital Advisors Blog, 2011).

Digital Signal Compression

Continued development of more efficient digital signal compression schemes will increase the quantity and quality of video distribution via the internet. Improvements in digital signal compression will allow OTT providers to stream more video content in a shorter period of time. The resulting improvements in video streaming quantity and quality will increase consumer cord cutting.

Unknown Technological Innovations

Development of currently unknown or undeveloped video distribution technological innovations can be expected to lead to increased consumer cord cutting at some point in the future. As Noll indicates, "We know from the past that clever advances will occur in the invention and development of unforeseen technologies. If there is anything that history teaches, it is that whatever is much in vogue today will most likely disappear tomorrow" (Noll, 1997, p. 186).

Opportunities

Regulatory Opportunities

Industry Self-Regulation

Engaging in self-regulation to "limit" the exercise of market power possessed by incumbent cable operators could reduce the probability that Congress and the FCC will reregulate the cable industry. The voluntary nature of such a self-imposed code of conduct necessarily reduces its effectiveness in controlling behavior. However, to the extent that major cable MSOs choose to follow the self-imposed regulations, Congress and the FCC are less likely to feel the need to reregulate cable (Hearn, 1990).

Intellectual Property Rights Protection

Working with copyright owners to convince Congress to maintain and/or increase the intellectual property rights protection enjoyed by video copyright holders (including working to prevent the establishment of a compulsory license for internet carriage of over-the-air TV and cable/MVPD programs/program networks) could allow cable to minimize "free/lower priced" consumer access to high quality video programming through over-the-top video providers (Convente, 2011). This could in turn limit certain types of cord cutting.

Regulatory Parity

Continuing to make the case for regulatory parity with respect to how cable is regulated relative to its MVPD and OTT video competitors could reduce the likelihood of reregulation of cable (through passage of new legislation/promulgation of new regulations) and increase the probability that existing regulations that limit cable's ability to compete will be eliminated. The FCC's Program Access Rules (established by Congress in the *Cable Television Consumer Protection and Competition Act of 1992*), which require cable MSO-owned program networks be made available to all of cable's MVPD competitors on a non-discriminatory basis (i.e., at "reasonable" rates), provide one example where cable faces restrictions not imposed on some of its MVPD competitors. The FCC is required to review its "program access rules" periodically to determine if they should be continued or allowed to sunset ("Court upholds FCC program access rules," 2010; "FCC to examine prohibition on exclusive contracts," 2001). If cable can convince the FCC that the MVPD marketplace is sufficiently competitive, the FCC will sunset the rules and cable MSOs will once again be able to gain market advantages by distributing exclusive content like DirecTV's NFL Sunday Ticket package (see http://en.wikipedia.org/wiki/NFL_Sunday_Ticket).

Telling Cable's Story

Increasing cable's public relations/lobbying/competitive research efforts to tell cable's story to Congress and the FCC could help the industry avoid significant reregulation. However, as cable MSOs found out in 1992, if Congress, the FCC, and the public are sufficiently unhappy because they believe the cable industry is "misbehaving," public relations and lobbying will not be enough to prevent regulators from taking significant action to protect consumers and competitors.

Serving the Public Interest

Making the additional investment needed to realize the full potential of cable's required public, educational, and governmental (PEG) access channels (along with any other franchise based public interest requirements) could help the cable industry fend off federal reregulation by demonstrating its commitment to serving the "public interest." It could also improve cable's relationship with local franchising authorities and local community leaders (Arnold, 2011).

Pricing and Regulation

Developing a strategic approach to limit price increases for video, data, and voice services could help the cable industry minimize undesirable reregulation. Annual basic cable rate increases that averaged more than three times the rate of inflation following passage of the *Cable Communications Act of 1984* played a large role in Congress's decision to re-establish basic rate regulation along with many other onerous regulations in the *Cable Television Consumer Protection and Competition Act of 1992* (Parsons, 2008).

Competitive Opportunities

First Mover Advantage

As Tables 2.1 and 2.5 illustrate, cable operators have the highest market share among all MVPD and CTT video providers. This gives them a first mover advantage. If cable operators are willing to continually innovate with services that meet consumers' changing needs, they will be able to slow the market development of OTT video providers. Cable's "TV Everywhere" efforts (Winslow, 2012a, January, p. 11), underscore the progress that has been made in responding to the desire of consumers for more content on more devices. Likewise, cable and telco operators can partner with OTT providers to deliver content to OTT video devices in the home. For example, in 2010, Comcast, AT&T's U-verse and Verizon's FiOS TV cut deals with Microsoft to deliver video content to the Xbox game console (Winslow, 2012b, January, p. 10). Additionally, Cablevision's Optimum Link PC-To-TV service enables consumers to stream over-the-top content from their computers to their TVs (Lawler, 2011).

Enhance the Price/Value Relationship for Consumers

If cable operators broaden their service offerings to include OTT video choices for consumers, in addition to their current "full service" video packages, they will meet the needs and budgets of more consumers. This will provide consumers with more choice and enhance cable's value proposition. This could also allow cable MSOs to grow their video customers and maintain their overall level of profitability.

New Revenue Streams

As cable operators move to partner with some OTT video providers, additional revenue streams are likely to develop. For example, cable operators may be able to charge OTT providers a service fee for the use of their networks. In effect, cable operators could charge a fee for the increased reliability of migrating the service delivery of OTT video providers from the unmanaged internet to a managed network. Likewise, OTT providers might contract with cable operators to provide billing and customer service support for their OTT video customers. Instead of service fees, cable operators may opt for a revenue sharing arrangement with OTT providers.

Usage Based Pricing

Implementation of a "carefully crafted" usage based approach to charging for bandwidth use will help cable operators minimize cord cutting. In today's current environment for OTT, many consumers have grown to expect access to unlimited bandwidth for a flat price along with "free" programming. As cable operators move to usage based pricing, consumers will begin to understand the realities of OTT video delivery (Moffett, Deo, Findlay, & Chan, 2012, February 29).

Consumer Demand Opportunities

Customer Service

Heavily investing in all things customer service to provide cable video/data/voice subscribers with the best service experience possible should significantly reduce cord cutting. Striving to be on top of the J.D. Power and Associates Power Circle Ratings for Residential Telecommunication Services (video/data/voice) could also be expected to have a very positive impact on the image of individual cable MSOs as well as the industry as a whole (Bookman, 2011).

Price Discrimination

Establishing a "revenue neutral" price discrimination scheme that reduces the price of multichannel video service tiers (where consumer demand is expected to be more elastic) and that increases the price of its broadband/high speed data tier through usage based pricing (where consumer demand is expected to be less elastic), could help cable operators minimize consumer cord cutting. Although the cable industry is in a better position to deal with OTT video competition through this type of strategy than any of its MVPD competitors, the industry's ability to increase broadband prices through usage based pricing could be regulatorily limited (Moffett, Deo, Possavino, & Weisgall, 2010, May 10).

Lower Income Consumers

Establishing and promoting affordably priced video/data/voice individual tiers and bundled packages to serve lower income consumers could reduce consumer cord cutting. This approach would also allow cable operators to demonstrate their commitment to the public interest by working to provide telecommunication services to as many members of the communities they serve as possible (Moffett, Deo, & Chan, 2011, September 13).

Connecting with Consumers

Establishing programs that "bond" cable companies to the local communities they serve should allow cable operators to do a better job of connecting with consumers. Cable companies that are successful in developing deeper and more meaningful partnerships with local institutions will be able to create stronger consumer oriented brands that build long term reputation and value with both subscribers and non-subscribers (Shayon, 2012). Local TV stations have been much more effective at doing this over the years than has cable. As a result, local TV stations have typically won the public relations battles with cable during retransmission consent disputes (Donahue, 2011; Stelter & Carter, 2010, October).

TV Everywhere

Developing even stronger relationships with cable programmers to promote and extend the "TV Everywhere" initiative could reduce cord cutting. If the cable industry is able to "seamlessly" deliver "all" video content to consumers when and where they want it at a "reasonable" price point, while protecting the intellectual property rights of copyright holders, OTT video distribution will be more complementary than competitive with cable's multichannel video service. The ultimate success of TV Everywhere from a consumer perspective depends on cable operators' ability to provide a "unified TV Everywhere interface for all devices" to minimize consumer confusion stemming from making content "available on some platforms, but not others; and the authentication process that grants them the right to view specific programs" (Franzese, 2012).

Technological Opportunities

Optimizing Delivery Infrastructures

Cable operators are in the process of migrating their network infrastructures from traditional pay-TV distribution networks to networks that will also provide internet TV. The prospect of OTT competition provides

> operators [with] a rare opportunity to step back and re-evaluate their delivery infrastructures. This includes their ability to add

new features that can be realized by augmenting their existing delivery infrastructure with new technologies in a hybrid network, or by replacing them altogether, to enable them to combine traditional media content with Internet-delivered content.

(Hawley, 2010, p. 39)

Migrating CPE Costs to Consumers

In order to become an OTT video customer, consumers must invest in such devices as game consoles, iPads, Roku or Boxee boxes, and Apple TV. Cable operators might be able to capitalize on this by reducing or eliminating the practice of providing cable subscribers with set-top boxes and other customer premises equipment (CPE). To the extent that consumer CPE expectations/behavior changes, cable's capital costs would be reduced and operators would have more flexibility to migrate service offerings as technology changes.

Service Platform Investment

Maintaining the most widely deployed "high capacity" broadband delivery platform is a technological opportunity for cable. As Hawley indicates, "the losers in the new IP Video world will include pay-TV network operators that do not invest in their service platforms in ways that will allow them to reach consumers across the full spectrum of devices and access" (Hawley, 2010, p. 10). By continuing to make economically viable incremental improvements to its broadband delivery system/platform, cable will minimize consumer cord cutting.

Investing in Technological Innovation

Continued focus on economically viable technological innovation by cable MSOs and CableLabs will help cable operators maintain their technological edge. It will also provide them with the most favorable economic approach for deploying new technology and help reduce consumer cord cutting.

Technology and TV Everywhere

"TV Everywhere" represents an attempt by large cable MSOs (multiple system operators) to strike back against OTT. If it can be made to work technologically, OTT video providers will struggle to gain market share at cable's expense. In addition, this initiative should increase customer loyalty by providing consumers with increased choice and eliminating the need for consumers to pay multiple times for content.

Future Viability of the Cable Telecommunications Industry

SNL Kagan predicts that 12.1 million US TV households (10 percent of TV households) will have substituted OTT video service for cable, DBS, or telco multichannel video service by 2015 (Olgeirson & Myers, 2011). Magna Global predicts 8.3 million OTT video households by 2015 (Viewer watch, 2012). In light of these predictions and the information provided in this chapter, we conclude with a brief discussion of the future viability of the cable telecommunications industry.

Overall, we are of the opinion that cable will continue to be the market leader with respect to multichannel video program distribution for the foreseeable future (i.e., over the next five to ten years). However, increased competition from OTT video providers, continued improvement in the quantity and quality of OTT video, and increased desire of consumers to have maximum control over when and where they consume video will result in a declining market share for cable's core video product.

In the area of residential broadband, we expect cable to maintain its market leadership position by increasing its market share during this same time period. Expansion of consumer demand for OTT video, which requires a bigger, faster "fat pipe," will play a major role in differentiating cable's broadband service from its competitors (except for FiOS and to some extent U-verse). As a result, cable's broadband service will replace its multichannel video delivery service as cable's "core" business.

Cable's VoIP wireline service market share will also continue to increase during the time period. Given the rate at which cable's VoIP wireline customers are increasing and telco access lines are declining, we anticipate that cable's VoIP wireline market share will approach the telcos wireline market share in the next five to ten years.

In addition, cable is in the process of expanding into new business areas such as business services, home networking, and home security. If any of these areas become significant new revenue streams, they could easily offset any losses cable might suffer as a result of increased OTT video competition.

Table 2.7 provides the authors' predictions regarding the most likely to occur threats from OTT video providers and opportunities for cable MSOs to stem the OTT video tide over the next few years.

Our list of threats suggests that cable will face some regulatory barriers as it attempts to respond to OTT video competition, particularly in the area of usage based price discrimination schemes that raise the cost of OTT video distribution on cable's broadband networks. We believe that Congress and the FCC will allow cable operators to engage in some usage based pricing but probably not enough to make up for all of the revenue it could eventually lose from OTT based consumer cord cutting. We also believe that a sustainable OTT video distribution business

Table 2.7 Predictions Regarding Cable's Future

Regulatory Threats	Regulatory Opportunities
• Cable's ability to competitively respond to OTT video providers will be somewhat regulated • Cable usage based price discrimination schemes will be somewhat regulated	• Cable will work with copyright owners to maintain/increase online video copyright protection in ways that do not significantly limit cable's broadband/ high speed data service • Cable will continue to work to achieve regulatory parity with its MVPD rivals and with OTT video providers • Cable will continue to ramp up its PR/lobbying/competitive research efforts to tell its story to regulators
Competitive Threats	Competitive Opportunities
• OTT video providers will develop sustainable business models that will enable the OTT business to grow • "Niche" programming genres that are developed exclusively for internet-only TV will grow significantly and provide growth opportunities for OTT video providers	• Cable operators will develop some new revenue streams by partnering with OTT video providers • Modest success with usage based pricing will help cable finance future capital requirements as well as slow the growth of OTT video providers
Consumer Demand Threats	Consumer Demand Opportunities
• Cable will only be partially successful in responding to consumer demand for TV everywhere • Cable will receive a disproportionate amount of the blame for keeping desired video content off of the internet • Cable will be slow to develop lower priced video tiers for low income consumers	• Cable will continue to work on improving its customer service and its customer service ratings • Cable will implement a carefully constructed usage based price discrimination scheme to limit OTT video providers' ability to use too much of cable's broadband capacity without paying their fair share • Cable will do everything it can to fully implement its TV Everywhere initiative
Technological Threats	Technological Opportunities
• Cable will need to make continuous investments to upgrade the downstream and upstream bandwidth available to its customers • Usage based pricing will help cable operators allocate the cost of network usage to "heavy users," however, this effort will likely not be totally successful. As a consequence, cable operators will bear a disproportionate share of the network costs	• Increasingly, cable will have to make fewer investments in CPE. More of these costs will be borne by cable customers • Cable will continue to make economically viable incremental improvements in its broadband delivery system/platform which will help minimize the impact of OTT video

Source: Authors' Compilation.

model will be developed in the next five to ten years along with exclusive internet-only niche programming. Additionally, we expect that cable will be only partially successful in responding to consumers' demand for TV everywhere, and that cable will continue to have to make significant capital expenditures to keep up with consumers' demand for greater amounts of bandwidth and higher speed service.

Our list of opportunities suggests that cable will be somewhat successful in slowing down OTT video competition by working with copyright holders to get Congress and the courts to prevent OTT video providers from using existing video content without permission of copyright holders. Cable operators will also find ways to partner with OTT video providers to create new revenue streams for cable and its OTT "partners." Cable will also continue to improve its customer service ratings and rankings. However, given the many challenges cable faces with trying to provide TV Everywhere and consumers' current unhappiness with cable, progress in this area is likely to be fairly modest for the foreseeable future. Finally, we expect that cable will make significant progress with respect to its TV Everywhere initiative and that it will be at least partially successful in stemming the tide of OTT video competition.

Although there are many uncertainties, we are of the opinion that, in spite of the competition that it faces from over-the-top video providers, the cable industry is well positioned to deal with the capitalistic winds of "creative destruction" represented by OTT. In fact, it is very possible that cable's overall market position will be even stronger in five to ten years as it continues to find new ways to reinvent itself through use of its high capacity broadband network.

References

Accessibility driving demand for content according to Deloitte's "state of the media democracy" survey. (2012, January). *Deloitte*. Retrieved on February 19, 2012 from http://www.deloitte.com/view/en_US/us/press/Press-Releases/3ef5d7108de84310VgnVCM1000001a56f00aRCRD.htm

Ammori, M. (2010, January). *TV competition nowhere: How the cable industry is colluding to kill online TV*. Retrieved December 15, 2011 from http://www.freepress.net/files/TV-Nowhere.pdf

Anderson, C. (2008). *The longer long tail*. New York: Hyperion.

Arnold, E. K. (2011, August 7). The cable TV access crisis. *AlterNet*. Retrieved on February 28, 2012 from http://www.alternet.org/media/151905/the_cable_tv_access_crisis?page=entire

AT&T U-verse. (2012). *Wikipedia*. Retrieved February 16, 2012 from http://en.wikipedia.org/wiki/AT%26T_U-verse

Berman, S. J. (2011). *Not for free: Revenue strategies for a new world*. Boston, MA: Harvard Business Review Press.

Bookman, S. (2011, August 24). Cable customer service struggles to climb. *FierceCable*. Retrieved February 28, 2012 from http://www.fiercecable.com/special-reports/cable-customer-service-struggles-climb

Bortz Media & Sports Group. (2010). *An analysis of the cable industry's impact on the US economy*. Retrieved February 15, 2012 from http://www.ncta.com/PublicationType/ExpertStudy/Bortz-Report-2011.aspx

Bothun, D. (2009, October). The mobile evolution, pp. 1–5. *PricewaterhouseCoopers*. Retrieved on February 19, 2012 from http://www.pwc.com/us/en/industry/entertainment-media/publications/consumer-intelligence-series.jhtml

Bothun, D., & Lieberman, M. (2010, October). Discovering behaviors and attitudes related to pirating content, pp. 1–7. *PricewaterhouseCoopers*. Retrieved on February 19, 2012 from http://www.pwc.com/us/en/industry/entertainment-media/publications/consumer-intelligence-series.jhtml

Bothun, D., & Lieberman, M. (2011). Premium content consumption: Responding to the "instant access" consumer, pp. 1–9. *PricewaterhouseCoopers*. Retrieved on February 19, 2012 from http://www.pwc.com/us/en/industry/entertainment-media/publications/consumer-intelligence-series.jhtml

Cable Communications Act of 1984. (1984, October 30). Pub Law No. 98–549, 98 STAT. 2780.

Cable Television Consumer Protection and Competition Act of 1992. (1992, October 5). Pub Law No. 102–385, 106 Stat. 1460.

Convente, M. (2011, November 17). SOPA: Could this be the end of YouTube? *Pnosker.com: tech news and reviews*. Retrieved February 28, 2012 from http://tech.pnosker.com/2011/11/17/sopa-could-this-be-the-end-of-youtube/

Copyright Revision Act of 1976. (1976). 17 U.S.C. Secs. 101–810.

Court upholds FCC program access rules. (2010, March 12). *The Hollywood Reporter*, Retrieved February 28, 2012 from http://www.hollywoodreporter.com/news/court-upholds-fcc-program-access-21583

Cox, W. M., & Alm, R. (2008). Creative destruction. *The concise encyclopedia of economics*. Retrieved February 10, 2012 from http://www.econlib.org/library/Enc/CreativeDestruction.html

Donahue, S. (2011, December 23). 2011 year in review: Retransmission consent battles get ugly. *FierceCable*. Retrieved February 28, 2012 from http://www.fiercecable.com/special-reports/2011-year-review-cable-goes-gaga-mobile/2011-year-review-retransmission-consent-batt

Eckert, H. C. (2011, June 16). Ninth Circuit rejects consumer antitrust challenge to cable television bundling. *Antitrust Law Blog*. Retrieved on February 19, 2012 from http://www.antitrustlawblog.com/2011/06/articles/article/ninth-circuit-rejects-consumer-antitrust-challenge-to-cable-television-bundling/

Economides, N. (2011, fourth quarter). Broadband openness rules are fully justified by economic research. *Communication & Strategies*, No. 84, pp. 1–25. Retrieved on December 15, 2011 from http://works.bepress.com/ecnomides/36

FCC acts to preserve internet freedom and openness. (2010, December 21). FCC News Release, Retrieved February 19, 2012 from http://www.fcc.gov

FCC to examine prohibition on exclusive contracts. (2001, October 11). FCC News Release, Retrieved February 28, 2012 from http://www.fcc.gov

Franzese, G. (2012, January 3). What smart TV viewers really want in 2012: Viewer watch report. *VideoMind*. Retrieved on February 29, 2012 from http://videomind.ooyala.com/blog/what-smart-tv-viewers-really-want-2012-viewer-watch-report

Grant, A. E., & Meadows, J. H. (2006). *Communication technology update* (tenth edn.). Boston: Focal Press.

Grant, A. E., & Meadows, J. H. (2010). *Communication technology update and fundamentals* (12th edn.). Boston: Elsevier Inc.

Harris, D. (2012, January). How P2P could save the set-top box by improving VOD. *Gigaom*. Retrieved on February 19, 2012 from http://gigaom.com/cloud/how-p2p-and-big-data-could-save-the-set-top-box/

Hawley, S. (2010, October). *TV anywhere: How the internet & mobile technologies will change the pay-TV industry*. Cambridge, MA: Pyramid Research.

Hearn, E. T. (1990, February 18). Cable TV industry takes crack at self-regulation. *Chicago Tribune*. Retrieved February 28, 2012 from http://articles.chicagotribune.com/1990-02-18/business/9001140469_1_cable-industry-national-cable-television-association-cable-users

Interactive Television Institute. (2012). List of over-the-top TV businesses. Retrieved February 23, 2012 from http://www.itvdictionary.com/index.php?ax=list&sub=58&cat_id=58

JSI Capital Advisors Blog. (2011, September 14). Why video cord cutting is bad for telcos—Even those that don't offer video. Retrieved February 27, 2012 from http://www.jsicapitaladvisors.com/the-ilec-advisor/2011/9/14/why-video-cord-cutting-is-bad-for-telcoseven-those-that-dont.html

Kirjner, C., Parameswaran, R., & Chan, A. (2012, February 15). YouTube economics—A riddle wrapped in a mystery inside an enigma. *Bernstein Research*.

Lawler, R. (2011, September 16). How over-the-top video actually helps the cable industry. Retrieved February 23, 2012 from http://gigaom.com/video/over-the-top-cablevision/

Moffett, C., Deo, N. D., & Chan, A. (2011, September 13). US telecom and US pay TV: The low end consumer, and the looming affordability crisis. *Bernstein Research*, 1–13.

Moffett, C., Deo, N. D., Findlay, M., & Chan, A. (2012, February 28). Time Warner Cable (TWC): The carrot and the stick ... usage based pricing comes (back) to Texas. *Bernstein Research*, 1–4.

Moffett, C., Deo, N. D., Possavino, R., & Chan, A. (2010, November 30). Video cord cutting: Urban myth or the beginning of the end? *Bernstein Research*, 1–32.

Moffett, C., Deo, N. D., Possavino, R., & Chan, A. (2010, December). US telecommunications and cable & satellite: Capital punishment. *Bernstein Research*, 1–251.

Moffett, C., Deo, N. D., Possavino, R., & Pan, P. (2009, June 11). US telecommunications, cable & satellite: The dumb pipe paradox, revisited. *Bernstein Research*, 1–22.

Moffett, C., Deo, N. D., Possavino, R., & Weisgall, A. (2010, February 16). The long view: Beyond video ... taking the measure of the broadband-centric cable MSO. *Bernstein Research*, 1–25.

Moffett, C., Deo, N. D., Possavino, R., & Weisgall, A. (2010, May 10). US cable: Pulling the plug ... regulatory uncertainty clouds terminal growth rates. *Bernstein Research*, 1–28.

Moffett, C., Deo, N. D., Possavino, R., & Weisgall, A. (2010, June 8). US satellite: The growth question ... and what valuations say about expectations. *Bernstein Research*, 1–34.

Moffett, C., Kirjner, C., Deo, N. D., Findlay, M., Parameswaran, R., & Chan, A. (2012, January 27). Why haven't we seen a virtual MSO yet? *Bernstein Research*, 1–6.

Moffett, C., Possavino, R., & Deo, N. D. (2010, October 18). US cable and US telecommunications: Broadband end game? *Bernstein Research*, 1–37.

Moffett, C., Possavino, R., & Deo, N. D. (2010, October 22). The poverty problem. *Bernstein Research*, 1–4.

Moyler, A., & Hooper, M. (2009, November 20). Over the top TV (OTT TV) platform technologies. Retrieved February 23, 2012 from http://www.bci.eu.com/category/white-papers/

National Cable Telecommunication Association. (Various). Retrieved from http://ncta.com/Statistics.aspx

Noll, A. M. (1997). *Highway of dreams: A critical view along the information superhighway*. Mahwah, NJ: Lawrence Erlbaum Associates.

Olgeirson, I., & Myers, D. (2011, July 15). Over-the-top substitution forecast to erode multichannel penetrations. *SNL Kagan Economics of Internet Media*. Retrieved December 5, 2011 from http://www.snl.com/InteractiveX/default.aspx?

Owen, B. M. (1999). *The internet challenge to television*. Cambridge, MA: Harvard University Press.

Parsons, P. R. (2008). *Blue skies: A history of cable television*. Philadelphia, PA: Temple University Press.

Pye, H., & Acker, C. (2011, January/February). The future of cable TV, part 5: Over-the-top video. *Broadband Properties*. Retrieved February 23, 2012 from http://www.bbpmag.com/2011mags/janfeb11/BBP_JanFeb11_OwnersCorner.pdf

Schumpeter, J. (1942). *Capitalism, socialism, and democracy*. New York: Harper and Brothers.

Shayon, S. (2012, January 27). Time Warner and Time Warner Cable bring future of tech to big apple. *Brandchannel*. Retrieved February 28, 2012 from http://www.brandchannel.com/home/post/2012/01/27/Time-Warner-Medialab-012712.aspx

Southwick, T. P. (1998). *Distant signals: How cable TV changed the world of telecommunications*. Overland Park, KS: Primedia Intertec.

Spangler, T. (2011, September 1). Starz to pull plug on Netflix deal. Retrieved February 27, 2012 from http://www.multichannel.com

Spangler, T. (2011, October 17). Telco, satellite-TV subs still happier than cable's. Retrieved December 15, 2011 from http://www.multichannel.com

Stelter, B., & Carter, B. (2010, October 16). In cable TV fights, consumers wait to see who blinks. *The New York Times*. Retrieved on February 28, 2012 from http://www.nytimes.com/2010/10/17/business/media/17cable.html

Tedesco, R. (1999, March 8). Who'll control the video streams? *Broadcasting*, 20–4.

Telecommunications Act of 1996. (1996, February 8). Pub Law 104–104, 110 STAT. 56.

The difference engine: Politics and the web. (2010, December 24). *The Economist*. Retrieved February 19, 2012 from http://www.economist.com/blogs/babbage/2010/12/net_neutrality

The "long tail" of video is about to get longer—What role will cable play? (2005, March). *Broadband Directions*. Retrieved on February 19, 2012 from http://www.broadbanddirections.com/0503.html

Verizon FiOS. (2012). *Wikipedia*. Retrieved February 16, 2012 from http://en.wikipedia.org/wiki/Verizon_FiOS

Viewer watch 2012: Annual report on consumer behavior. (2012, January 2). *Multichannel News*, pp. 9, 12–20. Retrieved on February 19, 2012 from https://www.multichannel.com

Wagging the video long tail. (2012, January 10). *Entertainment Marketing Media*. Retrieved on February 19, 2012 from http://entertainmentmarketingmedia.com/tag/the-long-tail/

Winslow, G. (2012a, January 2). Measuring TV everywhere's progress, p. 11. Retrieved on February 19, 2012 from http://www.multichannel.com

Winslow, G. (2012b, January 2). More content, less clarity, p. 10. Retrieved on February 19, 2012 from http://www.multichannel.com

Wirth, M., & Collette, L. (2001). Should Congress establish a compulsory license for internet video providers to transmit over-the-air TV station programming via the internet? In Compaine, B. M., & Greenstein, S. (Eds.). *Communications policy in transition: The internet and beyond*. Cambridge, MA: MIT Press, pp. 397–416.

Wirtz, B. W. (2011). *Media and internet management*. Germany: Gabler Verlag.

3

INNOVATION FAILURE
A Case Study Analysis of Eastman Kodak and Blockbuster Inc.

Richard A. Gershon, Ph.D.

Introduction

The lessons of business history have taught us that there is no such thing as a static market. There are no guarantees of continued business success for companies regardless of the field of endeavor. Schumpeter (1942) introduced the principle of *creative destruction* as a way to describe the disruptive process that accompanies the work of the entrepreneur and the consequences of innovation.[1] In time, companies that once revolutionized and dominated select markets give way to rivals who are able to introduce improved product designs, offer substitute products and services, and/or lower manufacturing costs. The resulting outcome of creative destruction can be significant including the failure to preserve market leadership, the discontinuation of a once highly successful product line or in the worse case scenario—business failure itself.

This chapter presents a unique opportunity to look at modern media and information technology and the problems associated with preserving market leadership. Specifically, it will address the following question: Why do good companies fail to remain innovative over time? This chapter will further consider some of the contributing reasons that lead to business failure. The arguments presented in this research inquiry are theory-based and supported by case-study evidence. Special attention is given to two media companies: Eastman Kodak Corporation and Blockbuster Inc. These companies were selected because they directly experienced the effects of a disruptive and changing technology that eventually resulted in business failure. A major argument of this chapter is that the warning signs of a troubled business often exist for long periods of time before they combine with enabling conditions to produce a significant business failure (Collins, 2009). Both Eastman Kodak and Blockbuster knew they were at risk of failing well in advance of their eventual decline. If two

Table 3.1 Successful Innovation: Feature Elements

The innovation is based on a <u>novel principle</u> that challenges management orthodoxy.	Sony: Walkman portable music stereo and Apple iPad computer tablet
The innovation is <u>systemic</u>; that is, it involves a range of processes and methods.	Dell Computer: Direct-to-home sales delivery, Just-in-time manufacturing, 24/7 customer support.
The innovation is part of an <u>ongoing commitment</u> to develop new and enhanced products and services.	Apple: iPod; iTunes; iPhone; iPad

Source: R. Gershon, adapted from Gary Hamel (2006).

such highly respected media companies can go from iconic to irrelevant, what might we learn by studying their downfall and how do other companies avoid a similar fate?

Innovation and Lasting Advantage

Innovation is important because it creates lasting advantage for a company or organization (Hamel, 2006). It allows a business to develop and improve on its existing product line as well as preparing the ground work for the future. Successful innovation occurs when it meets one or more of the following conditions. First, the innovation is based on a novel principle that challenges management orthodoxy. Second, the innovation is systemic; that is, it involves a range of processes and methods. Third, the innovation is part of an ongoing commitment to develop new and enhanced products and services. There is natural progression in product design and development (Hamel, 2006). Table 3.1 provides a clear illustration of the above principles.

While most organizations recognize the importance of innovation, there is a wide degree of latitude regarding the method and approach to innovation. For some business enterprises, innovation is deliberative and planned. It is built into the cultural fabric of a company's ongoing research and development efforts. Other times, innovation is the direct result of a triggering event; that is, a change in external market conditions or internal performance that forces a change in business strategy (Wheelen & Hunger, 1998).

Understanding Business Failure

We begin by asking the question: What is business failure? At first glance, business failure is typically associated with bankruptcy or poor financial performance. But at a deeper level, business failure is also about the proverbial "fall from grace." A company that once dominated an industry no longer finds itself the market leader. The company is faced with a public perception that it has lost all relevancy in an otherwise highly competitive business and technology environment (Charran & Useem, 2002). The fall from grace is best illustrated by a dramatic downturn in the company's stock value.

The consequences are very real, both symbolically and financially. There are several reasons that help to explain why companies experience business failure. They include:

- The Tyranny of Success;
- Organizational Culture;
- Lengthy Development Times and Poor Coordination;
- Risk Averse Culture;
- Executive Leadership Failures;
- The Challenges of a Disruptive Technology.

The Tyranny of Success

Past success can sometimes make an organization very complacent; that is, they lose the sense of urgency to create new opportunities (Tushman & O'Reilly, 1997). Collins (2001) makes the point unequivocally when he writes that, "good is the enemy of great" (p. 16). Companies, like people, can become easily satisfied with organizational routines. They become preoccupied with fine-tuning and making slight adjustments to an existing product line rather than preparing for the future. They are engaged in what MIT's Negroponte (1995) describes as the problem of "incrementalism." Says Negroponte, "incrementalism is innovation's worst enemy" (p. 188). The history of business is filled with examples of past companies where senior management failed to plan for the future. Such companies did not anticipate a time when a substitute product (or changing market conditions) might come along and dramatically alter the playing field.

IBM

As an example, IBM made its name and fortune in the development of mainframe computers. At the start of the 1980s, IBM recognized that the computing needs of the modern business organization were undergoing a major change. More and more, business computing was shifting away from the centralized mainframe towards the standalone desk top computer. Initially, IBM got it right with the development of the IBM PC. But the wild success of the IBM PC also began to undermine the company's core mainframe business. Instead of adjusting to the future,

IBM became a victim to its own corporate bureaucracy and past success (Carroll, 1993). In the end, the company could not let go of mainframe computer design principles despite the numerous studies commissioned by senior management arguing to the contrary.

Organizational Culture

Organizational culture (or corporate culture) refers to the collection of beliefs, values, and expectations shared by an organization's members and transmitted from one generation of employees to another (Schein, 1983). Organizations (even large ones) are human constructions. They are made and transformed by individuals. Culture is embedded and transmitted through both implicit and explicit messages such as formal statements, organizational philosophy, and adherence to management orthodoxies, deliberate role modeling, and behavioral displays by senior management (Pilotta, Widman, & Jasko, 1988).

But what happens when organizational culture stands in the way of innovation? What happens when being tied to the past (and past practices) interferes with a company's ability to move forward? The combination of past success coupled with an unbending adherence to management orthodoxy can seriously undermine a company's ability to step out of itself and plan for the future Suddenly, creative thinking and the ability to float new ideas gets caught up in a stifling bureaucracy. Sometimes what passes for management wisdom and experience is inflexibility masquerading as absolute truth (Hamel, 2006).

AT&T

Following the break-up of AT&T in 1984, one of the company's most salient issues was how to address the organization's own internal culture. The management at AT&T understood the external challenges. The problem was how to overcome the company's institutionalized bureaucracy dating back to the days of Alexander Graham Bell.

Business journalist Leslie Cauley (2005) irreverently refers to AT&T's organizational culture as "the Machine":

> Literally a century in the making, the culture was so omnipresent that it even had its own nickname: the Machine. It was an apt moniker. Almost impenetrable to outsiders ... the Machine steadfastly resisted change, and embraced those who did the same.
> (pp. 116–117)

The new AT&T was faced with competitive challenges on a number of fronts including competitive services from the Regional Bell Operating

Companies (RBOCs) Verizon and SBC as well as the advent of cellular telephony which proved insurmountable. Long distance telephony was fast becoming a commodity and was no longer a sustainable business. Talented employees who attempted to test the boundary waters of AT&T's organizational culture were met with such well worn corporate phrases as "that's not the AT&T way." It would only be a matter of time before AT&T would be sold off in pieces to the highest bidder. One of those companies was Southwestern Bell Corporation (SBC) which would later rename itself the new AT&T.

Lengthy Development Times and Poor Coordination

The combination of changing technology and shifting consumer demands makes speed to market paramount today. Yet companies often can't organize themselves to move faster. Too often, companies that are highly compartmentalized can become immobilized when it comes to fast turnaround times, given the entrenchment of existing departments and area silos. This, in turn, results in a lack of coordination that can seriously impair product innovation and development times. Lengthy development times and poor coordination are closely tied to the execution of strategy. The problem often starts with executive failure to properly articulate the goals of the strategic plan to the organization as a whole.

Microsoft Vista

In January 2007, after years of hype and anticipation, Microsoft unveiled its Windows Vista operating system (OS) to a decidedly lukewarm reception by the PC community, IT pros, and tech savvy users alike. Instead of a revolutionary next-generation operating system, Vista was plagued with performance and compatibility problems from the start.[2] Following its immediate launch, Vista proved significantly less stable than its predecessor XP OS. Computer users experienced more hard locks, crashes, and blue screens. In time, Windows Vista lost all credibility. It was not until Microsoft introduced its Windows 7 operating system that the company could effectively start over again and restore public confidence in its software products.

Risk Averse Culture

Successful businesses with an established customer base find it hard to change. There is a clear pattern of success that translates into customer clients, predictable revenue, and public awareness for the work that has been accomplished to date. The adage "why mess with a winning formula" slowly becomes the corporate norm. There are no guarantees of success when it comes to new project ventures. The difficulty, of course, is that playing it safe presents its own unique hazards. Even well managed companies can suddenly find themselves outflanked by changing market conditions and advancing new technologies.

Sony

Consider, for example, the impact that the Apple iPod had on the Sony Walkman portable music player. Sony's co-founder Akio Morita was the quintessential marketer. He understood how to translate new and interesting technologies into usable products (Nathan, 1999). Nowhere was this more evident than in the development of the original Sony Walkman portable music player in 1979. The Walkman created an entirely new market for portable music systems. By combining the features of mobility and privacy, the Walkman contributed to an important change in consumer lifestyle (Gershon & Kanayama, 2002).

But even a company as respected as Sony was not invulnerable to the problems associated with innovation failure. As illegal music downloads exploded in popularity in the late 1990s, Sony, like the rest of the music industry, was unable or unwilling to adapt to the changing technology environment. Instead, the company was committed to its existing mini-disk technology. The introduction of the Apple iPod in 2001 proved to be a watershed event in digital music. The Apple iPod in combination with its iTunes music store in 2004 created the first sustainable music downloading business model of its kind and redefined the music industry forever (Gershon, 2009). Sony, for its part, knew about the research and development work being done at Apple. Yet it was not prepared to move quickly enough and adjust strategy in order to preserve market leadership in the area of portable music.

Executive Leadership Failures

Leadership is a process that involves influence and the art of directing people within an organization to achieve a clearly defined set of goals and outcomes. Successful leaders know what they want to accomplish in terms of organizational outcomes. In his book, *Leading Change*, Kotter (1996), suggests that a leader's strategic vision should convey a picture of what the future will look like as well as appealing to the long term interests of organizational members, customers, and others who have a stake in the enterprise.

Celebrity Leaders

The challenge for a company occurs when the executive leader loses perspective on his/her own role within the organization. In time, the executive leader becomes bigger than the organization itself. They become an example of what Collins (2001) describes as celebrity leaders. Examples might include Ted Turner, former CEO of Turner Broadcasting and Steve Jobs, Apple. According to Collins, fellow managers and board members are less likely to challenge the strategic vision of a charismatic leader out of respect for the CEO's past success and/or by not wanting to appear contrary.

Corporate Governance

Closely tied to failures in executive leadership are the problems associated with corporate governance. The role of a corporate board of directors is to provide independent oversight and guidance to the CEO and company's staff of senior executives. This can include everything from approving new strategic initiatives to reviewing CEO performance. One of the important goals of corporate governance should be to prevent significant mistakes in corporate strategy and to ensure that when mistakes happen, they can be corrected quickly (Pound, 2002). The problem occurs when a corporate board of directors ignore their fiduciary responsibility by failing to challenge questionable corporate strategy and/or by permitting unethical business practices to occur. More problematic is when a corporate board loses its sense of independence. In the worst case scenario, failures in corporate governance can lead to a diffusion of authority, where neither company nor person is fully aware of or takes responsibility for the actions of senior management (Cohan, 2002).

Activist Shareholders

The opposite issue can be equally problematic. Instead of board members being too passive, they can sometimes become too active in their responsibilities.

Typically, such members tend to have an equity stake in the company and are sometimes referred to as activist shareholders. The reasons for shareholder activism can vary in size and purpose from differences in management strategy to disagreements concerning executive compensation. Shareholder activism can take different forms including proxy battles, publicity campaigns, shareholder resolutions, and litigation.

The Challenges of a Disruptive Technology

Rogers (1995) defines innovation as "an idea, practice or object that is perceived as new by an individual" (p. 11). In principle, there are two kinds of innovation; namely, sustaining technologies versus disruptive technologies. A sustaining technology has to do with product improvement and performance. The goal is to improve on an existing technology by adding new and enhanced feature elements (Christensen, 1997, 2003). In contrast, a disruptive (or breakthrough) technology represents an altogether different approach to an existing product design and process. A disruptive technology redefines the playing field by introducing to the marketplace a unique value proposition.

Authors Collins and Porras (1994) make the argument that highly successful companies are those that are willing to experiment and not rest on their past success. In time, tastes, consumer preference, and technology change. It's hard for even the most innovative companies to stay current. The decisions that lead to failure are sometimes made by executives widely regarded as the best in their field.

The Innovator's Dilemma

Researcher Clayton Christensen (1997) suggests that even the best managed companies are susceptible to innovation failure. In fact, past success can sometimes become the root cause of innovation failure going forward. The main reason is that such companies are highly committed to serving their existing customers and are often unable (or unwilling) to take apart a highly successful business in favor of advancing unfamiliar and unproven new technology and service. Christensen (1997) posits what he calls the *innovator's dilemma*; namely, that a company's very strengths (i.e., realizing consistent profits and being responsive to customer needs) now become barriers to change and the agents of a company's potential decline.

Accordingly, strength becomes weakness, and the same reasons that enabled a company to become successful are now responsible for its failure. Advancing new technologies and services requires expensive retooling and whose ultimate success is hard to predict. Such companies lose because they fail to invest in new product development and/or because they fail to notice small niche players who enter the market and are prepared to offer customers alternative solutions at better value. The anticipated profit margins in developing a future market niche can be hard to justify given the high cost of entry; not to mention the possible destabilization of an otherwise highly successful business. Therein lies the innovator's dilemma. As we shall see, the innovator's dilemma was a major contributing factor to the events that led to the downfall of Eastman Kodak and Blockbuster Inc.

The Eastman Kodak Company

The Eastman Kodak Company (commonly known as Kodak) is a pioneering company in the field of photography. The company was founded by

George Eastman in 1889 and is headquartered in Rochester, New York. Kodak is best known for a wide range of photographic and imaging equipment. Throughout most of the twentieth century, Kodak was singularly the most important company in the production and sale of film equipment. The company's visibility and dominance was evidenced by the phrase "Kodak moment" which became part of the public lexicon to describe a personal event worthy of being recorded for posterity (Jasper, 2012). On January 19, 2012, the 131-year-old company filed for bankruptcy. It was several years in the making, but Kodak steadily faltered beneath the wave of advancing digital media technology (DeLaMerced, 2012).

The Start of Kodak

Founded by George Eastman, Kodak became one of America's most notable companies, helping establish the market for film and instamatic cameras which the company dominated for most of the twentieth century. Eastman did not invent photography. He did, however, make it accessible to large numbers of people by introducing a simple camera called the Kodak. As Genzlinger (2000) points out,

> before Eastman, photography was like portrait painting. Subjects would sit prim and still while a photographer wielding a bulky camera, glass plates and assorted chemicals caught the moment. The moment, though, had to last some seconds to allow for exposure, and the life captured by these early photographers was one without spontaneity. Eastman changed all that
>
> (p. 15)

Eastman would eventually replace the wet-plate process, in which the photographer used chemical additives, to a dry-plate system which involved using a kind of precoated glass. Later, he replaced the glass plates with rolled paper film. The goal was to make shooting a photograph a much simpler process. By 1884, Kodak had become a household name. One of the company's first marketing campaigns contained the slogan, "You press the button, and we do the rest" (Gavetti, Henderson, & Giorgi, 2005).

Eastman's work led to the creation of the "Kodak" camera. The Kodak was a fairly expensive camera in the beginning stages of its design. It would eventually give way to the Brownie family camera designed by Kodak's Frank Brownell. Throughout the years, Kodak has led the way with an abundance of new products and processes, including the introduction of Kodachrome which set the stage for color photographs. Kodachrome became the color film standard throughout the 1950s and 1960s. In the 1960s, Kodak also introduced the "instamatic camera." The company achieved $1 billion in sales in 1962. By 1976, Kodak captured the majority of the US film and camera market (90 percent and 85 percent, respectively). Kodak's photofinishing process quickly became the industry standard for quality ("Kodak legacy," 2012). As a result, a major focus of the company was on its massive film-making plant. Traditionally, most of the company's CEOs had a strong manufacturing background.

The External Challenges: Rivalry with Fujifilm

Starting in the 1970s, Kodak was faced with a number of foreign competitors; most notably, Fujifilm of Japan, which undercut Kodak's prices. In the beginning, Kodak did not take the competitive threat seriously. That complacency proved to be costly when the company passed on the opportunity to become the official film sponsor of the 1984 Summer Olympics in Los Angeles. That decision gave Fuji high visibility, sponsorship rights, and a permanent foothold in the US film market. Soon thereafter, Fuji opened up a film plant in the US, cut prices, and aggressively marketed its film product. Fuji's US market share went from 10 percent to over 20 percent by the late 1990s. At the same time, Kodak was unsuccessful in penetrating the Japanese market; then considered the second largest market for film and paper after the US.

In 1995, Kodak filed a petition with the US Commerce Department (and later the World Trade Organization, WTO) arguing that its poor performance in the Japanese market was the direct result of unfair trade practices adopted by Fuji and the Japanese government. The WTO soundly rejected the Kodak petition. Kodak's financial results for fiscal year 1997 showed that corporate revenues dropped more than 10 percent from $15.9 billion to $14.3 billion. Kodak experienced a simultaneous drop in market share from 80.1 percent to 74.7 percent in the US, a one year drop of five percentage points (Finnerty, 2000). Kodak was rightly criticized for being slow to react and for underestimating its rivals.

Kodak also found itself at odds with its chief camera rival, the Polaroid Corporation. In October 1990, Kodak found itself on the losing end of the largest patent-infringement case of its kind. The company was forced to pay Polaroid $909.4 million for infringing on seven of Polaroid's instant photography patents. That decision forced Kodak out of the instant photography business ("Kodak legacy," 2012).

The Shift to Digital Cameras

As early as 1981, Kodak recognized that a shift in digital camera technology was underway. That year, Sony Corporation announced the launch of a new digital camera called Mavica. At the time, it was described as a filmless digital camera that would display pictures on a television screen

(Gavetti et al., 2005). Kodak had some prior experience with digital cameras, having invented one of the early prototype designs as early as 1975. Starting in the early 1980s, Kodak began the process of entering into digital cameras and film. Throughout most of that decade, Kodak introduced more than 50 products that were tied to digital photography and the storage of images. Yet the company was unable to successfully commercialize them (Lucas & Goh, 2009). At the same time, Kodak was fully committed to traditional film technology and processing. By the 1990s, the onset of digital photography started to erode the demand for conventional film and processing, thereby, putting a squeeze on Kodak's business.

The Advantages of Going Digital

Digital photography has many advantages over traditional film. Digital photos are convenient and allow the user to see the results instantly. Digital photos don't require the costs associated with film and development time. Digital cameras enable the user to take multiple shots at no additional cost. They can be stored on a variety of digital devices, including personal computers, smart phones, tablets as well as being uploaded on to the Internet. All this points to the fact that the transition to digital media is not just about a single product; but, rather, about significant changes to communication display and storage processes (Gershon, 2009). Digital photography proved to be the ultimate disruptive technology. It was only a matter of time before traditional film processing would become obsolete.

Executive Leadership Challenges

Between 1983 and 1993, Kodak underwent seven organizational restructurings. In 1993, Kay Whitmore (a Kodak insider) stepped down as CEO and was succeeded by George Fisher. Fisher was recruited from Motorola where he had successfully revitalized that company. As Kodak's newly appointed CEO, Fisher began steering the company to embrace a digital future. The goal was to enhance, not replace, conventional film. He brought more outsiders into the company and began investing heavily in China and other emerging markets. Fisher began the first in a set of new initiatives to reach out to companies like Microsoft and Apple. Most proved unsuccessful. Kodak executives could not imagine a world without traditional film (Gavetti et al., 2005). Despite a clear understanding of the problem, Kodak couldn't seem to shake off its complacency.

Fisher clearly recognized that the organizational culture at Kodak had to change. The importance of digital media and communication had to be understood and embraced at all levels of the organization. To that end, he hired Dr. John White, a former US government official with extensive private sector experience, to serve as one of his change agents. The challenge, however, would prove formidable. While Kodak recognized the importance of digital media to its future, the company wanted to engage the process in its own way while staying within the confines of its Rochester, New York headquarters. This was ultimately a recipe for failure. The creativity demands for producing digital media are so vastly different than traditional photography. Kodak's leadership was not prepared to impose the kind of disruptive changes on the organization that would have been required (Swasy, 1997).

Kodak eventually settled on a combination strategy whereby it created a separate digital and applied imaging division while still preserving its core capabilities in traditional film. By 1993, Kodak had spent $5 billion to research and develop digital cameras and imaging equipment.

While Kodak had the right intentions, the company's middle management resisted the move toward digital photography for a variety of reasons. At issue were the high costs associated with developing new production facilities as well as a genuine concern that such changes might result in a loss of jobs. In the meantime, Kodak continued to miss critical target dates and experienced multiple setbacks in research and development. The company was unable to bring significantly new products to market. Former Hewlett-Packard CEO Carly Fiorina made the following observation:

> Kodak sat on a mountain of cash and profitability in their traditional photography business and I believe their thinking was digital photography will eat into my traditional and most profitable business. I don't want that to happen ...
> Kodak miscalculated about [who was in charge] ... Consumers were in charge. Individuals were in charge.
> (quoted in Lucas & Goh, 2009, p. 54)

The Challenges of Staying Competitive

The year 2001 proved to be an important cutover point. The company experienced a significant drop in film sales. CEO Daniel Carp (Fisher's successor) continued the process of moving the company into digital cameras. It began by introducing the EasyShare family of digital cameras. Kodak spent tremendous resources studying customer behavior, finding out that women in particular loved taking digital photos but found it difficult to transfer them to their computers. This unmet need presented a major opportunity for Kodak. The goal was to manufacture multiple digital camera designs that made it easy for people to share photos with friends and family members via their PCs. One of their major innovations was a printer dock, where consumers could insert their cameras into this compact device, press a button, and watch their photos roll out. By 2005, Kodak became the number one digital camera manufacturer in the US with sales having risen 40 percent to $5.7 billion.

Despite its impressive start, Kodak's digital camera line became quickly copied by Asian competitors that could produce equivalent cameras at lower cost. Digital cameras soon proved to be a low profit margin item. In order to stay competitive, Kodak found itself losing money on every digital camera sold. Consumer electronics companies like Sony, Panasonic, and Canon could afford to be patient and lose money on select line items because they have hundreds of other products to offset potential losses. Not so for Kodak, which had a limited product line. The final *coup de grâce* came with the onset of cellphones equipped with cameras. In one sense, the cellphone camera represents the dumbing down of picture-taking since the quality is not as good as a camera. That said, a younger generation of users are willing to sacrifice picture quality for convenience. By 2010, Kodak ranked seventh behind Canon, Sony, Nikon, and others in digital camera sales. Today, cameras have become a standard feature on all smart phone devices.

Adjusting to Market Realities and Bankruptcy

At the time of writing, Kodak's financial reserves have reached a critical stage. The company has $5.1 billion in assets and nearly $6.8 billion in debts. Its biggest group of unsecured creditors were bondholders represented by the Bank of New York Mellon who are owed $658 million. Kodak filed for Chapter 11 protection in January 2012 and has exited select operations by closing 13 manufacturing plants and 130 processing labs while reducing its workforce by 47,000 employees (DeLaMerced, 2012). In a final effort to stabilize its finances, Kodak hired asset management firm Lazard Ltd. to sell its 1,100 digital imaging patents. This proved too little too late. Kodak had failed to generate enough potential interest, driven in part by fears of the company's deteriorating financial health.

In the end, George Fisher was unable to transform Kodak into a high-tech growth company (Lucas & Goh, 2009). Fisher's belief in the future of digital communication lacked urgency and did not permeate all levels of the organization. Nor were successors Daniel Carp (2000–2005) and Antonio Pérez (2005–2012) any more successful. Under Pérez's leadership, Kodak tried to reinvent itself by focusing on printers, packaging, and work force software. That strategy proved unsuccessful as well. The price of Kodak shares decreased from around $25 in 2005 to less than $1 by September 30, 2011. It was emblematic of the fall of a great American company.

Blockbuster

Blockbuster Inc. (currently Blockbuster LLC) is an American-based DVD and videogame rental service. Blockbuster was founded by David Cook, who used his experience with managing large database networks as the foundation for Blockbuster's retail distribution model. At its peak in 2009, Blockbuster had an estimated 7,100 retail stores in the US with additional locations in 17 countries worldwide, and had over 60,000 employees in the US and worldwide. The company is headquartered in McKinney, Texas (Blockbuster Inc., 2012).

Because of competition from other video rental services, most notably Netflix and RedBox, Blockbuster has sustained significant revenue losses in recent years. The company filed for bankruptcy just shy of its 25th anniversary on September 22, 2010. In April 2011, Blockbuster was acquired by satellite television service provider Dish Network at an auction price of $233 million and the assumption of $87 million in liabilities and other obligations.

The acquisition was completed on April 26, 2011 ("Dish network wins bidding," 2011).

The Start of Blockbuster Video

The first Blockbuster store opened October 1985 in Dallas, Texas. Shortly thereafter, the company's founder David Cook opened several additional stores and later built a $6 million warehouse in Garland, Texas that could service them all. The key to Blockbuster's early success was the convenience and ease of renting film entertainment for consumer use. Another important factor to Blockbuster's early success was its timely access to recently released feature films combined with films on VHS geared to the neighborhood demographics of its local retail outlets.

In 1987, Waste Management president Wayne Huizenga and his business partner John Melk paid Cook $18 million for a controlling interest in the new startup company. Together, they used the lessons from their experience with Waste Management to build Blockbuster into a global enterprise. Huizenga took the company public in 1989 and aggressively transformed it from a $7 million business with 19 stores to a $4 billion global enterprise with more than 3,700 stores in 11 countries. They also bought every video rental franchise they could reasonably acquire and spent the better part of the late 1980s acquiring several of Blockbuster's key rivals (DeGeorge, 1996).

Viacom Acquires Blockbuster Video

Despite Blockbuster's success, Huizenga felt that it was only a matter of time before technology advancements would directly challenge Blockbuster's bricks and mortar approach. In 1994, Huizenga sold Blockbuster to Viacom Inc. for $8.4 billion. The Blockbuster acquisition was seen as a way to use the company's healthy cash flow to service the massive $10 billion debt that Viacom incurred when it acquired Paramount Pictures. The idea was correct in principle but the Blockbuster business model had one serious flaw. The problem in part had to do with the high cost of acquiring videotapes from various Hollywood studios, which made it difficult to stock the shelves with an adequate level of inventory at Blockbuster's multiple store outlets. The movie studios sold VHS cassettes to rental companies for about $65 apiece. In practical terms, a rental store would have to rent out each tape about 30 times in order to be successful. That represents a significant upfront cost for a product whose consumer appeal is temporary; that is, the first few weeks after the movie has been released (Antioco, 2011). Add to the retail mix that stores like Blockbuster have to maintain a diverse inventory where the rental numbers are not likely to offset the cost of acquiring less popular titles. This, in turn, forced a strict limit on the number of tapes that Blockbuster was able to afford per store site. As a consequence, many customers would leave Blockbuster empty handed, unable to find the tapes they wanted. By 1997, this strategy fell apart as Blockbuster sustained a pre-tax loss of $323 million ("The vindication of Sumner Redstone," 1998). To make matters worse, Viacom had to write off two-thirds of Blockbuster's tape inventory valued at $315 million.

The untenable situation led to the firing of Blockbuster's then CEO, Bill Fields, who was replaced by John Antioco. During the next six months, Viacom President and CEO Sumner Redstone, working with Antioco and his management team, was able to redesign the company's business model. They came up with an alternative revenue sharing scheme, whereby Blockbuster would buy tapes from the studios at one to two dollars per tape. Blockbuster, in turn, would give back approximately 40 percent of the rental revenue per tape to the studios. The new revenue sharing model resulted in a dramatic turnaround at Blockbuster and, by 1998, the company saw a 17.6 percent increase in revenues. For the next six years, Blockbuster experienced steady growth and performance with revenues reaching in excess of $6 billion in 2003 and 2004 (Antioco, 2011).

Netflix and Business Process Innovation

Today, innovation is about much more than developing new products. It's about reinventing business processes and building entirely new markets to meet untapped customer needs. Business process innovation involves creating systems and methods for improving organizational performance (Gershon, 2011). The application of business process innovation can be found in a variety of settings and locations within an organizational structure, including product development, manufacturing, inventory management, customer service, and distribution (Davenport, 1993). It renders two important consequences. First, a highly successful business process is transformative; that is, it creates efficiencies that benefit the organization as well as the end user. Second, it sets into motion a host of imitators who see the inherent value in applying the same business process to their own organization (Gershon, 2011).

Blockbuster was the right technology for the time. It was a 20-year interim technology that provided a practical solution in meeting the needs for home television viewing. As early as 1994, Wayne Huizenga understood the limitations of Blockbuster's bricks and mortar approach when he sold the company to Viacom. His concerns were shared by any number of observers throughout the industry. The Blockbuster retail model was going to be difficult to sustain in the wake of advancing technology (DeGeorge, 1996). On the immediate horizon was cable television and its promise of video-on-demand service. Less obvious was the future of e-commerce and the disruptive technologies made possible by the Internet. One of those disruptive technologies would take the form of a unique business process innovation and a company called Netflix.

Netflix

Netflix is an online subscription-based DVD rental service. Netflix was founded by Reed Hastings in 1997 during the emergent days of electronic commerce (EC) when companies like Amazon and Dell Computer were starting to gain prominence. The challenge for Hastings was whether he wanted to duplicate the traditional retail model that was currently in place. The alternative was to utilize the power of the Internet for placing video rental orders and providing online customer service (Shih, Kaufman, & Spinola, 2007).

Neflix offers its customers a great value proposition; namely, two to three DVDs per week (depending on the service plan) for a fixed monthly price. In practical terms, Neflix provides greater value to the consumer when compared to a traditional video rental store which charges by the individual DVD rental unit. Second, Netflix offers consumers greater convenience in the form of "no late fees." The subscriber is free to hold on to a specific video as long he/she wants (E-Business Strategies, Inc. 2002).

Third, a big part of Netflix's success is the direct result of personalized marketing which involves knowing more about the particular interests and viewing habits of one's customers. Netflix utilizes the power of the

Internet to promote a proprietary software recommendation system. A common complaint with Blockbuster was the experience of renting an unfamiliar movie and being dissatisfied with the viewing experience later on. The Netflix software recommendation system, on the other hand, makes suggestions of other films that the consumer might like based on past selections and a brief evaluation that the subscriber is asked to fill out. Netflix's interactive capability and proprietary recommendation system changed the basic relationship between retailer and consumer by shifting the emphasis from traditional retail sales to relationship building (Gershon, 2011).

Moreover, the proprietary software recommendation system has the added benefit of stimulating demand for lesser known movies and taking the pressure off recently released feature films where demand sometimes outstrips availability. This is in keeping with Anderson's (2006) long tail principle.[3] Finally, Netflix has adapted to changing technology by offering a "watch instantly" feature which enables subscribers to stream near-DVD quality movies and recorded television shows to those subscribers equipped with a computer and high speed Internet connectivity. The "watch instantly" feature is delivering in real time and in greater numbers what cable television failed to achieve in terms of its video-on-demand system feature (Gershon, 2011). Netflix has proven to be the ultimate game changer by revolutionizing the DVD rental business through the use of business process innovation and its EC technology platform.

Blockbuster's Failure to React

Blockbuster had more than sufficient time to react to the competition and revise its business model. As early as 2001, Blockbuster was in a position to strategically reposition itself. The company could have possibly acquired Netflix or modified its strategy by duplicating many of the same EC efficiencies that Netflix's business model had already demonstrated. Alternatively, it could have opened kiosks (i.e., similar to RedBox) and begun closing stores. This would have reduced capital costs and improved convenience (Woloszynowicz, 2010). Instead, Blockbuster chose to ignore the competitive threat posed by Netflix. They were doing quite well for the moment and didn't want to destabilize an otherwise successful business enterprise (i.e., the innovator's dilemma). In practical terms, Netflix was allowed to go unchallenged for six years before Blockbuster launched its own EC service in 2004. By then, Netflix had brand recognition, 3 million customers, and a strong business momentum ("How Blockbuster failed," 2010). Critics point to the fact that CEO John Antioco should have taken the Netflix threat more seriously. Blockbuster's business complacency coupled with a failure to appreciate the future of electronic commerce would prove costly in securing the company's long term future.

Blockbuster's Executive Leadership and Activist Board

John Antioco proved to be a capable CEO for the first six years of his tenure at Blockbuster. Between 1998 and 2004, the company achieved steady revenue growth. Most outside observers, however, were convinced that Blockbuster was a flawed business model that had reached the climax of its business run. This is reflected in a 1999 IPO offering where Blockbuster stock received a lukewarm reception on the first day of trading.

In 2004, Blockbuster finally launched its own online DVD rental service to compete directly with Netflix. In a bid to slow the competition, Blockbuster introduced a flat monthly fee and later eliminated late fees as well. Subscriptions did increase, but not enough to offset the $300 million loss the company absorbed by eliminating late fees. The combined strategy wound up costing the company an estimated $400 million (Poggi, 2010).

In 2004, Viacom (which still owned 80 percent of the company) chose to sell its stake in Blockbuster and took a $1.3 billion charge to reflect the declining value of the business. Later that same year, a second major change occurred that affected the company's organizational dynamics when activist investor Carl Icahn bought nearly $10 million shares of Blockbuster stock. The goal was to leverage his investment at a time when Blockbuster was trying to negotiate the purchase of its chief rival, Hollywood Video. The Federal Trade Commission, for its part, rejected the proposed merger. Shortly thereafter, Icahn began giving interviews to the press and writing letters to Antioco as well as shareholders claiming that Blockbuster had spent too much money on developing its online business and eliminating late fees. He was critical of Antioco's attempted merger strategy and claimed that the CEO was making too much money. Icahn proceeded to launch a proxy fight. At the 2005 shareholders meeting, Icahn proposed two new directors to the company's board of directors, which won approval. Blockbuster's eight board of directors now consisted of Icahn and the two newly elected activist board members (Antioco, 2011).

For Antioco and his management team, a set of contentious directors meant having to constantly justify and explain each business decision. To the public, Blockbuster's evolving business strategy seemed disjointed, almost random. First, Blockbuster offered a no late fee policy, but charged the consumer a restocking fee if the movie was returned too late. The company then excluded certain products, like video games, from the offer. Eventually, Blockbuster did away with the no late fees policy altogether, but without really telling anybody or making any announcements. All this points to the fact that Blockbuster was a company in trouble. The problem was made worse by the fact that Antioco and the company's board of directors were at serious odds with one another. Icahn routinely battled with Antioco about how to revive the company. Antioco wanted to keep the company independent while Icahn wanted to sell it to a private-equity firm (Poggi, 2010).

In December 2006, the situation came to a head over executive compensation. The board decided to significantly reduce Antioco's bonus compensation. Antioco chose to negotiate a severance deal with Blockbuster rather than accept the reduced bonus amount (Antioco, 2011). Set against the backdrop of some highly intense corporate infighting, the board approved the hiring of Jim Keyes who was the former head of 7-Eleven. He had a difficult assignment that included quelling the unrest at Blockbuster while trying to develop a strategy for the future. Unfortunately, the hiring of Jim Keyes was too little, too late. By now, it was clear to everyone that Blockbuster was in a slow death spiral. In the end, Blockbuster failed because the company chose not to change ("How Blockbuster failed," 2010). It was too slow in reacting to the competitive challenges posed by Netflix and RedBox. This, in combination with a highly contentious board of directors, proved to be a toxic mixture. Reflecting on Blockbuster's Chapter 11 filing, former CEO John Antioco (2011) concludes: "The day the company's failure will hit me hardest is probably when my own neighborhood store closes" (p. 42).

Discussion

A major argument of this chapter is that the warning signs of a troubled business often exist for long periods of time before they combine with enabling conditions to produce a climactic business failure. Collins (2009) refers to this as "the silent creep of impending doom" (p. 1). The business failures at both Kodak and Blockbuster share one thing in common. Each failed to recognize the early warning signs of advancing technological change. Kodak was paralyzed by an organizational culture that was highly resistant to change. While Kodak had the right intentions, the company was not prepared to make the costly changes needed to fully embrace the business of digital media and information technology. As Lucas and Goh (2009) point out, when a business is confronted with a highly disruptive technology, senior management has to be a catalyst for change at all levels of the organization. Although Kodak recognized the external threats, the company's organizational culture prevented it from moving forward. Kanter (2012) suggests that Kodak was very Rochester-centric and never really developed an innovation presence in other parts of the world that were developing leading edge media technologies. Instead, Kodak adhered to a kind of old-line manufacturing mentality. It was in the film business plain and simple. It was, after all, what made them profitable in the past.

In retrospect, it seems clear that the practice of driving to a store to rent a movie was a business process destined to fail as the Internet became more of a factor in the world of electronic commerce. For years, business analysts and professional observers have recognized that Blockbuster was a flawed business model that would be difficult to sustain in the wake of advancing technology. As early as 1994, Wayne Huizenga understood the limitations of a bricks and mortar approach when he sold Blockbuster to Viacom Inc. Ten years later, Viacom CEO Sumner Redstone came to the same conclusion when he sold his 80 percent stake in the company as well. Both Huizenga and Redstone operated at a time when the conventional wisdom and smart money was on cable television and its highly touted video-on-demand service. Despite many attempts, video-on-demand television has never realized its full potential (Gershon, 2009). It too has failed. The Internet, however, is an entirely different story. Joseph Schumpeter (1942) long ago noted that entrepreneurs disrupt. For Blockbuster, the disrupter indeed was a company called Netflix. The situation at Blockbuster was further complicated because of failures in executive leadership coupled with a highly contentious board of directors. The standoff between CEO John Antioco and the company's board resulted in business strategy gridlock and a public loss of confidence in the company.

The lessons of business history have taught us that there is no such thing as a static market. This is especially true in the field of media and telecommunications where today's high-flying company can quickly become yesterday's news; supplanted by the next communication start-up with a good idea. Think America OnLine (AOL), the Sony Walkman, AT&T long distance telephone service, Kodak film, and of course Blockbuster video. The resulting effects of creative destruction can be significant, including the failure to preserve market leadership, the discontinuation of a once highly successful product, and ultimately business failure itself. Both Eastman Kodak and Blockbuster were highly successful companies that once dominated their respective specialty area. Their previous strengths and one-time success ultimately laid the groundwork for their eventual decline. Each was susceptible to the innovator's dilemma. In the end, the requirements for change proved too formidable an obstacle.

Notes

1 The principle of disruptive technology owes its aegis to the work of Joseph Schumpeter who argued that innovation leads to the gales of "creative destruction" as new innovations cause old ideas, technologies and skills to become obsolete.

In Schumpeter's view, creative destruction, however difficult and challenging, leads to continuous progress moving forward. A good example of this is the impact that personal computers had on mainframe computers. In doing so, entrepreneurs created one of the most important technology advancements of the twentieth century.

2 Work on Vista began in 2001 under the code name Longhorn. The release of Windows Vista occurred more than five years after the introduction of Windows XP, thus making it the longest time interval between two releases of Microsoft Windows. Even still, Vista became the subject of numerous criticisms by various user groups who claim that Vista is hard to load and can make computers less stable and run slower.

3 The focus on lesser known films is in keeping with Anderson's (2006) principle of the "long tail." The term describes the niche strategy of businesses, such as Amazon or Netflix, that sell a large number of unique items, in relatively small quantities.

References

Anderson, C. (2006). *The long tail: Why the future of business is selling less of more*. New York: Hyperion.
Antioco, J. (2011, April). How I did it? Blockbuster's former CEO on sparring with an activist shareholder. *Harvard Business Review*, 39–44.
Blockbuster Inc. (2012). *Fundinguniverse*. Available at: http://www.fundinguniverse.com/company-histories/Blockbuster-Inc-Company- History.html Retrieved: March 7, 2012.
Carroll, P. (1993). *Big blues: The unmaking of IBM*. New York: Crown Publishers.
Cauley, L. (2005). *End of the line: The rise and fall of AT&T*. New York: Free Press.
Charran, R. & Useem, J. (2002, May 27). Why companies fail. *Fortune*, pp. 50–62.
Christensen, C. (1997). *The innovator's dilemma*. Boston, MA: Harvard Business School Press.
Christensen, C. (2003). *The innovator's solution*. Boston, MA: Harvard Business School Press.
Cohan, J. (2002). I didn't know and I was only doing my job: Has corporate ethics governance careened out of control? A case study of Enron's information myopia. *Journal of Business Ethics*, 40(3), 275–299.
Collins, J. (2001). *Good to great*. New York: Harper Collins.
Collins, J. (2009). *How the mighty fall*. New York: Harper Collins.
Collins, J. & Porras, J. (1994). *Built to last*. New York: Harper Collins.
Davenport, T. (1993). *Process innovation*. Boston, MA: Harvard Business School Press.
DeGeorge, G. (1996). *The making of a Blockbuster: How Wayne Huizenga built a sports and entertainment empire from trash, grit, and videotape*. New York: John Wiley & Sons.
DeLaMerced, M. (2012, January 19). Eastman Kodak files for bankruptcy. *New York Times*. Available at: http://dealbook.nytimes.com/2012/01/19/eastman-kodak-files-for-bankruptcy/ Retrieved: February 20, 2012.

Dish network wins bidding for assets of bankrupt Blockbuster. (2011, April 7). *Los Angeles Times*. Available at: http //articles.latimes.com/2011/apr/07/business/la-fi-ct-dish-blockbuster-20110407 Retrieved: March 7, 2012.

E-Business Strategies, Inc. (2002, October). Netflix: Transforming the DVD rental business. *Published Report*, 1–10.

Finnerty, T. (2000). Kodak v. Fuji: The battle for global market share. Unpublished report. New York: Lubin School of Business, Pace University.

Gavetti, G., Henderson, R., & Giorgi, S. (2005). *Kodak and the digital revolution*. Cambridge, MA: Harvard Business School Press.

Genzlinger, N. (2000, May 22). Television review: He changed photography and transformed society. *New York Times*. Available at: http://www.nytimes.com/2000/05/22/arts/television-review-he-changed-photography-and-transformed-society.html Retrieved: March 5, 2012.

Gershon, R. (2009). *Telecommunications and business strategy*. New York: Taylor & Francis.

Gershon, R. (2011). Business process innovation and the intelligent network. In Z. Vukanovic & P. Faustino (Eds.), *Managing media economy, media content and technology in the age of digital convergence* (pp. 59–85). Lisbon, Portugal: Media XXI / Formal press.

Gershon, R. A. & Kanayama, T. (2002). The SONY corporation: A case study in transnational media management. *The International Journal on Media Management*, 4, 44–56.

Hamel, G. (2006, February). The what, why and how of management innovation. *Harvard Business Review*, 72–87.

How Blockbuster failed at failing. (2010, October 11). *Time*, pp. 38–40.

Jasper, R. (2012, January 20). The end of our Kodak moment. *The Telegraph*. Available at: http://www.telegraph.co.uk/family/9025257/The-end-of-our-Kodak-moment.html. Retrieved: February 20, 2012.

Kanter, R. (2012, January 14). The last Kodak moment? *The Economist*. Available at: http://www.economist.com/node/21542796. Retrieved: February 20, 2012.

Kodak legacy. (2012, January 19). *New York Times*. Available at http://www.nytimes.com/interactive/2012/01/19/business/dealbook/dbgfx-kodaks-legacy.html Retrieved: February 20, 2012.

Kotter, J. (1996). *Leading change*. Boston, MA: Harvard Press.

Lucas, H. & Goh, J. M. (2009). Disruptive technology: How Kodak missed the digital photography revolution. *Journal of Strategic Information Systems*, 18, 46–55.

Nathan, J. (1999). *Sony: The private life*. New York: Houghton-Mifflin.

Negroponte, N. (1995, April). The balance of trade of ideas, *Wired*, 188.

Pilotta, J., Widman, T., & Jasko. S. (1988). Meaning and action in the organizational setting: An interpretive approach. *Communication Yearbook*, 11, 310–334.

Poggi, J. (2010, September 23). Blockbuster's rise and fall: The long. rewinding road. Available at: http://www.thestreet.com/story/10867574/1/the-rise-and-fall- of-blockbuster-the-long-rewinding-road.html Retrieved: March 8, 2011.

Pound, J. (2002). The promise of the governed corporation. *Harvard Business Review on Corporate Governance*. Boston, MA: Harvard Business School Press.

Rogers, E. (1995) *Diffusion of innovation*. Fourth edn., New York: Free Press.
Schein, E. (1983). The role of the founder in creating organizational culture. *Organizational Dynamics*, 11, 13–28.
Schumpeter, J. (1942). *Capitalism, socialism and democracy*. New York: Harper & Row.
Shih, W., Kaufman, S., & Spinola, D. (2007, November). Netflix: *Harvard Business School Case Study Series* (9–607–138), 1–15.
Swasy, A. (1997). *Changing focus: Kodak and the battle to save a great American company*. New York: Times Business—Random House.
The vindication of Sumner Redstone. (1998, 15 June). *Forbes*, pp. 105–111.
Tushman, M. & O'Reilly, C. (1997). *Winning through innovation*. Boston, MA: Harvard Business School Press.
Wheelen, T. & Hunger, D. (1998). *Strategic management and business policy*. Reading, MA: Addison Wesley Longman, Inc.
Woloszynowicz, M. (2010, September 22). Business Lessons from Blockbuster's Failure. *Web 2.0 business and development lessons*. Available at: http://www.w2lessons.com/2010/09/business-lessons-from-blockbusters.html Retrieved: March 7, 2012.

Section II

MME RESEARCH FROM JUNIOR SCHOLARS

4

APPLICATION OF THE LONG TAIL ECONOMY TO THE ONLINE NEWS MARKET IN TAIWAN

Civic Participation Matters

J. Sonia Huang, Ph.D. and Wei-Ching Wang, Ph.D.

The news industry as a whole is undergoing a transformation brought on by the emergence of digital technologies that have impacted all media. With audiences dispersing across ever more media outlets, nearly every media industry is losing popularity. Many news media have tried to redefine their appeal and their purpose (e.g., hyper-local or crowd-sourcing) based on the diminished capacity of each medium. For traditional media, the challenge is how to manage decline. However, in the case of Internet media, some doubt that Internet revenue will grow to the point where it can pay for journalism on the scale to which media are accustomed.

That is, even though the Internet has become the main news source for many and Internet advertising revenue grows over time (Interactive Advertising Bureau, 2011), the highest portion (28 percent) goes to search engines and Internet service providers rather than to news-related sectors such as newspaper websites (5 percent) or other news and current events sites (less than 3 percent) (Project for Excellence in Journalism, 2010). Moreover, general news online has become increasingly open to charging for at least part of its content as paywall experiments by pioneers like London's *Times* and *The New York Times* (Lefkow, 2011, May 17), but the fear that paywalls will result in a loss of traffic and of online advertising revenue is still omnipresent. The downward drift in profits has lately afflicted media publishers, as Gannett, A.H. Belo, Washington

---

This study was made possible through research grants from the National Science Council of Taiwan: [NSC 98-2410-H-009-001-] and [NSC 100-2410-H-003-075-]. The authors would also like to acknowledge Ai-Chieh Lin, Yi-Chen Lin, and Pin-Chun Chen for their data entry contributions.

Post Company, and the New York Times Company all saw profits shrink in 2011 (Kaplan, 2011, July 28).

To explore alternative business models for news media's competitive market capacity, economic theories are applied in this chapter. As opposed to the conventional 80/20 principle, Anderson (2006) introduced *The Long Tail: Why the Future of Business is Selling Less of More* as an entirely new business model that showed how successful Internet businesses were expanding their tails to reach previously unreachable customers with the help of new information technologies. Anderson used Amazon.com as an example: about a quarter of Amazon's book sales came from outside its top 100,000 titles, around the number that the average brick and mortar bookstore carries. If the Amazon statistics are any guide, we wondered, is there a long-tail economy for the Internet media and to what extent can the online news sector be sustainable for a variety of players? Specifically, the authors seek to uncover a relationship between the long tail forces and the performance of the online news market in our home country—Taiwan, where dozens of national online news media compete for user attention.

The Online News Market in Taiwan

In the 1960s, McLuhan (1964) saw different media working together, while he predicted the attainment of a global village in which information and experience would be freely available for all to share. The idea of a global village became most explicit over the past two decades. There were no online news services in the world before 1993 but nowadays thousands of daily and non-daily newspapers (see onlinenewspapers.com) are available to interested users. In a similar vein, the first Taiwanese news site launched in September 1995, published by a major newspaper company, China Times Inc. Thereafter, most legacy news media established their online presences. A high-profile news site udn.com, affiliated with another major newspaper in Taiwan, *United Daily News*, went online in 1999 and surpassed *China Times* after four years of innovative operations such as monetization of all offline content produced by the United Daily News Co. since 1951 (see udndata.com). At the time of the study, more than a dozen Taiwan-based news sites had substantial market share but no one charged users a fee for news access; that is, all online news were offered to Taiwan's residents for free except for news archives.

With regard to market competition, news portals and newspaper sites have dominated Taiwan's online news market for years. News portals (e.g., Yahoo! Kimo News and MSN News) and newspaper sites (e.g., the online editions of the *United Daily News* and *Apple Daily*) have always been among the top 100 popular sites in Taiwan (Luo, Yang, &

Zhao, 2011). However, news portals outperform most newspaper sites in audience share. According to an online news survey of 1,485 respondents, 79.6 percent of all Internet users obtained news from portal sites whereas only 18.1 percent accessed news directly from newspaper sites. More critically, a quarter of those who got news from portal sites did not visit newspaper sites at all (Brain.com, 2009). The online advertising revenue data also confirm this situation. Most of the Internet advertising revenue went to portals. For example, in 2008, the portal site advertising revenue accounted for 90.23 percent of the total online advertising revenue. The most successful portal Yahoo! Kimo earned 3.38 billion New Taiwan (NT) dollars; however, the most successful newspaper site, the *United Daily News*, only got 180 million NT dollars (see Table 4.1). The advertising profit of Yahoo! Kimo is 18.7 times higher than that of the United Daily News website. Beside portals, social media (e.g., Facebook and Google+) have also become critical players in news on the Internet. Social media's audience is vastly larger than any single news organization and their role has evolved from a network for friends to a way for people to share, recommend, and link together all kinds of information, including news (Nielsen Company and PEJ Research, 2011). Overall, the entry of a variety of players into the online news market in Taiwan in the past two decades brought about renewed competition which provides a unique context for the examination of a long tail economy.

The Long Tail Economy

Conventionally a business analysis would show that the Pareto Law or the 80/20 principle holds; i.e., 80 percent of total revenue will be generated from just 20 percent of the total product line (Koch, 1998). With rapid advances in Internet technologies and limitless space on the Internet, however, online news sites are currently able to offer audiences more segmented news and create more viewership niches; audiences and customers today also are increasingly favoring the media with the most choices (Li, 2001; Morton, 2004; Wicks, 1989). Drawing from Anderson's (2006) long tail model, the business that can offer more niche products is expected to be most successful. The long tail idea is based on several phenomena: the tail of available variety (i.e., the product line) is far longer than before and more extensive than we realize; the variety is now economically within reach of the average person due to the help of Internet technology; all of these niches, when aggregated, can make up a significant market share. None of the aforementioned phenomena can happen without a reduction in the cost of reaching niches. At least three powerful forces cause those costs to fall: democratization of the tools of production; democratization of the tools of distribution; and the connection of supply and demand. However, these forces were not newly

Table 4.1 Online Advertising Revenue in Taiwan

News Site/Year	1997	1998	1999	2000	2001	2002	2003	2004	2005	2006	2007	2008
Yahoo! Kimo	3	26	90	290	300	423	760	1,050	1,750	2,500	3,350	3,380
Yam	0	5	60	100	97	189	252	313	322	250	264	198
PChome	4	22	55	130	120	120	204	310	229	240	180	165
China Times	0	21	50	80	85	72	90	126	152	130	160	128
United Daily	0	0	0	12	38	60	120	135	146	164	179	180
MSN	0	0	0	25	40	75	120	230	380	370	422	498
Total	35	120	360	700	860	1,020	1,710	2,330	3,190	3,580	4,700	4,700

Unit: Million New Taiwan dollars.

Source: Adopted and modified from Brain.com.

invented; the ideas are similar to some older concepts which communication scholars have talked about a lot. Anderson only systematically linked them together.

Democratization of Production Tools, Product Segmentation, and Civic Participation

The first force, democratizing the tools of production, has two implications: one is the incremental variety of products; the other is new producers in production (Anderson, 2006). When considering product variety, "In an era without the constraints of physical shelf space and other bottlenecks of distribution, narrowly targeted goods and services can be as economically attractive as mainstream fare" (p. 52). The majority of relevant media studies consider such issues as the reasons for and the phenomenon of news "segmentation" on the radio or TV or in newspapers. They also examine online industries, mainly regarding consumer products, their product segmentation, and the industries' market performance (e.g., Li, 2001; Maynard, 1995; Wicks, 1989).

In addition to product segmentation, democratizing the tools of production promotes civic or public participation in content creation. Due to the incremental interactivity capacity of information technologies, today's online news websites can offer many more opportunities for the audience to interact with news providers, to participate in online news and content production, and also to personalize the channels and kinds of news that they prefer. There are several opportunities by which readers interact with news websites and participate in news processes (Briggs, 2007; Foust, 2005; Stovall, 2004). The first is by offering news websites feedback or discussion through information tools like email, forums, chat rooms, sharing, bulletin boards, news website blogs, or polls. The second is when the audience directly submits news articles, photos, video, audio, or any other type of media material to online news sites as news resources, such as crowd-sourcing and distributed, collaborative, or open-source reporting. The third is by personalizing or customizing news or news platforms. The last but not least kind of audience participation includes participating in online games and using databases.

Democratization of Distribution Tools and Versioning

The second force that bolsters the long tail economy is the democratization of the tools of distribution. Information technologies have dramatically lowered the costs of delivering and enlarging output channels, thus considerably and effectively raising sales. Considering movie release windowing as an example, current movie output channels largely use a combination of theaters, paid cable, DVD, web-based VOD, commercial television, etc. This phenomenon of varying output channels is similar to the idea of "versioning," by which a company offers a product line of variations on the same underlying good (Varian, 2000, pp. 137–138). According to Varian's idea of "versioning," the product line is designed so as to appeal to different market segments, thereby selling at a high price to those who place a high value on the product and at a low price to those who value it less. This results in the phenomenon of price discrimination. The flexibility of information technologies nowadays offers many alternative forms of versioning and thus price discrimination.

Connection of Supply and Demand and Collaborative Filtering

The third force of the long tail model is connecting supply and demand by introducing consumers to available goods and services. More powerful search engines and recommendation lists are effective tools for enabling consumers to easily find desired niche products. Thus, the incremental use of new information technologies to connect consumers to products or services is what drives consumer demand from the head to the tail. Although websites themselves offer tools to help consumers filter information and locate their preferred products and content, consumers also help each other to screen, filter, and organize content, a process that Wertime and Fenwick (2008) call "collaborative filtering" (p. 23). Collaborative filtering enables consumers to help each other by pooling information about consumer behavior or by recommendation. Some examples include most viewed news, most recommended news, most emailed news, and most searched news.

Previous Studies with Mixed Results

Those who explicitly tested the long tail phenomena on an empirical basis have produced mixed results as far as various industries are concerned. The model has been validated by a variety of new media applications such as online book stores, search engines, digital music and movie services, and online news. For example, Brynjolfsson, Hu, and Smith (2006a, 2006b) investigated a multi-channel retailing company and found that the Internet channel exhibited a significantly less concentrated sales distribution when compared with traditional channels. Carpenter's (2010) research on content diversity in online citizen journalism and online newspaper articles also confirmed the long tail effect in terms of diversity of topics, use of outbound hyperlinks, and number of multimedia and interactive elements. Not all studies have reached the same conclusion. In Smyrnaios, Marty, and Rebillard's (2010) research on the long tail of French-speaking news websites, the authors argue that it is the 80/20 principle, not the long tail phenomenon, that rules the online news market; that is, the spectrum of issues that websites deal with is highly concentrated on a few major and redundant issues. Besides, Elberse and Oberholzer-Gee (2008) examined competing hypotheses between the "long tail" idea and the "superstars" theory in video sales both online and offline and found that the popularity of niche titles went hand in hand with a significant concentration of success on ever fewer items and the video sales declined across all quantiles of the distribution. Results imply that the top end of distribution draws smaller audiences and the tail end appears incredibly flat.

Objectives of the Study

This diversity of viewpoints leads the present study to examine a long tail economy in a more comprehensive way. First, the study takes the entire products and services which a news website can offer into consideration, rather than looking solely at news stories. Second, the study explores the driving forces of the long tail (democratizing the tools of production, the democratization of the tools of distribution, and connecting supply and demand), rather than analyzing content diversity, which constitutes only a fraction of the long tail concept. Third, the above-mentioned studies reach different conclusions because they make different comparison (past vs. present or online vs. offline), use different elements of observation (topics, headlines, sales), or examine different media sectors (news, music, film, video). In contrast to these studies, the present study explores *The Long Tail*'s most crucial implication, that the long tail benefits market performance (Anderson, 2006); that is to say, a determination of whether there is a long tail economy should rely on a linkage between the long tail forces (which are new information technologies incorporating product segmentation, civic participation, versioning, and collaborative filtering) and their effects (i.e., market performance) in any given business. Accordingly, we address the following research questions:

RQ1: To what extent are the long tail forces adopted by Taiwan's news sites?

RQ2: What are the most frequent long tail forces adopted by Taiwan's news sites?

RQ3: What are the links between the long tail forces and market performance among Taiwan's news sites?

Methods

To zero in on the long tail economy of the online news market from several independent directions, this study collected market performance data from a third party company, InsightXplorer, and long tail's three

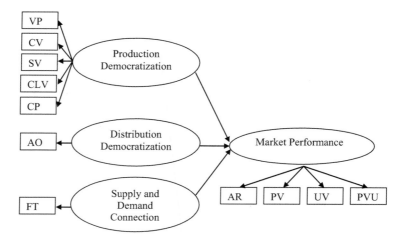

Figure 4.1 Analytical Framework of the Long Tail Economy for Online News

Note: VP = volume of production, CV = content variety, SV = service variety, CLV = classified variety, CP = civic participation, AO = access options, FT = filter tools, AR = average reach, PV = monthly page views, UV = monthly unique visitors, and PVU = page views per user.

Source: Authors' compilation.

forces information from a content analysis of news websites. The analytical framework of the present study and the multi-method approach to collect data are detailed above (Figure 4.1).

Market Performance

Operationalization

Market performance, the key concept of dependent measures, is defined as the result of a firm or industry's activities considered in terms of the efficiency, equity, progress, and externalities created (Albarran, 2002; Picard, 1989). To evaluate market performance from a microeconomic perspective, most empirical studies have instead examined financial performance or business performance. Financial performance centers on the use of simple financial indicators such as profit or revenue, assumed to reflect the fulfillment of the economic goals of a firm (Dess & Robinson JR., 1984; Zou & Cavusgil, 2002). Business performance, in addition to indicators of financial performance, emphasizes non-financial but business-related factors such as market share, product quality, or marketing effectiveness (Venkatraman & Ramanujam, 1986, 1987). Various media-related studies have already used newspaper circulation or broadcast rating as a proxy of media performance (e.g., Chan-Olmsted & Ha, 2003; Stavitsky, 2000). Due to media companies' unwillingness to disclose financial records, the present study proposed online traffic in the form of average reach, monthly page views, monthly unique visitors. and page views per user as indicators of media's business performance (also see Figure 4.1).

Third Party Data

The traffic data used in this analysis were collected by a third party company, InsightXplorer (IX), which has a syndicated service (i.e., Access Rating Online, also known as ARO) like NetRatings provided by Nielsen and MediaMetrix by comScore for the Taiwanese Internet market. IX maintains a panel of more than three thousand online users for Taiwan's cybermarket and tracks panelists' every online clickstream across websites that they visit by installing proprietary client-side software on panelists' major computers either at home or at work (InsightXplorer, 2009). Besides, panel participants allowed IX to track their every clickstream online and in return were compensated by regular sweepstakes programs. Data in the present study were collected from the first quarter of 2010. According to IX's ARO report, 20 national news sites generated substantial traffic in Taiwan with an average reach ranging from 1.22 percent to 81.59 percent of total online users (see Table 4.2). Among the top 20 news sites, 15 are based in Taiwan, 3 in China, 1 in the United States, and 1 in the United Kingdom. In terms of affiliations, 7 are newspaper-affiliated, 6 are aggregators, 3 are television-affiliated, 3 are pure-plays, and 1 is a news agency.

Long Tail's Three Forces

Operationalizations

Once the sample list had been finalized, the study performed a detailed content analysis to examine the long tail's three forces about the 20 most popular news sites in Taiwan. According to the aforementioned literature reviews, the three-force strategy applied by any company results in more products (which lengthens the tail), more access (which fattens the tail), and/or more filters (which drives businesses from hits to niches) (Anderson, 2006, pp. 54–56). Overall, we are interested in whether a news site with more products, more access, and/or more filters performs better in the online news market.

Coding Scheme

Few, if any, studies have empirically tested Anderson's three long tail forces, so the present study developed a coding scheme mostly based on

Table 4.2 Top 20 Most Popular News Sites in Taiwan

News Site (URL)	Average Reach	Monthly Page Views	Monthly Unique Visitors	Page Views per User
Yahoo! Kimo News (tw.news.yahoo.com)	81.59%	799,206.41	10,267.15	77.84
United Daily News (udn.com)	41.64%	126,522.60	5,240.37	24.14
NOW News (nownews.com)	34.80%	54,651.61	4,379.73	12.48
Apple Daily (tw.nextmedia.com)	18.17%	93,101.46	2,287.13	40.71
China Times (news.chinatimes.com)	17.49%	31,555.40	2,200.82	14.34
MSN News (news.msn.com.tw)	15.65%	31,783.84	1,969.04	16.14
Liberty Times (libertytimes.com.tw)	13.08%	17,919.53	1,646.08	10.89
Yam News (n.yam.com)	7.86%	6,382.12	989.28	6.45
PChome News (news.pchome.com.tw)	6.95%	11,570.00	874.40	13.23
Epoch Times (epochtimes.com)	6.69%	1,534.30	841.52	1.82
Google News (news.google.com.tw)	4.67%	4,159.13	587.58	7.08

CTS News (news.cts.com.tw)	4.65%	1,202.64	585.21	2.06
HiNet News (times.hinet.net)	4.57%	3,205.94	575.02	5.58
Sina News (news.sina.com.tw)	4.12%	1411.66	519.05	2.72
Central News Agency (cna.com.tw)	4.01%	1,330.44	504.27	2.64
People's Daily (people.com.cn)	2.66%	686.48	334.76	2.05
China News (big5.china.com.cn)	2.11%	492.49	265.65	1.85
China Daily News (cdns.com.tw)	1.79%	346.55	225.47	1.54
China Radio International (big5.cri.cn)	1.65%	1,074.40	207.29	5.18
BBC News (bbc.co.uk)	1.22%	779.34	153.39	5.08

Source: Adopted and modified from InsightXplorer (2009).

examples provided in Anderson's book and on our professional experience in the news industry. To examine the evidence of production democratization, we constructed five indicators by accumulating scores assigned to volume of production, content variety, service variety, classified variety, and civic participation (also see Figure 4.1). By measuring both volume and variety, the study is able to detect how many products and how many product lines are produced by each news site.

First, the volume of production was generated by website downloading software, WebSite Downloader, which produced several statistics including speed, downloaded size, number of files, and elapsed time while downloading an entire site. The present study only selected the number of files to represent the volume of production for each news site. Content, service, and classified variety were indexed by counting categories provided by the site menu. For example, the content index might include home, news, weather, sports, traffic, entertainment, health, and lifestyle; the service index might include register, login, site help, contact us, subscribe, and advertise; and the classified index might include jobs, homes, autos, rentals, community, and coupons. To ensure that the categories in the three variety indices were mutually exclusive and exhaustive (Babbie, 2008), we first assigned the categories on the homepage to content, service, and classified indices, and categories on subsequent pages were counted under the designated index. Last, the civic participation index measured whether users were able to comment, recommend, rate, and share stories or whether users were provided with personalized pages, blogs, polls, and forums.

The second force, democratizing the tools of distribution, is evaluated on the number of users with access to niches. To calculate the access options, coders were instructed to record whether news sites took advantage of various ICT options to attract users through not only the Internet but also newsletters/email, mobiles, RSS, instant messaging, Twitter, and iPods/podcasts. In a similar vein, for the third force, connecting supply and demand, coders were instructed to record whether the news sites provided filters such as headlines, latest news, most popular, most recommended, most commented, most emails, most searched, most blogged, and news search to increase demand for niches and flatten the demand curve. For the indices of civic participation, access options, and filter tools, open-ended questions were provided to achieve exhaustiveness because it may not be possible to create a coding scheme for all the activities happening on the Internet.

Training and Reliability

A code sheet was developed to record information on how and what news sites were presented in terms of the long tail forces. The extensive

Table 4.3 Inter-coder Reliability of the Long Tail Indices among Taiwan's News Sites

	Inter-coder Reliability	
	Spearman rho	*Pearson r*
Production volume	1.0	0.72
Content variety	0.33	0.96
Filter tools	0.31	0.84
Classified variety	–	–
Service variety	0.65	–0.03
Civic participation	0.82	0.78
Access options	0.74	0.84

Note: 19 out of 20 news sites in Taiwan did not provide classified ads which made the variable a constant, so Spearman *rho* and Pearson *r* could not be computed.

code sheet included topics of content variety, service variety, classified variety, civic participation, access options, and filter tools. Three coders (students majoring in communications and technologies) were trained on how to code the news sites and what definitions corresponded to each variable on the code sheet. It is noteworthy that the entire site was coded, including all links and pages associated with each particular variable of interest but not going beyond the main root address (e.g., http://www.buffalonews.com/). This method has been used in previous studies to obtain the most comprehensive snapshot of a website (Chan-Olmsted & Park, 2000; Macias & Lewis, 2003). Overall, 10 percent of the news sites were randomly selected and independently coded to establish inter-coder reliability. Because our variables were metric and in many instances precise agreement was unlikely, the level of co-variation of coders' total counts was accessed by Spearman *rho* and the Pearson correlation coefficient (Neuendorf, 2002). The coefficients of reliability are listed in Table 4.3, ranging from –0.03 for the service variety to 1.0 for the production volume. As reliability coefficients of 0.80 or greater are acceptable, service variety and classified variety had coefficients that were too low to be considered reliable within the sample. As a result, we dropped the two indices from further statistical analyses.

Data Analysis

The long tail economy, defined as the link between each long tail index and market performance indicator, was measured by both zero-order correlation and partial correlation since previous studies indicated several factors which had great influence on market performance. As mentioned in the literatures, empirical research has documented the superior performance of news portals over newspaper sites not only in the US market (Chyi & Lewis, 2009) but also in Taiwan (Luo et al., 2011; Yang, Huang, & Chyi, 2011). Besides, the role of geography also has been identified as a major factor in the online news market: the local market still outweighs the long-distance market in terms of audience share (Chyi & Sylvie, 2001). If their finding holds true in Taiwan's online news market, Taiwan-based news sites (e.g., tw.news.yahoo.com or libertytimes.com. tw) are expected to perform better than foreign news sites (e.g., china. com.cn). Therefore, this study attempts to compare the links between long tail forces and market performance controlling for whether a news site is a portal or has a local nature. Since the study used a non-probability sample and our sample size was small, no inferential and multivariate statistics were used. Instead, we applied Pearson product-moment correlation and reported correlation coefficients to describe direction and strength between variables. As a rule of sum, a coefficient less than 0.20 is a slight, almost negligible correlation; 0.20–0.40 is a low, definite-but-small correlation; 0.40–0.70 is a moderate, substantial correlation; 0.70–0.90 is a high, marked correlation; more than 0.90 is a very high, very dependable correlation (Weaver, 1981).

Results and Discussion

The Extent of Long Tail Tools Adopted by Taiwan's News Sites

RQ1 sought to explore the extent of long tail tools adopted by Taiwan's news sites. According to Anderson (2006), the long tail idea reflects several phenomena: more products, more access, and more filters. Overall, we found that the top news sites in Taiwan produced an average of 3.5 million files, 164 content categories, 15 filters, 5 civic participation opportunities, and 4 access options in 2010 (see Table 4.4). To provide an overview, we collapsed the metric data into categories and found the majority of news sites supplied less than 1 million files (53 percent), less than 100 content categories (60 percent), less than 5 opportunities for civic participation (65 percent), and less than 5 access options (85 percent). The only exception comes from 70 percent of the news sites providing more than 10 filter tools (e.g., news search, latest news, top stories, etc.) for their users. Possible reasons include the ease of filter creations and the copycat effect among competitors. For example, filter tools like latest news and top stories are created by automatic aggregation algorithms which do not require discrete editorial efforts so they are easy to create and simple to copy.

The categories were built mandatorily for comparison purposes since the study partly replicated a previous study by the authors about the United States' online news market (see Huang & Wang, 2010 and

Table 4.4 The Extent of Long Tail Tools Adopted by Taiwan's News Sites

Index	Frequency	Valid Percent
Production volume ($M=3,533,205$, $SD=6,011,885.44$, $N=15$)		
0–1,000,000 files	8	53
1,000,001–10,000,000 files	5	33
More than 10,000,000 files	2	13
Content variety ($M=164.15$, $SD=154.05$, $N=20$)		
0–100 categories	12	60
101–200 categories	1	5
More than 200 categories	7	35
Civic participation ($M=5$, $SD=3.65$, $N=20$)		
0–5 opportunities	12	60
6–10 opportunities	7	35
More than 10 opportunities	1	5
Access option ($M=3.55$, $SD=2.56$, $N=20$)		
0–5 options	17	85
6–10 options	2	10
More than 10 options	1	5
Filter tools ($M=14.75$, $SD=9.69$, $N=20$)		
0–5 tools	3	15
6–10 tools	3	15
More than 10 options	14	70

Note: Due to dynamic pages and corporate firewalls, the numbers of production volume of five news sites (i.e., tw.news.yahoo.com, libertytimes.com.tw, news.google.com.tw, china.com.cn, and cri.cn) are missing. Bold numbers represent the percentages of the mode.

Appendix Table 4.1A). Compared to data drawn from the US, Taiwan's news sites are stronger in terms of content variety and filter tools, weaker regarding civic participation and access options, and similar in their skewness to the low end. The results suggest a great opportunity for, and a great threat to, the online news market. In contrast to traditional media, Internet media present a way to eliminate most of the physical barriers to unlimited choices; however, not many news sites are taking full advantage of the so-called "long tail market."

The Most Frequent Long Tail Tools Adopted by Taiwan's News Sites

RQ2 sought to explore the most frequent long tail tools adopted by Taiwan's news sites. Anderson (2006) has addressed at least three powerful forces which cause the emergence of a long tail economy: democratization of production tools, democratization of distribution tools, and connection of supply and demand. It is essential to understand the tools of the long tail forces used in Taiwan's news sites. With regard to content variety, more than half of Taiwan's news sites featured entertainment (90 percent), sports (85 percent), business (80 percent), world (65 percent), politics (55 percent), society (55 percent), and life (55 percent) in their regular sections (see Table 4.5). A news service is supposed to promote political engagement, community knowledge, and social trust, but the trend toward tabloidization (Grabe, Zhou, Lang, & Bolls, 2000; Wang & Huang, 2011) and infotainment (Graber, 1994) appeared to be more salient in the present sample. In terms of civic participation, share a story (85 percent), forum (55 percent), and poll (50 percent) were adopted by most news sites (see Table 4.5). Although many civic participation opportunities such as building readers' blogs, making comments directly below a story, and recommending good stories, were not frequently adopted, production tools were never available to users in traditional media. The traditional line between producers and consumers has blurred, so civic participation could be a useful production tool to make consumers more active and producers more cost-effective.

Access options, traditionally also known as versioning, is a way to offer a product line of variations on the same underlying good. Our results show that all Taiwan's news sites offer Internet access (a default function) and 70 percent of the news sites provided RSS, which published frequently updated works such as news headlines and blog entries in a standardized format (see Table 4.5). In the past, the Web 1.0 strategy was to pull people to sites either for content or for business; the Web 2.0+ approach now sends messages to crowded places. Once the crowds find the sites' information engaging, they will become more likely to visit the sites in the future. However, some popular social networking services such as Facebook or Plurk were still lowly adopted as access points for content at the time when the study was conducted.

Filters, a catch-all phrase for recommendations, present users with the recommendations that are most relevant for them. The main effect of filters is to help people move from the world they know ("hits") to the world that they don't know ("niches") via a route that is both comfortable and tailored to their tastes (Anderson, 2006, p. 109). According to Table 4.5, the most commonly used filter for online news sites is news search (100 percent). News search functions as a filter to bring back just the news stories that are most relevant to users' search terms. Other filters like latest news/most recent (95 percent), top stories/headlines (85 percent), and most viewed (65 percent) also were commonly adopted

Table 4.5 The Most Frequent Long Tail Tools Adopted by Taiwan's News Sites

Index	Frequency	Valid Percent
Content Variety		
Entertainment	18	90
Sports	17	85
Business	16	80
International	13	65
Politics	11	55
Society	11	55
Life	11	55
Technology	9	45
Local	8	40
Travel	7	35
China	7	35
Health	6	30
Education	5	25
Arts	2	10
Civic Participation		
Share a story	16	80
Forum	11	55
Poll	10	50
Reader blog	9	45
Comment	9	45
Recommend	7	35
Customize	5	25
Discussions	4	20
Correction	3	15
Rate	3	15
Access Options		
Internet	20	100
RSS	14	70
Newsletter	9	45
Mobile	5	25
Plurk	3	15
Facebook	2	10
Twitter	2	10
Podcasts	2	10
iGoogle	2	10
Filter Tools		
News search	20	100
Latest news/most recent	19	95
Top stories/headlines	17	85
Most viewed	13	65
Featured stories	9	45
Photo galleries	8	40
Most blogged	5	25
Most commended	4	20
Most recommended	3	15
Rankings	3	15
Most searched	3	15
Most emailed	2	10

Note: Bold numbers represent percentages more than 50.

by news sites. Filters serve a function to give users lower search costs of finding niche content.

Links Between the Long Tail Tools and Traffic Performance

RQ3 examined links between each long tail index and each market performance indicator among Taiwan's news sites. Before going to the bivariate relationships, descriptive statistics of the traffic data are reported. According to IX's ARO report, the 20 Taiwan's news sites on average attracted 59,446 monthly page views, 1,733 monthly unique visitors, 14 percent reach, and 13 page views per user in one month. However, the standard deviation values of the four traffic variables are very large, indicating imbalanced distributions; because a few news sites performed extremely well whereas others were not able to attract much attention. The phenomenon also serves as a good reason for conducting this study: why some news sites are very successful; but others aren't. Is a news site that can offer more niche products and services expected to be most successful?

To obtain an overall picture of the relationship, we conducted both zero-order and partial correlations. In the zero-order correlations, results indicated five definite-but-small correlations: production volume and average reach (0.21); production volume and monthly unique visitors (0.21); civic participation and average reach (0.22); civic participation and monthly unique visitors (0.22); and access options and page view per user (0.20) (see Table 4.6). After controlling for whether a news site is a portal or has a local nature, seven definite-but-small correlations and two substantial correlations popped up. The two substantial and positive correlations lie in the relationships between civic participation and average reach (0.41) and between civic participation and monthly unique visitors (0.41). Six of them were unveiled after control: content variety and average reach (0.27), content variety and monthly unique visitors (0.27), civic participation and monthly page views (0.24), civic participation and page view per user (0.35), filter tools and average reach (0.22), filter tools and monthly unique visitors (0.22) (see Table 4.6). Although two original coefficients were weaker, the substantial increases in other relationships represent that the long tail forces have some impact on news sites' market performance in the form of traffic generation after relevant variables were held constant. Specifically, among the long tail forces, civic participation appeared to have the strongest and most positive relationships with market performance. The relationship uncovered by the present study may not be as surprising because social media which enable everyone to create and disseminate content are gaining ground as a powerful media platform and civic participation plays a big part in it.

Table 4.6 Correlations between the Long Tail Tools and Traffic Performance among Taiwan's News Sites

	Production Volume		Content Variety		Civic Participation		Access Options		Filter Tools	
	Zero-order (N)	Partial (N)	Zero-order (N)	Partial (N)	Zero-order (N)	Partial (N)	Zero-order (N)	Partial (N)	Zero-order (N)	Partial (N)
Average Reach	**0.21** (15)	0.17 (20)	0.08 (20)	**0.27** (20)	**0.22** (20)	**0.41** (20)	0.14 (20)	0.10 (20)	-0.08 (20)	**0.22** (20)
Monthly Page Views	-0.04 (15)	-0.14 (20)	-0.07 (20)	0.07 (20)	0.09 (20)	**0.24** (20)	0.02 (20)	0.09 (20)	0.08 (20)	0.12 (20)
Monthly Unique Visitors	**0.21** (15)	0.17 (20)	0.08 (20)	**0.27** (20)	**0.22** (20)	**0.41** (20)	0.14 (20)	0.10 (20)	-0.08 (20)	**0.22** (20)
Page Views per User	-0.08 (15)	-0.18 (20)	-0.07 (20)	0.11 (20)	0.15 (20)	**0.35** (20)	**0.20** (20)	**0.24** (20)	-0.14 (20)	0.14 (20)

Note: Partial correlations controlling for portal news sites and Taiwan-based news sites. Bold numbers between 0.20 and 0.40 represent low, definite-but-small correlations; those between 0.40 and 0.70 represent moderate, substantial correlations.

Conclusion

Today's online news sites, which represent the latest and most promising news media and news technology, are the media source with the most potential to aggregate the benefits of the long tail for news consumption. To explore whether online news sites have exploited the long tail economy to improve their market performance, we examined the links between the long tail forces and the market performance of the top 20 national news sites in Taiwan through a comprehensive content analysis correlated with third party traffic data. Four key points conclude the study. First, the results generally suggest that Taiwan's news sites were not taking full advantage of the long tail forces with the frequent use of filter tools being the only exception. Second, Taiwan's news sites have developed a trend toward greater infotainment. Third, when correlating with traffic data, filter tools and content variety did not contribute much to each news site's market performance. Lastly, on the other hand, news sites that formulated civic or public participation opportunities have gained more substantial traffic rewards. Since civic participation empowers an individual who has something to tell with the tools to express his/her opinion to the world, online news sites that recognize and respond to this ongoing trend favoring public participation may earn a competitive advantage.

It is also important to address limitations in our study and directions for future research. In terms of product variety for production democratization, the indices were created by counting categories and subcategories provided by each news site, but the method might have suffered due to different website structures (flat or deep). Further, the uncustomized third party traffic metrics limit us to discussion of the bivariate association between each long tail tool and each market performance indicator. Nevertheless, having established at least an initial connection between long tail forces and market performance data, we believe it makes sense for future studies to consider the effectiveness of specific long tail tools in terms of audience adoption, an ultimate criterion of a successful or unsuccessful strategy and business model.

Appendix

Table 4.1A The Extent of Long Tail Tools Adopted by News Sites in the United States (N=204)

Index	Frequency	Valid Percent
Production Volume		
0–1,000,000 files	–	–
1,000,001–10,000,000 files	–	–

Table 4.1A (cont.)

Index	Frequency	Valid Percent
More than 10,000,000 files	–	–
Content Variety		
0–100 categories	153	75
101–200 categories	45	22
More than 200 categories	6	3
Civic Participation		
0–5 opportunities	100	49
6–10 opportunities	98	48
More than 10 opportunities	6	3
Access Options		
0–5 options	133	65
6–10 options	71	35
More than 10 options	2	1
Filter Tools		
0–5 tools	69	34
6–10 tools	75	37
More than 10 options	59	29

Note: Production volume was not calculated in the US study.

References

Albarran, A. B. (2002). *Media economics: Understanding markets, industries, and concepts* (second edn.). Ames: Iowa State University Press.

Anderson, C. (2006). *The long tail: Why the future of business is selling less of more.* New York: Hyperion.

Babbie, E. (2008). *The practice of social research.* Belmont, CA: Wadsworth.

Brain.com. (2009). Do portal news sites matter? Impacts on newspapers. Retrieved from http://www.brain.com.tw/News/RealNewsContent.aspx?ID=13200

Briggs, M. (2007). Journalism 2.0: How to survive and thrive. Retrieved from http://www.kcnn.org/images/uploads/Journalism_20.pdf

Brynjolfsson, E., Hu, Y. J., & Smith, M. D. (2006a). From niches to riches: Anatomy of the long tail. *MITSloan Management Review*, 47(4), 67–71.

Brynjolfsson, E., Hu, Y. J., & Smith, M. D. (2006b). Goodbye Pareto principle, hello long tail: The effect of search costs on the concentration of product sales. Retrieved from http://www.scribd.com/doc/3542250/Goodbye-Pareto-Principle-Hello-Long-Tail

Carpenter, S. (2010). A study of content diversity in online citizen journalism and online newspaper articles. *New Media & Society*, 12(7), 1064–1084.

Chan-Olmsted, S., & Ha, L. S. (2003). Internet business models for broadcasters: How television stations perceive and integrate the Internet? *Journal of Broadcasting & Electronic Media*, 47(4), 597–617.

Chan-Olmsted, S., & Park, J. S. (2000). From on air to online world: Examining the content and structures of broadcast TV stations' Web sites. *Journalism & Mass Communication Quarterly*, 77(2), 321–339.

Chyi, H. I., & Lewis, S. (2009). Use of online newspaper sites lags behind print editions. *Newspaper Research Journal*, 30(4), 38–53.

Chyi, H. I., & Sylvie, G. (2001). The medium is global, the content is not: The role of geography in online newspaper markets. *Journal of Media Economics*, 14(4), 231–248.

Dess, G. G., & Robinson JR., R. B. (1984). Measuring organizational performance in the absence of objective measures: The case of the privately-held firm and conglomerate business unit. *Strategic Management Journal*, 5, 265–273.

Elberse, A., & Oberholzer-Gee, F. (2008). Superstars and underdogs: An examination of the long-tail phenomenon in video sales. Harvard Business School Working Papers Series, Available at http://www.people.hbs.edu/aelberse/papers/hbs_07–015.pdf.

Foust, J. C. (2005). *Online journalism: Principles and practices of news for the web*. Scottsdale, AZ: Holcomb Hathaway Publishers, Inc.

Grabe, M. E., Zhou, S. H., Lang, A., & Bolls, P. D. (2000). Packaging television news: The effects of tabloid on information processing and evaluative responses. *Journal of Broadcasting and Electronic Media*, 44(4), 581–598.

Graber, D. A. (1994). The infotainment quotient in routine television news: A director's perspective. *Discourse in Society*, 5(4), 483–508.

Huang, J. S., & Wang, W. (2010, June). *The application of the long tail economy on the online news industry*. Paper presented at the 9th World Media Economics and Management Conference (WMEMC), Bogota, Colombia.

InsightXplorer. (2009). ARO Internet audience measurements. Retrieved from http://www.insightxplorer.com/en/product_aro.html

Interactive Advertising Bureau. (2011, April). IAB Internet advertising revenue report: 2010 full-year results. Retrieved from http://www.iab.net/insights_research/530422/adrevenuereport

Kaplan, D. (2011, July 28). McClatchy profits fall amid industrywide declines. *paidContent.org*. Retrieved from http://paidcontent.org/article/419-mcclatchy-profits-fall-amid-industrywide-declines/

Koch, R. (1998). *The 80/20 principle: The secret of achieving more with less*. New York: Currency Doubleday.

Lefkow, C. (2011, May 17). NY Times unveils plan to charge readers on the Web. *AFP News Agency*. Retrieved from http://www.taipeitimes.com/News/biz/archives/2011/03/19/2003498535

Li, S. S. (2001). New media and market competition: A niche analysis of television news, electronic news, and newspaper news in Taiwan. *Journal of Broadcasting & Electronic Media*, 45(2), 259–276.

Luo, Z.-Y., Yang, X.-L., & Zhao, D.-A. (2011). 2011 Web 100. *Business Next*, 202, 79–89.

Macias, W., & Lewis, L. S. (2003). A content analysis of direct-to-consumer (DTC) prescription drug web sites. *Journal of Advertising*, 32(4), 43–56.

Maynard, N. H. (1995). Diversity, democracy and niche markets. *Media Studies Journal*, 9(3), 141–148.

McLuhan, M. (1964). *Understanding media: The extensions of man*. New York: McGraw-Hill.

Morton, J. (2004). Nouveau niche. *American Journalism Review*, 26(1), 64.

Neuendorf, K. (2002). *The content analysis guidebook*. Thousand Oaks, CA: Sage Publications.

Nielsen Company and PEJ Research. (2011). Facebook is becoming increasingly important. Retrieved from http://www.journalism.org/analysis_report/facebook_becoming_increasingly_important

Picard, R. G. (1989). *Media economics: Concepts and issues*. Beverly Hills, CA: Sage.

Project for Excellence in Journalism. (2010). The state of the news media 2010: An annual report on American journalism. Retrieved from http://stateofthemedia.org/previous-reports/

Smyrnaios, N., Marty, E., & Rebillard, F. (2010). Does the long tail apply to online news? A quantitative study of French-speaking news websites. *New Media & Society*, 12(8), 1244–1261.

Stavitsky, A. G. (2000). By the numbers: The use of ratings data in academic research. *Journal of Broadcasting & Electronic Media*, 44(3), 535–539.

Stovall, J. G. (2004). *Web journalism: Practice and promise of a new medium*. Boston, MA: Pearson Education, Inc.

Varian, H. R. (2000). Market structure in the network age. In Brynjolfsson, E. & Kahin, B. (Eds.), *Understanding the digital economy: Data, tools, and research*. Cambridge, MA: The MIT Press.

Venkatraman, N., & Ramanujam, V. (1986). Measurement of business performance in strategy research A comparison of approaches. *Academy of Management Review*, 11(4), 801–814.

Venkatraman, N., & Ramanujam, V. (1987). Measurement of business economic performance: An examination of method convergence. *Journal of Management*, 13(1), 109–122.

Wang, W., & Huang, J. S. (2011). The Taiwanese press in the Internet age: Business strategies, revenue models, long tail economy, and their impacts on journalism. *JRE Online Journal*, 28–54.

Weaver, D. H. (1981). Basic statical tools. In G. H. Stempel III & B. H. Westley (Eds.), *Research methods in mass communication* (pp. 48–85). Englewood Cliffs, NJ: Prentice Hall.

Wertime, K., & Fenwick, I. (2008). *Digimarketing: The essential guide to new media and digital marketing*. Singapore: John Wiley & Sons Pte., Ltd.

Wicks, R. H. (1989). Product matching in television news using benefit segmentation. *Journal of Advertising Research*, 29(5), 64–68.

Yang, M. J., Huang, J. S., & Chyi, H. I. (2011, June). *Friend or foe? Examining the relationship between portal news and newspaper sites in Taiwan*. Paper presented at the International Telecommunication Society's Asia-Pacific Regional Conference, Taipei, Taiwan.

Zou, S., & Cavusgil, T. (2002). The GMS: A broad conceptualization of global marketing strategy and its effect on firm performance. *Journal of Marketing*, 66(October), 40–56.

5

ORDER OF MARKET ENTRY
Examining First Mover Advantages among Social Networking Sites

Jiyoung Cha, Ph.D.

Literature Review

First Mover Advantages

Many different factors may affect the success of a firm. In business literature, order of market entry has been regarded as one of the determinants of success. Order of market entry refers to the time a business first enters its market (Robinson, 1988). In business theory, it has been commonly believed that being first in marketing a new product or technology provides advantages (Hoppe & Lehmann-Grube, 2001). First mover advantage theory posits that first movers have a competitive advantage because successful followers must overcome barriers to entry that are formed by early entry (Denstadli, Lines, & Grønhaug, 2005). Prior research suggested various sources of barriers to entry. One is learning effects. That is, first movers' experience, accumulated from the learning curve, can pose a substantial barrier to entry to later entrants (Lieberman & Montgomery, 1988). Another source of barriers to entry is that first movers can secure R&D and patents (Mellahi & Johnson, 2000). Other sources of barriers to entry include cost advantages (Robinson & Fornell, 1985), switching costs (Lieberman & Montgomery, 1988; Porter, 1985), and economies of scale (Kerin, Varadarajan, & Peterson, 1992). In addition, the acquisition of quality resources by first movers is a source for barriers to entry for followers (Barney, 1991).

Over the past several decades, researchers have examined the relationship between order of market entry and performance of organizations in different goods sectors. The empirical research shows contradicting results. One group of researchers found that surviving early entrants or market pioneers appear to have substantially greater shares than surviving later entrants in both consumer and industrial markets

(Bond & Lean, 1977; Kalyanaram & Urban, 1992; Lambkin, 1988; Robinson & Fornell, 1985; Spital, 1983; Whitten, 1997). However, empirical research on first mover advantages has suffered from survivor bias. The problem is that many empirical studies on first mover advantages tended to identify pioneers among survivors. For instance, Amazon and AOL (America Online) are often referred to as first movers in their respective product categories, but in fact they were followers, not pioneers, in the markets. The first movers in each product category were Bookstacks and OnSale, respectively (Ankney & Hidding, 2005; Hidding & Williams, 2003).

During the late 1980s and early 1990s, another group of researchers challenged the first mover advantage theory, arguing that the theory is outdated and inapplicable in a dynamic, hypercompetitive environment (Golder & Tellis, 1993). Literature on imitators versus first mover innovators suggests that imitation surpasses innovation as a business strategy in industries, such as online businesses, with weak intellectual property rights protection, technological interdependence, market and technical uncertainties, rapid rates of technical innovation, and the swift movement of information (Mellahi & Johnson, 2000). Scholarly research on early followers' advantages also emphasizes the critical role of product quality improvements for the relative performance of firms. The quality of a new product improves over time (Dutta, Lach, & Rustichini, 1995) and thus early followers enjoy advantages derived from increased product quality. Nevertheless, Lieberman and Montgomery (1998) argued that followers' advantages may not be as important as those of pioneers.

Some empirical studies supported early followers' advantages. Shankar, Carpenter, and Krishnamurthi (1998) analyzed 13 brands in 2 pharmaceutical product categories and found that product innovation enables second movers to overtake the pioneers. Similarly, Berndt, Bui, Reily, and Urban (1995) also found that second movers benefit from better quality than pioneers in the US anti-ulcer drug market. Cho, Kim, and Rhee (1998) showed how latecomers can leapfrog over pioneers in an examination of the semiconductor industry in Korea and Japan. Keohane and Nye (1998) found that a fast follower can outperform a first mover in some commercial situations.

Information technology is one of the product markets where fast followers have advantages over a first mover. Specifically focusing on e-business technology product categories, Hidding and Williams (2003) examined 27 IT-driven product categories, and found that fast followers sustained market leadership on average 60 percent of the time, whereas only 3–17 percent of first movers in the IT product categories maintained advantages. Tellis and Golder (2002) also found similar results using a sample of 67 consumer product categories, including 17 information technology products.

Considering the conflicting findings regarding first mover advantages and early follower advantages, this study addresses the following research question:

RQ1: Do first movers of social networking service perform better than early followers?

Resource-Based View

The framework of the resource-based view informs the design of more sophisticated studies on timing of entry (Frawley & Fahy, 2006). The first mover advantage or disadvantage is conceptually linked with the resource-based view (Barney, 1991; Lieberman & Montgomery, 1998). The majority of the first mover advantage literature suggests that pioneers have advantages because they are more likely to acquire valuable resources and capabilities before other firms enter the market. On the other hand, pioneers may not be efficient in determining what are good resources or capabilities in the market because of lack of experience, knowledge, and consumer preferences (Lieberman & Montgomery, 1998). The resource-based view links how firms possess valuable resources and capabilities with time of market entry.

The resource-based view arose from the frustration with the structure-conduct-performance paradigm of the industrial organization (IO) view, which posits that a firm's performance is determined by its external environment (Bain, 1959; Porter, 1985). Contrary to the IO view, the resource-based view posits that resources and capabilities possessed by a firm sustain its competitive advantage (Dierickx & Cool, 1989; Prahalad & Hamel, 1990) and differentiate the firm from its competitors (Bharadwaj, 2000). Researchers suggested that the value, inimitability, and non-substitutability of a firm's resources and capabilities secure its competitive advantage in the market (Barney, 1991; Wernerfelt, 1989).

Broadly speaking, a firm's resources are either tangible-based or intangible-based. Tangible resources refer to "the physical assets that an organization possesses and include physical resources and financial resources" (Henry, 2011, p. 128). Intangible resources refer to "intellectual/technological resources and reputation" (Henry, 2011, p. 128). Technological resources encompass an organization's ability to innovate and how rapidly the firm innovates. Intellectual resources include patents and copyrights that are based on the organization's technological resources (Henry, 2011). Along with technological and intellectual resources, reputations of firms among customers and suppliers are another type of intangible resource that enable firms to sustain competitive advantage (Porter, 1985). Possessing good resources does not, however, directly translate into good performance of a firm. Maximizing a firm's performance by utilizing the resources requires capabilities—the abilities to assemble, integrate, and manage these bundles of resources (Russo & Fouts, 1997).

Applying the resource-based view, researchers of information systems further identified various resources that can sustain competitive advantage. Information technology (IT) infrastructure is one type of resource that helps a firm to sustain competitive advantage (Keen, 1991; McKenney, 1995). IT infrastructure of a firm consists of the computers and communication technologies as well as the shareable technical platforms and databases (Ross, Beath, & Goodhue, 1996). It is widely perceived that information systems can be easily purchased and duplicated by competitors, which lowers the value of IT infrastructure as a resource that sustains competitive advantage (Mata, Fuerst, & Barney, 1995). This perception assumes that it is easy to separate IT assets. The perception also disregards the synergistic benefits of integrated systems. Much time, effort, and experiential learning is needed for an IT firm to create synergistic benefits of integrated systems (Bharadwaj, 2000).

Teece (1998) argues that the competitive advantages of firms are attributed not to market position but to difficulty of replicating knowledge assets and the way they are deployed. Know-how refers to knowledge assets that a firm can build. The critical dimension of IT resources includes technical IT skills and managerial IT skills. Technical and managerial IT skills typically require the accumulation of experience, and thus it takes time for them to evolve (Katz, 1974). The reason why technical and managerial skills need the accumulation of time and experience is because those skills often depend on strong interpersonal relationships, which may take years to develop (Chatfield & Bjorn-Andersen, 1997; Mata et al., 1995). Firms can develop valuable, inimitable, and non-substitutable resources and capabilities internally, or they can acquire them through strategic alliances/partnerships or acquisitions of other entities. Corporate reputations benefit from possessing technical and managerial IT skills because a good corporate reputation enables the firm to more strongly attract talent and investors (Vergin & Qoronfleh, 1998). Strong reputations bring more opportunities for alliances/partnerships.

Empirical studies examining the first mover advantage through the lens of the resource-based view found that first mover firms possess strong research and development (R&D) skills and financial resources. On the other hand, late-mover firms possess strong manufacturing and marketing resources (Robinson, Fornell, & Sullivan, 1992; Schoenecker & Cooper, 1998; Thomas, 1996). Although early entrants may have the benefit of R&D, it might be also risky for firms to enter a market earlier than others due to the uncertainty of the market (Mellahi & Johnson, 2000; Wernerfelt & Karnani, 1987).

Based on the prior research examining a relationship between the order of market entry and possessing resources, this study addresses a second research question:

RQ2: To what resources do first movers and early followers in the US social networking service market gain access?

Network Externalities

When examining first mover advantages in the social networking service market, network externality is an important concept. Network externalities refer to the change in a product's value as its installed user base (i.e., size of the network) grows (Frels, Shervani, & Srivastava, 2003; Katz & Shapiro, 1985). Along with resources and capabilities, first movers may be likely to capitalize on the opportunity to attract a large user base prior to the entrant of other firms into the market. First movers have the chance to observe network behavior and capture information before later entrants. Privileged access to information about transactions and product-usage patterns can provide opportunities for identifying similar members, connecting new members to current members, and to strengthen and expand the network (Varadarajan, Yadav, & Shankar, 2008). As the users of the first movers' products increase, potential users perceive the first movers' products more favorably because of their user base (Varadarajan et al., 2008). Prior studies examined the role of network externalities as a potential source of competitive advantage. In light of network externalities, the battle between Betamax and VHS format video cassette recorders has been examined (Cusamano, Myllonadis, & Rosenbloom, 1992; Varadarajan, 1999). The competition between Nintendo and Sega videogame systems has also been investigated (Shankar & Bayus, 2003).

Network externalities are critical in predicting adoption of innovations, particularly communication technologies, because the value of a communication technology is directly linked to the number of prior adopters (e.g., Ilie, Van Slyke, Green, & Lou, 2005; Nysveen, Pedersen, & Thorbjornsen, 2005; Song, Parry, & Kawakami, 2009; Strader, Ramaswami, & Houle, 2007). In the context of social networking sites, network externalities may be important for firms in achieving competitive advantages. Regarding adoption of a new technology or product, researchers suggest that companies with the largest installed network bases will dominate the market (Arthur, 1996; Brynjolfsson & Kemerer, 1996; Katz & Shapiro, 1985; Lee & O'Connor, 2003).

Unlike physical product markets, it is relatively easy for a new firm to enter the social networking service market because the market does not require high upfront fixed costs. However, if a new firm enters the market too late, it might be difficult for the firm to attract users within

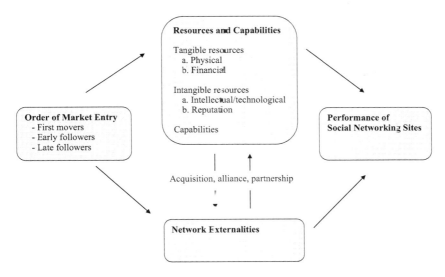

Figure 5.1 Framework for Performance of Social Networking Sites
Note: Created by Jiyoung Cha

a short period of time compared to incumbents, if incumbents have a large installed user base. Over the past decade, the number of social networking sites operating in the US has grown. When taking the importance of network externalities of social networking sites into account, the social networking service market may be eventually highly concentrated. The dominance of a few social networking sites may compel other social networking sites to exit the market. Figure 5.1 illustrates the theoretical framework of this study.

Applying network externalities to the social networking service market, this study addresses a third research question:

RQ3: How does the network size of a dominant social networking site influence strategic decisions of other social networking sites in the market?

Method

A qualitative research approach was chosen to investigate the research questions. A qualitative study approach is used to examine complex situations and problems (Hoepfl, 1997). The current study includes comprehensive longitudinal data that show histories of social networking sites operating in the US. A qualitative research approach is appropriate when a holistic investigation is needed (Feagin, Orum, & Sjoberg, 1991) and when the phenomenon of interest should be understood within the context (Yin, 2003). Therefore, the qualitative longitudinal research approach is widely used in the field of management (e.g., Benner & Tripsas, 2012). Some prior research that examined first mover advantages also conducted qualitative studies (e.g., Geroski & Vlassopoulos, 1991; Rosenbloom & Cusumano, 1987; Sutton, 1991). A qualitative research approach is often taken when existing research has barely explored the topic (Eisenhardt, 1989). The majority of order of market entry literature has focused heavily on physical product markets, but the effect of order of market entry has not been investigated in the context of social networking sites.

This study focused on US-based social networking sites that target *mass markets* from the US population. Social networking sites are defined as web-based services that (1) focus primarily on connecting individuals with others through sharing their daily lives and thoughts, (2) electronically link registered users, and (3) are open to general Internet users without specific interest orientation. Under the definition, blogs focusing on primary services such as recording opinions and information, dating sites, online communities focusing on bringing together people with the same interests, and niche social networking sites were not included for the analysis. The selection of social networking sites was based on their *initial* offerings and positioning. This study identified 24 general social networking sites that were launched and operated in the US (see Table 5.1). The time frame for the analysis ranged from 1995 to 2012. The beginning year was selected because one of the first US-based social networking sites was launched in 1995. To remain free of the survival bias, this study avoided the feature-centric definition of social networking sites (e.g., Boyd & Ellison, 2007) because the definition merely reflects the features of *popular* or *dominant* social networking sites.

After all the general social networking sites are identified, they were classified into three categories: first movers, early followers, and late followers. Classmates, PlanetAll, and SixDegrees, which were launched in 1995, 1996, and 1997 respectively, were categorized as first movers because they were the first three entrants in the US social networking service market. There was a significant time gap between the time SixDegrees entered the social networking service market in 1997 and the time the next entrant, Friendster, entered the market in 2002. Following the three first movers, 17 social networking sites entered the market between 2002 and 2007; they were categorized as early followers. Early followers include Friendster, MySpace, Facebook, Twitter, Hi5, Tagged, Orkut, and Cyworld USA. Once Facebook outperformed MySpace in 2008, Facebook experienced phenomenal and accelerated growth and began to exert a great deal of market power in the US social networking service market. Subsequently, the 4 social networking sites launched after 2007 were categorized as late followers and included Plurk, WeOurFamily,

Table 5.1 Social Networking Sites Operated in the US (1995–present: February 2012)

Classification	Market entry – Status	SNS	Estimated no. of registered users (2012)+	Estimated daily time on the site (2012)**	Estimated daily page view per user (2012)**
First movers	1995–present	Classmates	60 million	03:39	3.44
	1996–2000	PlanetAll	1.5 million*	N/A***	N/A***
	1997–2001	SixDegrees	1.3 million*	N/A***	N/A***
Early followers	2002–present	Friendster	115 million	02:48	2.77
	2002–present	Reunion	41 million	01:37	1.91
	2003–present	Hi5	230 million	04:55	8.35
	2003–present	MySpace	12.5 million	02:56	2.80
	2003–present	Multiply	11 million	05:31	5.59
	2004–present	Facebook	800 million	24:05	12.48
	2004–present	Tagged	100 million	24:40	18.41
	2004–present	Orkut	15.5 million	01:49	2.30
	2005–present	Bebo	117 million	03:50	5.09
	2005–present	myYearbook	33 million	21:31	13.20
	2005–present	Ning	65 million	05:14	4.65
	2006–present	Badoo	130 million	16:29	15.16
	2006–2010	Cyworld USA	Unknown	N/A***	N/A***
	2006–present	Twitter	300 million	06:58	4.81
	2006–2011	Windows Live Spaces	120 million*	N/A***	N/A***
	2007–2008	Pownce	45,000*	N/A***	N/A***
	2007–present	Virb	Unknown	04:19	3.40
Late followers	2008 present	Plurk	6 million	05:19	2.85
	2009–present	WeOurFamily	Unknown	01:34	1.8
	2010–2011	Google Buzz	Unknown	N/A***	N/A***
	2011–present	Google+	90 million	01:30	1.53

+ *Source*: Various newspapers/industry journals.
* The numbers were based in the year of closing.
** *Source*: Alexa.com.
*** Estimated daily time and page views were not available for the sites closed.

Google Buzz, and Google+. To answer the research questions, the analysis focused on first movers and early followers.

This study drew upon a broad range of industry sources and archival data. To measure performances of social networking sites, this study tracked relevant information regarding year of market entry, year of market exit, market position, number of registered users, daily time spent on each site, and daily page view per user. To identify resources and capabilities of social networking sites, information regarding the sites' acquisition of other entities and alliances/partnerships was collected. In addition, patent data were sourced from the United States Patent and Trademark Office (USPTO). With respect to critical strategic decisions, this study focused on ownership and positioning changes. Data came from a combination of company websites, newspapers, trade publications, published executive interviews, and industry resources (e.g., Crunchase.com, Alexa.com). To ensure reliability and accuracy, multiple sources were used and the information presented in the paper was cross-checked. The analysis consisted of three steps. First, information was collected for each of the social networking sites focused on by this study. Second, commonalities within each social networking site group—first movers and early followers—were examined. Third, discrepancies between first movers and early followers were identified.

Results

Order of Market Entry and Survival

Three social networking sites, Classmates, PlanetAll, and SixDegrees, were the pioneers of the US social networking service market. Classmates was the first, debuting in 1995 (Goldsborough, 2002). The other two first movers, PlanetAll and SixDegrees, were launched in 1996 and 1997, respectively (Adweek, 1997; Riedman, 1998). Classmates was originally designed to help people reconnect with high-school classmates. Classmates required registrants to enter their real names, instead of pseudonyms, and their education history so that members could easily locate the people they wanted to find. Users could also display other information, such as hobbies, career, and marital status.

The other first mover, PlanetAll, was launched with the mission to harness the power of the Internet to help people build and maintain personal and professional relationships. A typical profile page included names of friends, business associates, classmates, other contacts, and affinity groups—such as schools attended, professional association memberships, and fraternity or sorority affiliations (Business Library, 1996). The site also offered other services such as a web-based address book, calendar, and reminder services, enabling users to organize and schedule contact information with other members (Bloomberg Businessweek, 2012).

The third entrant, SixDegrees, was named after the "Six Degrees of Separation" theory that people are connected through a maximum of six relationships. Six Degrees registrants entered their personal information, such as where they live and what they do, to connect with others. The site required users to indicate the email addresses of at least two people they know, and then those identified people were invited to join the site (Snider, 1997). A series of mutual acquaintances enabled one member to connect to all the site members. Members had control over who could see their personal information (Freierman, 1998).

All three first entrants were acquired by other firms. Two years after PlanetAll's launch, Amazon purchased PlanetAll in exchange for 800,000 shares (Silicon Valley/San Jose Business Journal, 1998). SixDegrees was acquired by YouthStream Media for $125 million in 2001 (*The New York Times*, 1999). In 2004, the Internet service provider United Online, which is known for its NetZero and Juno Internet subscriptions, purchased Classmates for $100 million in cash (Cook, 2004). After the acquisitions, PlanetAll and SixDegrees did not survive in the market and were closed in 2000 and 2001, respectively. Classmates survived, but it became part of a nostalgic content sharing site, MemoryLane, in 2011 (Elliott, 2011, March 18).

A host of early followers entered the US social networking service market between 2002 and 2008. The time period is bookended by 2001, when the two first movers PlanetAll and SixDegrees exited the market, and 2008, when the registered users of Facebook exceeded those of MySpace. Examples of early followers include Friendster, MyLife, Hi5, MySpace, Multiply, Facebook, Tagged, Orkut, Bebo, MyYearbook, Ning, Badoo, Cyworld USA, Twitter, Windows Live Spaces, and Virb (see Table 5.1). Notably, many of the early followers fueled the surging popularity of social networking sites inside or outside the US and increased the awareness of social networking services as a new media product category among consumers, educators, advertisers, and investors.

Early followers performed better than first movers with respect to survival and the number of registered users. As seen in Table 5.1, more than three-fourths of the early followers survived in the market. Exceptions include Pownce, Cyworld USA, and Window Live Spaces; they exited the market in 2008, 2010, and 2011, respectively (Brian in Jeollanam-do, 2010; McCarthy, 2008; Paul, 2010). Pownce stayed in the market for about one year. The other two early followers survived in the market for approximately four years. Overall, the network sizes of early followers were also much larger than those of first movers. Two first movers, PlanetAll and SixDegrees, had 1.5 million and 1.3 million registered users respectively when they were shut down (Erickson, 2012;

Wolverton, 2000). On the other hand, many early followers had more than 100 million registered users in 2011. Facebook, Twitter, and Hi5 had 800 million, 300 million, and 230 million registered users respectively in 2011 (Tagged, 2011; Taylor, 2011; Wortham, 2011) (see Table 5.1). With respect to the network size, early followers appeared to benefit from longer survival rates, better Internet infrastructure, and higher Internet penetration than first movers.

Resources and Capabilities of First Movers and Early Followers

The primary resources of first movers are social networking technologies and technological skills. In order for members to look up contacts without Internet connections, PlanetAll integrated phone access into its Virtual Address Book, which automatically updates the changes in friends' personal information. The technology allowed PlanetAll to form a syndication partnership with firms such as Unisys and Harris Publishing (Telecomworldwide, 1997). SixDegrees developed a personal bulletin board service and syndicated it to several job sites and special interest online communities, including Job Direct, CollegeBeat, and Online Career Center (Snyder, 1998).

Despite innovative technology and increase of registered users, first movers lacked the know-how to leverage their technologies and technological skills effectively to generate stable traffic on the sites. For instance, users of PlanetAll received updates on developments and pending events in their personal spheres through the Daily PlanetAll, a daily email message. If a member did not have email access, a fax was sent (Business Library, 1996). While providing convenience to users, these updates reduced the need for members to revisit the site repeatedly to get updates.

Although first movers introduced social networking technologies, they did not have adequate capabilities to secure their technologies. None of the first movers gained a direct benefit from patents of their social networking technologies. Classmates did not patent any of its technologies. Ten years after PlanetAll was closed, Amazon won a patent for a "social networking system" in 2010 from the United States Patent and Trademark Office (USPTO) because it acquired PlanetAll in 1998. Another first mover, SixDegrees, won a patent for a method and apparatus to build a networking database and system in 2001. But in that same year, the site ceased to operate. YouthStream Media took control of the patent when it acquired SixDegrees, then sold the patent to another social networking site.

In contrast, early followers were able to establish market competence based on the mistakes of the first movers. As seen in Table 5.2, some early followers have several patents. Between 2006 and 2010, the

Table 5.2 Social Networking Sites' Alliances/Partnerships (1995–2012)

SNS	Patents*	Alliances/Partnerships**
Classmates	0	Marketing (20th Century Fox, CBS, Vertrue, Webloyalty, Affinion)
		Online dating (PerfectMatch.com)
		Public records service (PeopleFinders.com)
PlanetAll	1	Branding (GeoCities, Lycos, Bernard C. Harris Publishing Company, InfoSpace, MonsterBoard, PlanetDirect, Four11, 4th Network, WhoWhere, Worldview/ITN, Unisys)
		Mobile data exchange software (Puma Technology)
		Search (Lycos)
SixDegrees	1	Marketing (Job Direct, CollegeBeat, Netcom, Online Career Center, Wall Street Links, Surfcaster, Worldwide Jewish Web, News America Digital Publishing)
Friendster	7	Branding (Big Sky Communication)
		Search and advertising (Yahoo!, Google, Eurekster)
		Classified ads (OLX)
		Online dating (eHarmony)
Reunion	0	Branding (Red Cross Services, LinkConnector, Bender/Helper Impact)
		Business information search (ZoomInfo)
		People search (Wink, TGN)
		Advertising (Microsoft)
Hi5	0	Game (Mochi Media, RockYou, RotoHog)
		Mobile ads (InMobi)
		Virtual currency monetization (PlaySpan)
MySpace	1	Game (Oberon Media, Zynga)
		Music content (Universal Music Group, Sony BGM Music Entertainment, Warner Music Group, IODA)
		Music distribution (TuneCore, Textango)
		Video content (Paramount, Gaumont, Endemol, Walt Disney)
		Online music publishing rights management (Songtrust)
		Mobile platforms (Microsoft, Vodafone, Cingular Wireless)
		Social music videos and TV shows (Panasonic)
		Merchandising products (Zazzle)
		Data portability (Facebook, Yahoo!, Twitter, eBay)
		Search and advertising (Google, Orange, Ad.ly)
		Contests/Events (NBC News, MSNBC, MTV, Comcast)
		Online city guide (Citysearch)
		Dance content (Electus, Sprite)
		Internet communications (Skype, UStream)
		Social television platform (Panasonic)
Multiply	0	Content (ABS-CBN)

Table 5.2 (cont.)

SNS	Patents*	Alliances/Partnerships**
Facebook	20	Game (Zynga, TrialPay, TGN)
		Music service (Spotify, Slacker Radio, Rhapsody, Rdio, MOG, Soundcloud, Deezer, Shazam, AudioVroom)
		Music distribution (Apple)
		Video content (Warner Brothers)
		Retail information service (WalMart, eBay, Harrah's Entertainment)
		Internet communication (Skype)
		Search (Bing, Google, Yahoo!)
		Web security (McAfee, Websense, Web of Trust)
		Social web browsing (RockMelt)
		Mobile payment (Bango)
		Mobile location service (Foursquare)
		Web analytics (Omniture, Nielsen)
		Data portability (MySpace)
		Event (CBS News, Washington Post, Slate, New York Times, CNN)
Tagged	3	Game (FlowPlay)
		Mobile music platform (Razz)
		Virtual goods monetization (Social Gold)
Orkut	0	Game (Viximo)
Bebo	5	Branding (Unilever)
		Music content (Apple)
		Online financing platform for recording artists (Slicethepie)
		Online video distribution (Brightcove)
		Mobile platform (Samsung Mobile UK, Intercasting, NewBay Software)
		Search and ads (Yahoo!)
		Instant messenger service (Microsoft)
		Video content (CBS, MTV, BBC, Channel 4, BSkyB)
myYearbook	0	Game (OMGPOP, Meez, Viximo)
		Online video platform (VideoEgg Inc)
		Virtual currency exchange service (WeeWorld)
		Security (ThreatMatrix)
Ning.com	3	Domain name registration (eNom)
		Education-focused publishing (Pearson)
		Cloud photo service (Aviary)
Badoo	0	Online dating (DailyStar)
Cyworld USA	0	Branding (United Talent Agency, Carat Brand Experience)
		Game (Mochi Media)
		Image editing (FotoFlexer)
		Video content (NBC Universal)
		Video platform (Eyespot)
		Media mixing platform (Eyespot)
		Advertising (Double Fusion)

Table 5.2 (cont.)

SNS	Patents*	Alliances/Partnerships**
Twitter	0	Music data services (The Echo Nest, Gracenote, Rovi)
		Video content (Fox News, Disney Pictures, Current TV)
		Search (Bing, Yahoo! Japan, Yandex)
		Browser (Mozilla)
		Social media content aggregation (Mass Relevance, Mediasift, Tweetmeme)
		Data on demand (Datasift)
		Web analytics (Gnip)
		Computing and mobile platform (Apple, O2)
		Advertising (Mixi, Sky)
		Data portability (LinkedIn, MySpace)
		Photo-sharing (Photobucket)
		Mobile social media aggregation service (Orange)
		Mobile platform (HeyWire)
		Event (American Express, Burberry)
Windows Live Spaces	0	Blog (WordPress)
Pownce	0	
Virb	0	Web analytics (Reinvigorate)

* *Source:* United States Patent and Trademark Office (USPTO).
** *Source:* Various newspapers/industry journals.

USPTO awarded a total of seven patents to Friendster, including multimedia aggregation in an online social network, proximity search methods using tiles to represent geographical zones, methods for sharing relationship information stored in a social network database with third party databases, and method of inducing content uploads in a social network. MySpace was also granted one patent for a video downloading and scrubbing system and method in 2011. Tagged possesses three patents, including user-created tags for online social networking. Another early follower, Facebook, was granted a patent for its news feed in 2010. Facebook also purchased all of Friendster's social networking-related patents in 2010 (Gannes, 2010). Facebook has a total of 20 patents awarded by the USPTO as of 2012. Other early followers, Bebo and Ning, have five and three patents, respectively, from the USPTO. By securing their social networking technologies, early followers raised barriers to entry in the social networking service market.

First movers tended to establish their core competencies by leveraging their own resources and capabilities. On the other hand, early followers strengthened and expanded their technologies and IT infrastructure through acquisitions. As seen in Table 5.3, many early followers acquired social networking technologies and platform firms. MySpace acquired Threadbox, Imeem, and iLike, providing group messaging and social music platform technologies. Facebook acquired more than 20 startups that specialized in mobile platform technologies and Web applications. Tagged acquired another social networking site, Hi5. The acquisition provided Tagged with social game and virtual world creation technologies, because Hi5 previously purchased two firms providing those services. In addition, Tagged purchased firms that specialized in automatic skimming of cloud documents. Twitter purchased more than 10 firms that provided mobile services, security, and social media data analytics services. In contrast, first movers did not acquire any entities, but focused on developing technologies in-house.

First movers failed to lure registered users back to their sites regularly or for long periods of time. Realizing this, early followers focused their resources and capabilities on developing multimedia services. While first movers tended to center their services on networking per se, early followers expanded the horizon and heavily invested in three multimedia service areas: (1) music; (2) video/images; and (3) games (see Table 5.2). Early followers produced almost no multimedia content themselves. Rather, they were aggressive in forming strategic alliances/partnerships to gain access to multimedia content. Early followers could offer their partners platforms with established, large user bases. In return, partners offered early followers certain types of content or service technologies they could distribute. Many early followers in social networking services have partnered with game developers or game platforms. For example, Facebook has been partnering with game application developers since 2007. Zynga offered Facebook users the ability to play card games like poker and blackjack, to add the online games to their profile pages and to play them with their Facebook friends. Facebook attracted a huge number of other social game developers, including Zynga, Playdom, EA, Buffalo Studios, Playtika, DoubleDown Interactive and Wooga. Other early followers such as Hi5, Tagged, Orkut, and myYearbook also have partnerships with game providers like Mochi Media, RockYou, RotoHog, FlowPlay, and OMGPOP. They also partner with virtual currency monetization firms, such as PlaySpan, Social Gold, and WeeWorld (see Table 5.2).

Music and video services are other strong resources that early followers possess compared to first movers. Facebook has partnerships with multiple audio and music service providers, including Spotify, Slacker Radio, Rhapsody, Rdio, and MOG. The partnerships allow Facebook users to share song catalog lists with their Facebook friends and to listen to the songs with their friends. Bebo partnered with the music review and finance service provider Slicethepie. Twitter also has partnerships with The Echo Nest, Gracenote, and Rovi. The partnerships allow the music

Table 5.3 Early Followers' Acquisitions (1995–2012)

SNS	Acquisitions by SNS
Reunion	Contact list service (MyAddressBook.com, GoodContacts)
	Offering deals on the stuff to do, eat, and buy (Dealometer/CitizenLocal)
	Online community (PlanetAlumni.com, Highschoolalumni.com)
	People search engine (Wink)
Hi5	Social game (Big Six)
	Virtual world creation (PixVerse)
MySpace	Group messaging platform (Threadbox)
	Social music platform (Imeem, iLike)
Tagged	Automatic skimming of cloud document (Topicmarks, dotSyntax)
	Social networking platform (Hi5)
Facebook	Email (MailRank)
	Internet service (Chi Labs)
	Local/travel recommendations (Nextstop)
	Message platform (drop.io)
	Mobile and web application technologies (Gowalla, Strobe, Snaptu, Zenbe)
	Mobile video and image app (Digital Staircase, Instagram)
	Mobile book publishing (Push Pop Press)
	Mobile group messaging (Beluga)
	Mobile advertising/marketing platform (Rel8tion, Tagtile)
	Mobile file sharing (Sendoid)
	Photo sharing (Divvyshot)
	Rich online conversation platform (ShareGrove)
	Social job search (Pursuit)
	Social network aggregator (FriendFeed)
	Social networking software (Whoglue)
	Social Q&A site (Friend.ly)
	Software (Sofa)
	Viral invite scripts (Octazen solutions)
	Web platform (Farakey)
Bebo	Online TV service (SeeSaw)
Twitter	Internet security (Dasient)
	List making service (Bagcheck)
	Location service (Mixer Labs)
	Mobile security provider (Whisper Systems)
	Mobile software (Atebits)
	Mobile messaging (Cloudhopper)
	Online database (Smallthought systems, Dabble DB)
	Online marketing (AdGrok)
	Online review search (Summize)
	Organizing the display of tweets (TweetDeck)
	Peer search Q&A (Fluther)
	Social aggregation service (Summify)
	Social information analytics (BackType, Julpan)
	Social software design (Values of n)

Source: Crunchbase.com (2012).

service providers to display tweets from artists as their songs play (Music Ally, 2012).

Unlike the other early followers that focus mainly on access to music *platforms*, MySpace focused its resources additionally on music *content*. MySpace offers music platforms along with a wide selection of music content, enabling the users to easily stream music on their profile pages. To that end, MySpace created a joint venture, MySpace Music, with major music labels such as Sony BMG, Universal Music Group, EMI Music, Sony ATV/Music Publishing, and Warner Music Group in 2008 (Arrington, 2008). To further expand its music catalog, MySpace Music has inked deals with Nettwerk Music Group, INgrooves, IRIS Distribution, and RoyaltyShare (Crum, 2009). Thanks to these efforts and investments, MySpace owns a library of 42 million tracks, far exceeding those of Spotify and Rhapsody (Sisario, 2012). MySpace also partners with Songtrust, an online music publishing rights management firm.

Competencies of early followers are also based on their reputations as social networking sites, a distinctive media product category. Since it was a new product/service, first movers had to build awareness of the new media product category among consumers, media, advertisers, and investors. The term "social networking site" first appeared in the media in 2003, referring to the early follower Friendster (e.g., Aragon, 2003). The use of the term "social networking site" boosted the awareness of the media product category among the public. This improved awareness enabled early followers to focus on building their own brands. According to a survey by Techdivine.com, Facebook and Twitter are two out of the top ten online brands that are based on recall, connect, and user experience (Social Media Marketing, 2010). Other early followers, MySpace, Friendster, Orkut, and Hi5, also have better brand awareness, recognition, and recall as social networking sites than those of the first movers.

Strong brand reputations of early followers directly influenced their ability to expand into foreign markets. While the three first movers among social networking sites limited their geographic markets to the US, early followers have been aggressive in expanding overseas. MySpace is particularly well known for its aggressive targeting of foreign markets, although it has been downsizing international expansion since it was overtaken by Facebook (Cha, 2011). Facebook, Twitter, Orkut, Friendster, Hi5, and Bebo registered more users living outside the US than within the US. According to Alexa.com's data regarding visitors by country (2012), Bebo and Friendster have more visitors in India than in the US. Bebo has attracted a huge numbers of users in India ever since it was launched there in 2009, following international expansions into France, Germany, Italy, Spain, and the Netherlands (Bebo, 2009). Meanwhile, Hi5 and Badoo attract more visitors in Thailand and Italy, respectively, than inside the US. Orkut, Facebook, Window Live Space, Twitter, Ning, and Multiply are also listed among the top ten social networking sites by unique visitors in Brazil (ComScore, 2012; Lardinois, 2010). The strong brand presence in international markets allows many early followers to stay relatively stable in the social networking service market, whereas the weaker brands of first movers fluctuated in the market.

Network Externalities and Strategic Decisions

Since November 2008, when Facebook overtook MySpace with respect to the number of unique visitors (Kazeniac, 2009), Facebook has continued to expand its market power in the US social networking service market. Facebook's network size surpasses that of any other US-based social networking site, and this fact has influenced the strategic actions of other social networking sites. First, the majority of the early followers that entered the market earlier than Facebook repositioned themselves (see Table 5.4). In 2010, MySpace repositioned itself as a social entertainment site (Barnett, 2010). Friendster and Hi5 shifted their focus from social networking to social gaming in 2011 (Baribeau, 2011; Wauters, 2011). Multiply repositioned itself as a social shopping site in 2010 (Dizon, 2010). Classmates became a part of the nostalgic content-sharing site MemoryLane in 2011 (Elliott, 2011, March 18). Networking is still a factor in the equation for these repositioned sites, but they placed more emphasis on the entertainment aspect of the services than on networking. Virb transformed into a web hosting service provider in 2010. Second, many early followers restructured their organizations between 2008 and 2011. As shown in Table 5.4, some early followers were acquired by other entities. Cyworld USA and Window Live Spaces closed their US operations in 2010 and 2011, respectively.

Discussion

This study examined how order of market entry influences the success of US-based social networking sites by integrating network externalities and the resource-based view. Findings of this study suggest that order of entry may not directly relate to whether social networking sites survive or perform better. Rather, order of entry determines which resources and capabilities social networking sites can acquire to sustain a competitive advantage, which eventually influences the success of social networking sites. The findings of this study provide empirical evidence of an interrelationship between timing of entry and acquisition of superior resources and capabilities as suggested by Lieberman and Montgomery (1988).

Specifically focusing on social networking sites operating in the US, the present study found that first movers had more disadvantages than

Table 5.4 Social Networking Sites' Strategic Decisions (1995–present: February 2012)

Entry Status	SNS	Ownership Change	Critical Strategic Decisions
1995–present	Classmates	Acquired by United Online in 2004	Became part of MemoryLane.com, nostalgic content sharing site in 2001
1996–2000	PlanetAll	Acquired by Amazon in 1998	Closed in 2000
1997–2001	SixDegrees	Acquired by YouthStream Media Networks in 2000	Closed in 2001
2002–present	Friendster	Acquired by MOL Global in 2009	Repositioned as social game site in 2011
2002–2009	Reunion	Owned by Reunion from the launch	Changed its name to MyLife.com in 2009
2003–present	Hi5	Acquired by Tagged in 2011	Repositioned as social game site in 2011
2003–present	MySpace	Acquired by News Corp. in 2005	Repositioned as social entertainment site in 2010
2003–present	Multiply	Acquired by Naspers in 2010	Repositioned as social shopping site in 2010
2004–present	Facebook	Owned by Facebook from the launch	Remains a social networking site
2004–present	Tagged	Owned by Tagged from the launch	Remains a social networking site
2004–present	Orkut	Owned by Google from the launch	Remains a social networking site
2005–present	Bebo	Acquired by AOL 2008	Remains a social networking site
		Acquired by Criterion Capital Partners in 2010	
2005–present	myYearbook	Acquired by Quepasa in 2011	Remains a social networking site
2005–present	Ning	Merged with Glam Media in 2011	Required paid subscriptions since 2010
2006–present	Badoo	Owned by Badoo from the launch	Remains a social networking site
2006–2010	Cyworld USA	Owned by SK communications from the launch	Closed in 2010
2006–present	Twitter	Owned by Twitter from the launch	Remains a social networking site
2006–2011	Windows Live Spaces	Owned by Microsoft from the launch	Closed in 2011
2007–2008	Pownce	Acquired by Six Apart in 2008	Closed in 2008
2007–present	Virb	Acquired by Media Temple in 2008	Repositioned as a web hosting site in 2010

advantages. First movers of social networking services suffered from a public lack of awareness of the product category; each site suffered from weak brand awareness among consumers, suppliers, advertisers, and investors. The heavy investment needed to raise awareness of the social networking product category caused first movers to entirely focus on the service of networking and connecting users. Their social networking technologies succeeded in attracting new users, but not in retaining existing users. First movers failed to offer a variety of products or services that could keep registered users coming back and staying on the sites for significant periods of time. In contrast, early followers of social networking sites benefited from the improved awareness of the product category. The increased awareness of the product category due to the efforts made by first movers gave early followers more room to establish their own unique and strong firm brands. Recognizing the failure of first movers to retain users, the early followers heavily invested in developing superior music, game, and video content and platforms. Those resources of early followers in the social networking service market enabled their users to *share fun and information with other users*, whereas first movers merely focused their resources on *connecting with other users*.

While first movers were free from threats of network externalities because they entered the market first, early entrants of social networking services were heavily influenced by network externalities. Lieberman (2007) suggested that the potential for network effects translates into a strong first mover advantage in Internet markets. Yet we note that the effect of network externalities did not come from the first movers but from a few early entrants in the US social networking service market. This study found that network externalities play a substantial role in strategic decisions of social networking sites. The exponential growth of Facebook's network size compelled many early followers to reposition from social networking to social games, social entertainment, or social shopping in 2010 and 2011. Despite the repositioning, they did not completely shut down, as did two of the first movers. It is worth noting that this study found that early followers were more flexible in expanding their product lines and redefining their initial positions than were first movers. Early followers also had the capabilities to expand into foreign markets. The strong presence of those sites in foreign markets helped the sites survive longer in the US market as well.

First movers of social networking services also lacked the capabilities and experiences needed to secure their technologies. While first movers theoretically have an advantage of winning patent races (Lieberman & Montgomery, 1988), the findings of the present study found that first movers of social networking services missed the opportunity to secure their social networking technologies through patents. This failure to preemptively secure social networking technologies lowered the barrier to entry. Furthermore, the time lag between first movers and early followers enabled early followers to leapfrog over first movers with respect to social networking technologies that can move across multiple platforms. Along with technologies and technological skills, early followers had superior capabilities of turning their technological resources into intellectual resources. The findings suggest that capabilities of leveraging valuable resources are as important as acquiring the resources.

This study is one of the first to examine social networking sites through the lens of the first mover advantage theory and resource-based view. Although the data relied on a variety of sources and were cross-checked to ensure reliability and validity, the data were still limited to published sources. Some alliances/partnerships and acquisitions may not be reported in publications. As one of the initial studies on the topic, this study focused on general social networking sites that target US Internet users. Considering that order of market entry and network externalities critically influence strategic decisions of social networking sites, future studies can examine niche social networking sites that target a specific customer segment, e.g., LinkedIn and MiGente, to examine how order of market entry and network externalities influence emergence and strategic decisions of niche social networking sites.

References

Adweek. (1997, February 10). Six degrees of separation. *Adweek*, 38(6), 9.
Alexa.com. (2012). Alexa. Retrieved February 20, 2012 from http://www.alexa.com/
Ankney, K. R., & Hidding, G. J. (2005). Fast-follower advantages and network externalities in IT-driven markets. *Journal of Information Science and Technology*, 2(2), 1–24.
Aragon, L. (2003, November 24). Mayfield ushers tribe into social software schmoozefest. *Private Equity Week*.
Arrington, M. (2008, April 2). Confirmed: MySpace to launch new music joint venture with big labels. Retrieved March 5, 2011 from http://techcrunch.com/2008/04/02/myspace-to-launch-new-music-joint-venture-with-big-labels/
Arthur, B. (1996). Increasing returns and the new world of business. *Harvard Business Review*, 74(4), 100–109.
Bain, S. (1959). *Industrial organization*. New York: Wiley.
Baribeau, T. (2011, February 23). Social game platform Hi5 launches SocioPay for cross-platform game monetization. *Inside Social Games*. Retrieved January 10, 2012 from http://www.insidesocialgames.com/2011/02/23/social-game-platform-hi5-launches-sociopay-for-cross-platform-game-monetization/
Barnett, E. (2010, November 14). MySpace surrenders to Facebook in battle of social networks. *The Telegraph*. Retrieved January 10, 2012 from http://www.telegraph.co.uk/technology/myspace/8130097/MySpace-surrenders-to-Facebook-in-battle-of-social-networks.html

Barney, J. (1991). Firm resources and sustained competitive advantage. *Journal of Management*, 17(1), 99–120.
Bebo. (2009, March 19). Bebo launches in India. *Bebo*. Retrieved February 20, 2012 from http://www.bebo.com/Press.jsp?PressPageId=8906862812
Benner, M. J., & Tripsas, M. (2012). The influence of prior industry affiliation on framing in nascent industries: The evolution of digital cameras. *Strategic Management Journal*, 33(3), 277–302.
Berndt, E. R., Bui, L., Reily, D. R., & Urban, G. L. (1995). Information, marketing, and pricing in the US antiulcer drug market, *American Economic Review, Papers and Proceedings*, 85(2), 100–105.
Bharadwaj, A. S. (2000). A resource-based perspective on information technology capability and firm performance: An empirical investigation. *MIS Quarterly*, 24(1), 169–196.
Bloomberg Businessweek. (2012). Company overview of PlanetAll, Inc. *Bloomberg Businessweek*. Retrieved January 14, 2013 from http://investing.businessweek.com/research/stocks/private/snapshot.asp?privcapId=33058
Bond, R. S., & Lean, D. F. (1977). Sales promotion and product differentiation in two prescription drug markets. Washington, DC: Federal Trade Commission.
Boyd, D. M., & Ellison, N. B. (2007). Social network sites: Definition, history, and scholarship. *Journal of Computer Mediated Communication*, 13(1). Retrieved December 20, 2011 from http://jcmc.indiana.edu/vol13/issue1/boyd.ellison.html
Brian in Jeollanam-do. (2010, February 3). Cyworld America shutting down on February 19th. *Brian in Jeollanam-do*. Retrieved February 19, 2012 from http://briandeutsch.blogspot.com/2010/02/cyworld-america-shutting-down-on.html
Brynjolfsson, E., & Kemerer, C. F. (1996). Network externalities in microcomputer software: An econometric analysis of the spreadsheet market. *Management Science*, 42(12), 1627–1647.
Business Library. (1996, November 13). PlanetAll plans to make a world of difference in busy lives; New interactive service keeps people connected, coordinated and clued-in. *Business Library*. Retrieved February 10, 2012 from http://findarticles.com/p/articles/mi_m0EIN/is_1996_Nov_13/ai_18858755/
Cha, J. (2011). *Business models of most-visited US social networking sites*. Paper presented at the annual meeting of the Association of Education in Journalism and Mass Communication, Saint Louis, MO.
Chatfield, A. T., & Bjorn-Andersen, N. (1997). The impact of IOS-enabled business process change on business outcomes: Transformation of the value chain of Japanese airlines. *Journal of Management Information Systems*, 14(1), 13–40.
Cho, D., Kim, D., & Rhee, D. (1998). Latecomer strategies: Evidence from the semiconductor industry in Japan and Korea. *Organization Science*, 9(4), 489–505.
ComScore. (2012, January 17). Facebook blasts into top position in Brazilian social networking market following year of tremendous growth. *ComScore*. Retrieved February 20, 2012 from http://www.comscore.com/Press_Events/Press_Releases/2012/1/Facebook_Blasts_into_Top_Position_in_Brazilian_Social_Networking_Market

Cook, J. (2004, October 25). Classmates online sells for $100 million. *Seattlepi.com.* Retrieved January 3, 2012 from http://www.seattlepi.com/news/article/Classmates-Online-sells-for-100-million-1157617.php

Crum, C. (2009, January 15). MySpace music makes some deals to bolster catalog. *WebProNews.* Retrieved March 10, 2011 from http://www.webpronews.com/myspace-music-makes-some-deals-to-bolster-catalog-2009-01

CrunchBase.com. (2012). *CrunchBase.* Retrieved February 20, 2012 from http://www.crunchbase.com/

Cusamano, M. A., Myllonadis, Y., & Rosenbloom, R. S. (1992). Strategic maneuvering and mass-market dynamics: The triumph of VHS over Beta. *Business History Review,* 66(1), 51–94.

Denstadli, J. M., Lines, R., & Grønhaug, K. (2005). First mover advantages in the discount grocery industry. *European Journal of Marketing,* 39(7/8), 872–884.

Dierickx, I., & Cool, K. (1989). Asset stock accumulation and sustainability of competitive advantage. *Management Science,* 35(2), 1504–1511.

Dizon, D. (2010, May 18). Multiply shifts gears, focuses on social shopping. *ABS CBN News.* Retrieved January 10, 2012 from http://www.abs-cbnnews.com/lifestyle/05/18/10/multiply-shifts-gears-focuses-social-shopping

Dutta, P. K., Lach, S., & Rustichini, A. (1995). Better late than early: Vertical differentiation in the adoption of a new technology. *Journal of Economics and Management Strategy,* 4(4), 563–589.

Eisenhardt, K. M. (1989). Building theories from case study research. *Academy of Management Review,* 14(4), 532–550.

Elliott, S. (2011, March 18). Classmates will now stroll along MemoryLane. *New York Times.* Retrieved February 10, 2012 from http://mediadecoder.blogs.nytimes.com/2011/03/18/classmates-will-now-stroll-along-memory-lane/

Elliot, S. (2011, September 11). Report details rise of social media. *New York Times.* Retrieved December 20, 2011 from http://mediadecoder.blogs.nytimes.com/2011/09/11/report-details-rise-of-social-media/

Erickson, C. (2012, May 17). 7 companies that could have been Facebook. *Mashable.* Retrieved February 20, 2012 from http://mashable.com/2012/05/17/companies-before-facebook/

Feagin, J., Orum, A., & Sjoberg, G. (1991). *A case for case study.* Chapel Hill: University of North Carolina Press.

Frawley, T., & Fahy, P. J. (2006). Revisiting the first mover advantage theory: A resource-based perspective. *Irish Journal of Management,* 27(1), 273–295.

Freierman, S. (1998, June 4). Screen grab: 6 degrees of networking. *New York Times,* p. G10.

Frels, J., Shervani, T., & Srivastava, R. K. (2003). The integrated networks model: Explaining resource allocations in network markets. *Journal of Marketing,* 67(1), 29–45.

Gannes, L. (2010, August 4). Facebook buys Friendster Patents for $40M. *Gigaom.* Retrieved January 20, 2012 from http://gigaom.com/2010/08/04/facebook-buys-friendster-patents-for-40m/

Geroski, P., & T. Vlassopoulos (1991). The rise and fall of a market leader: Frozen foods in the UK. *Strategic Management Journal,* 12(6), 467–478.

Golder, P. N., & Tellis, G. J. (1993). Pioneer advantage: Marketing logic or marketing legend. *Journal of Marketing Research,* 30(2), 158–170.

Goldsborough, R. (2002, October 10). Using the net to find old classmates. *The Philadelphia Inquirer*, p. C7.

Henry, A. (2011). *Understanding strategic management*. New York: Oxford University Press.

Hidding, G. J., & Williams, J. R. (2003). Are there first-mover advantages in B2B eCommerce technologies? In R. Sprague, & J. F. Nunamaker Jr. (Eds.), *Proceedings of the 36th Hawaii international conference on System Sciences*, (pp. 179–188). Waikaloa Village, Hawaii: IEEE.

Hoepfl, M. (1997). Choosing qualitative research: A primer for technology education researchers. *Journal of Technology Education*, 9(1), 47–63.

Hoppe, H. C. & Lehmann-Grube, U. (2001). Second-mover advantages in dynamic quality competition. *Journal of Economics & Management Strategy*, 10(3), 419–433.

Ilie, V., Van Slyke, C., Green, G., & Lou, H. (2005). Gender differences in perceptions and use of communication technologies: A diffusion of innovation approach. *Information Resources Management Journal*, 18(3), 16–31.

Kalyanaram, G., & Urban, G. L. (1992). Dynamic effects of the order of entry on market share, trial penetration, and repeat purchases for frequently purchased consumer goods. *Marketing Science*, 11(3), 235–250.

Katz, M. L., & Shapiro, C. (1985). Network externalities, competition and compatibility. *The American Economic Review*, 75(3), 424–440.

Katz, R. L. (1974). Skills of an effective administrator. *Harvard Business Review*, 52(5), 90–102.

Kazeniac, A. (2009, February 9). Social networks: Facebook takes over top spot, Twitter climbs. *CompetePulse*. Retrieved February 10, 2012 http://blog.compete.com/2009/02/09/facebook-myspace-twitter-social-network/

Keen, P. G. W. (1991). *Shaping the future: Business design through information technology*. Boston, MA: Harvard Business Press.

Keohane, R. O. & Nye, J. S. (1993). Power and interdependence in the information age. *Foreign Affairs*, 77(5), 81–94.

Kerin, R. A., Varadarajan, P. R., & Peterson, R. (1992). First mover advantage: A synthesis, conceptual framework and research propositions. *Journal of Marketing*, 56(3), 33–52.

Lambkin, M. (1988). Order of entry and performance in new markets. *Strategic Management Journal*, 9(S), 127–140.

Lardinois, F. (2010, October 7). Facebook growing fast in Brazil, but Orkut still far ahead. *Read Write Web*. Retrieved February 20, 2012 from http://www.readwriteweb.com/archives/brazil_facebook_is_growing_fast_but_orkut_still_far_ahead.php

Lee, Y., & O'Connor, G. C. (2003). New product launch strategy for network effects products, *Journal of the Academy of Marketing Science*, 31(3), 241–55.

Lieberman, M. B. (2007). Did first mover advantage survive the dot-com crash? Working paper, UCLA Anderson School of Management, Los Angeles, CA.

Lieberman, M. B., & Montgomery, D. B. (1988). First mover advantages. *Strategic Management Journal*, 9(S), 41–58.

Lieberman, M. B., & Montgomery, D. B. (1998). First-mover (dis)advantages: Retrospective and link with the resource-based view. *Strategic Management Journal*, 19(2), 1111–1125

Mata, F. J., Fuerst, W. L., & Barney, J. B. (1995). Information technology and sustained competitive advantage: A resource-based analysis. *MIS Quarterly*, 19(4), 487–505.

McCarthy, C. (2008, December 1). Pownce to shut down after Six Apart sale. *CNET*. Retrieved February 20, 2012 from http://news.cnet.com/8301-13577_3-10110443-36.html

McKenney, J. L. (1995). *Waves of change: Business evolution through information technology*. Cambridge, MA: Harvard Business School Press.

Mellahi, K., & Johnson, M. (2000). Does it pay to be a first mover in e.commerce? The case of Amazon.com. *Management Decision*, 38(7), 445–452.

Music Ally. (2012, January 11). Twitter inks tweet deals with the Echo Nest, Gracenote, and Rovi. Music Ally. Retrieved January 20, 2012 from http://musically.com/2012/01/11/twitter-inks-tweet-deals-with-the-echo-nest-gracenote-and-rovi/

The New York Times. (1999, December 16). Youthstream to acquire Sixdegrees for $125 million. *The New York Times*, p. C4.

Nysveen, H., P. E. Pedersen, & H. Thorbjornsen (2005). Intentions to use mobile services: Antecedents and cross-service comparisons. *Journal of the Academy of Marketing Science*, 33(3), 330–346.

Paul, I. (2010, September 28). Microsoft Live Spaces moves to WordPress: An F&Q. *PC World*. Retrieved February 20, 2012 from http://www.pcworld.com/article/206455/Microsoft_Live_Spaces_Moves_to_WordPress_An_FAQ.html

Porter, M. (1985). *Competitive advantage*. New York: Free Press.

Prahalad, C. K., & Hamel, G. (1990). The core competence of the corporation. *Harvard Business Review*, 68(3), 79–91.

Riedman, P. (1998, January 12). PlanetAll seeks a niche for networking services. *Advertising Age*. Retrieved February 20, 2012 from http://adage.com/article/news/planetall-seeks-a-niche-networking-services/632/

Robinson, W. T. (1988). Sources of market pioneer advantages: The case of industrial goods industries. *Journal of Marketing Research*, 25(February), 87–94.

Robinson, W. T., & Fornell, C. (1985). Sources of market pioneer advantages in consumer goods industries. *Journal of Marketing Research*, 22(3), 305–317.

Robinson, W. T., Fornell, C., & Sullivan, M. (1992). Are market pioneers intrinsically stronger than later entrants? *Strategic Management Journal*, 13(8), 609–624.

Rosenbloom, R., & Cusumano, M. (1987). Technological pioneering and competitive advantage: The birth of the VCR industry. *California Management Review*, 29(4), 51–76.

Ross, J. W., Beath, C. M., & Goodhue, D. L. (1996). Develop long-term competitiveness through IT assets. *Sloan Management Review*, 38(1), 31–45.

Russo, M. V., & Fouts, P. A. (1997). A resource-based perspective on corporate environmental performance and profitability. *Academy of Management Journal*, 40(3), 534–559.

Schoenecker, T. S., & Cooper, A. C. (1998). The role of firm resources and organizational attributes in determining entry timing: A cross-industry study. *Strategic Management Journal*, 19(12), 1127–1143.

Shankar, V., & Bayus, B. L. (2003). Network effects and competition: An empirical analysis of the video game industry. *Strategic Management Journal*, 24(4), 375–394.

Shankar, V., Carpenter, G. S., & Krishnamurthi, L. (1998). Late mover advantage: How innovative late entrants outsell pioneers. *Journal of Marketing Research*, 35(1), 54–70.

Silicon Valley/San Jose Business Journal. (1998, August 5). Amazon.com buys Junglee, PlaneAll. *Silicon Valley/San Jose Business Journal*. Retrieved January 13, 2012 from http://www.bizjournals.com/sanjose/stories/1998/08/03/daily10.html

Sisario, B. (2012, February 12). MySpace to announce one million new users. *New York Times*. Retrieved February 20, 2012 from http://mediadecoder.blogs.nytimes.com/2012/02/12/myspace-to-announce-one-million-new-users/

Snyder, B. (1998, June 8). SixDegrees pushes hot buttons with new syndicated partners. *Advertising Age*, p. 36.

Snider, M. (1997, March 6). Easing new users onto the Internet. *USA Today*, p. D6.

Social Media Marketing. (2010, January 13). Top 10 brands: Brand power: Going global, staying online with your user. *Social Media Marketing*. Retrieved February 10, 2012 from http://www.techdivine.com/tdblog/2010/01/top-10-brands-brand-power-going-global-staying-online-with-your-user/

Song, M., Parry, M. E., & Kawakami, T. (2009). Incorporating network externalities into the technology acceptance model. *Journal of Product Innovation Management*, 26(3), 291–307.

Spital, F. C. (1983). Gaining market share advantage in the semiconductor industry by lead time in innovation. In R. S. Rosenbloom (ed.). *Research in Technical Innovation. Management and Policy* (pp. 55–67). Greenwich, CT: JAI Press.

Strader, T., Ramaswami, S. N., & Houle, P. A. (2007). Perceived network externalities and communication technology acceptance. *European Journal of Information Systems*, 16(1), 54–65.

Sutton, J. (1991). *Sunk costs and market structure: Price competition, advertising, and the evolution of concentration*. Cambridge, MA: MIT Press.

Tagged. (2011, December 14) Tagged pumps up social discovery efforts with acquisition of hi5. *Tagged*. Retrieved February 11, 2012 from http://about.tagged.com/press-releases/tagged-pumps-up-social-discovery-efforts-with-acquisition-of-hi5/

Taylor, C. (2011, June 27). Social networking 'utopia' isn't coming. *CNN Tech*. Retrieved February 11, 2012 from http://articles.cnn.com/2011-06-27/tech/limits.social.networking.taylor_1_twitter-users-facebook-friends-connections?_s=PM:TECH

Teece, D. J. (1998). Capturing value from knowledge assets. The new economy, markets for know-how, and intangible assets. *California Management Review*, 40(3), 55–79.

Telecomworldwide. (1997, October 3). PlanetAll looks to future with new interface.

Tellis, G. J., & Golder, P. N. (2002). *Will and vision: How latecomers grow to dominate markets*. New York: McGraw-Hill.

Thomas, L. A. (1996). Brand capital and entry order. *Journal of Economics and Management Strategy*, 5(1), 107–129.

USPTO (The United States Patent and Trademark Office) (2012). *USPTO*. Retrieved February 20, 2012 from http://www.uspto.gov/

Varadarajan, R. (1999). Strategy content and process perspectives revisited. *Journal of the Academy of Marketing Science*, 27(1), 88–100.

Varadarajan, R., Yadav, M. S., & Shankar, V. (2008). First mover advantage in an Internet-enabled market environment: Conceptual framework and propositions. *Journal of the Academy of Marketing Science*, 36(3), 293–308.

Vergin, R. C., & Qoronfleh, M. W. (1998). Corporate reputation and the stock market. *Business Horizons*, 41(1), 19–26.

Wauters, R. (2011, June 29). From social network pioneer to yet another gaming site: Friendster reboots. *TechCrunch*. Retrieved January 10, 2012 from http://techcrunch.com/2011/06/29/from-social-network-pioneer-to-yet-another-gaming-site-friendster-reboots/

Wernerfelt, B. (1989). From critical resources to corporate strategy. *Journal of General Management*, 14(3), 4–13.

Wernerfelt, B. & Karnani, A. (1987). Competitive strategy under uncertainty. *Strategic Management Journal*, 8(2), 187–194.

Whiddon, R. L. (1998, November 9). Sixdegrees separates $10m from investors. *Private Equity Week*.

Whitten, I. T. (1997). *Brand preference in cigarette industry*. Washington, DC: US Federal Trade Commission.

Wolverton, T. (2000, June 8). Amazon to shut PlanetAll, absorb features. *CNET*. Retrieved February 20, 2012 from http://news.cnet.com/2100-1017-241648.html

Wortham, J. (2011, December 13). The Facebook resisters. *The New York Times*. Retrieved February 20, 2012 from http://www.nytimes.com/2011/12/14/technology/shunning-facebook-and-living-to-tell-about-it.html?_r=0

Yin, R. (2003). *Case study research: Design and methods*. Thousand Oaks, CA: Sage.

6

AN ARGUMENT FOR NEWS MEDIA MANAGERS TO DIRECT AND USE AUDIENCE RESEARCH

Rachel Davis Mersey, Ph.D.

An Argument for News Managers to Discuss and Study the Audience

Market research emerged as a major force in the news business in the 1970s but has since been both under-utilized and mis-utilized to the detriment of news organizations. Media managers, especially those within news media companies, have allowed marketing departments within their organizations and advertising companies outside their organizations to dictate their understanding of the audiences they serve. This has resulted in a shallow conception of the audience and, even worse, weak relationships among consumers and their news media products whether they are print, broadcast, digital, or mobile.

The fact is that marketing departments at news companies and advertisers have tended to measure audience by pure counts. Media kits tend to be indictors of this inclination. Included in the media kit of a strong news-based brand like *The New Yorker*, for example, are total audience by age, median household income, gender, education, and employment and marital status, with additional attention to the brand's "affluent audience" count (*The New Yorker*, 2011). Daily newspapers and television news are generally no better. The *Los Angeles Times*' list of audience traits in its media kit are age, household income, gender, ethnicity, education, and number of children (*Los Angeles Times*, 2011). From both CNN and Headline News: age, education, gender, home ownership, household income, and households with children (Comcast Spotlight, 2012a, 2012b).

This is not to say that the editorial teams at these news organizations do not know their audiences. It is to point out "you are what you measure" (Ariely, 2010). News managers must shift the conversation away from counting audience members by demographics (or number of eyeballs, minutes, or click-throughs) and reframe the industry's approach on the psychographic targeting of high-quality, relevant news products and audiences' engagement with them. This is the argument that a smaller number of consumers who you know and serve well make for a more profitable business model in news than a mass, faceless under-served audience.

The purpose of this chapter is to review the research that has been done on news audiences for print, television, and online, and to examine the cultural differences and varying motivations between market researchers and journalists. From this basis, this chapter asserts an argument that news managers must retake the lead of the conversation related to the news consumers to raise the quality of consumers' experiences with news, to preserve the democratic value of the Fourth Estate, and to reinforce a strong and vibrant Fifth Estate. Such concern has been raised regarding the degradation of news in America that in spring 2009 there was a Senate hearing on the Future of Journalism and Newspapers convened by Senator John Kerry, chairman of the commerce subcommittee on communications and technology. The driving question, according to Senator Kerry, was "How might we preserve the core societal function that is served by an independent and diverse news media?" Figuring out how to preserve journalism's community-service function has consumed the industry's attention. The preponderance of this attention has focused on how to fund the vital work of the Fourth Estate, monetizing content on the web being the key issue. In summer 2009 the Newspaper Association of America solicited several technology companies, including Google, to develop strategies for success with paid content on the web. However, these conversations neglect the fundamental issue at the crux of the news media and an economic model for their survival: the audience and its engagement with news.

Research on News Audiences

Among journalism scholars, issues of use (Johnson & Kaye, 2000; Thorson, 2008), media choice (Baum, 2003; Bennett, 2003a; Boczkowski & Peer, 2011; Delli Carpini & Williams, 2001; McManus, 1994; Mindich, 2005; Prior, 2007; Schudson, 2003), and fragmentation (Hamilton, 2004; Tewksbury, 2005; Underwood, 1993) have garnered the most attention in the area of news audiences. Johnson and Kaye (2000), for example, found that those with an interest in political affairs tend to use the Internet rather than the television for news. Boczkowski and Peer (2011) focused on the divergent news preferences between journalists and consumers, and reaffirmed earlier findings (Althaus & Tewksbury, 2002; Hamilton, 2004; Tewksbury, 2003; Tewksbury & Althaus, 2000).

An examination of the contrast between journalists' and consumers' choices shows a sizable and uniform gap in terms of what stories are selected—which is consistent with studies that have shown reduced interest in public affairs among online news consumers.

(Boczkowski & Peer, 2011, p. 867)

Recent research, as might be expected, has focused on news users and online news readership. Hoffman, Kolsbeek, and Novak (1996) focused on the role of demographic variables in Internet use but much of the research has addressed issues related to use preferences and practices. Chyi and Lasorsa (1999) determined that users of local newspapers online tended to read those print newspapers as well, while national newspapers online were more attractive than their print counterparts. According to the researchers, "This pattern of demand for different types of newspapers suggest that users do not view print and online versions of the same newspaper as competitive, an assumption from which many newspaper owners and editors appear to be operating" (Chyi & Lasorsa, 1999, p. 11). This idea of online news as a supplement to print news uses has since been expanded upon (Althaus & Tewksbury, 2000), while issues of exactly how online newsreaders scan and read have also garnered attention (Davis, 2000; Johnson, 2001; Tewksbury, 2003).

Academics in marketing have lent psychographics—and specifically VALS (Values and Lifestyle Segmentation) or the Rokeach Value Survey (RVS)—significantly more attention. This area of research has covered the general idea that consumers buy products at least in part to reflect their values and to meet their lifestyle demands (e.g., Connor & Becker, 1975; Rokeach, 1979). The work on psychographics has less commonly addressed news consumption but what has been done is worth noting.

In early work in this area, Becker and Connor (1981) undertook a study of personal values and the use of television, magazines, and newspapers and determined that demographic research on media use had failed to detect underlying motivators of media use. "In other words, it is not education or age or social class that determines one's attitudes and behaviors," according to the researchers. "These are merely correlates of values possessed by individuals, values that actually underlie people's behavior" (Becker & Connor, 1981, p. 41). Leung (1998) since expanded on this area of work to address the construct of social identity but he only dealt with the area of entertainment media use. Bringing it back to the news context, Chan and Leung (2005) determined that psychographics, or lifestyle orientations, were important predictors of the types of online news that people read and their enjoyment of interactive capabilities of online news. Chan and Leung concluded, "To provide services tailored to newsreaders' interests, online news publishers should consider offering personalized editions targeting online newsreaders with different lifestyles and values" (2005, p. 376).

Mersey (2010a, 2010b) expanded on this early work, bringing together the scholarship of social identity and the study of news use, arguing that if news managers better understood the identities of their target audience members, they could provide thoughtful and intelligent news and news products of interest to them. As Mersey argues to media managers,

> How can you mobilize your audience's chemistry? Find a focus relevant to your audience by studying them, their interests, and their media use. Use quantitative and qualitative techniques and primary and secondary research that can lead to the fullest understanding of your audience. You may begin with your intuition, but you should not end up there; this is about evidence-based research. Of course, your audience should be desirable and sizable enough to constitute a business opportunity; at this point, however, the key is to identify a constituency that shares experiences strongly enough to be loyal to a product you might generate to serve and lead them. Your aim is to develop a product that satisfies your audience's needs with regard to editorial content and tone, design, delivery, timeliness, usability, interactivity, and related services because you truly understand them, and in doing so you fill a gap in the marketplace.
>
> (2010b, p. 91)

The fact is that the more specialized a media outlet is, the more successful it tends to be at creating strong identity-based experiences in comparison to general-circulation media.

The Control of Market Researchers

If understanding psychographics, or identity, can lead to crafting news products people want to use and perhaps pay for, why have news managers ignored this research? First, we know that there has been concern on the part of journalists about the psychographic targeting of news. Much of this consternation has focused on the concept of ideological segregation. What happens, for example, when people watch only news that reinforces their preexisting beliefs? This is, on its face, a legitimate issue. However, research conducted by Gentzkow and Shapiro (2010) suggests that there is significantly less ideologically driven news consumption than people assume. Further, the consequence of news managers abandoning the necessity of their roles in studying and working for the audience because of their nervousness about ideological segregation has far greater negative implications. The troubled news business of the past ten years, including the cutbacks and editorial layoffs at most metropolitan dailies and the shuttering of others, are all too clear.

Still, as was pointed out at the outset of this chapter, news managers have allowed market researchers to dictate much of the conversation about the audience. One could argue that the dominance by market researchers is to be expected not only because marketing professionals are unlikely to share the previously discussed ideological concerns, but also because both market research practitioners and scholars have long realized the essential nature of the consumer in the retail and sales experiences. However, by putting the responsibility for understanding and communicating about the audience in the hands of market researchers, news organizations have permitted an overemphasis on serving the audience with exactly what it wants, which has been widely criticized (e.g., Bennett, 2003b; Carr, 2009; Gans, 2004; Patterson, 2003). The oft-heard examples of "giving them what they want" tend to usually involve a pseudo-celebrity on the front page of a newspaper, while a story about an important local issue like the school board or city council runs inside or goes uncovered entirely.

What is important to a discussion of why news managers should insert themselves into a leadership role in conversations about the audience is the understanding of exactly why market researchers would differ in their execution of audience-based research and the utilization of their findings. The fact is that market researchers are, by virtue of their positions, trained to be focused on a different end than journalists. Market researchers are not motivated by common or community good, democratic needs, or preservation of the Fourth or Fifth Estates. This is not a criticism of market researchers, nor their profession. Market research is a skill, and there are many talented practitioners working for news and non-news companies alike. But the key question motivating much of the market research news managers undertake and listen to is: What do consumers, and potential consumers, say would motivate them to purchase a newspaper or magazine, watch a television news program, or use a website? Let us first set aside one of the most often critiqued elements of this consumer-based approach to study. It predicates that consumers are cognizant enough of their behaviors to provide valuable information to such questions. This issue of self-awareness has been a key factor in the stream of uses and gratifications research. However, the face validity of uses and gratifications and related approaches remains clear. As Stone (1987) argued, "People will not attend to messages that have no perceived interest value for them. They will choose among media content offering those items they deem valuable, even if that value is only momentary enjoyment" (p. 129).

But editing to enjoyment—not that this is what Stone (1987) was arguing for—is the cause of market researchers trying to increase use, not the cause of journalists trying to inform the citizenry. To understand the motivations of journalists we have evidence from the Committee of Concerned Journalists. In 1997 the committee began a national conversation on the core principles of journalism, which became the basis of Kovach and Rosenstiel's (2001) book, *The Elements of Journalism*.

1. Journalism's first obligation is to the truth.
2. Its first loyalty is to citizens.
3. Its essence is a discipline of verification.
4. Its practitioners must maintain an independence from those they cover.
5. It must serve as an independent monitor of power.
6. It must provide a forum for public criticism and compromise.
7. It must strive to make the significant interesting and relevant.
8. It must keep the news comprehensive and proportional.
9. Its practitioners must be allowed to exercise their personal conscience.

To this point, news managers have been ineffective at reconciling these values with the need to be audience focused. Instead, they have left audience work to market researchers who are detached from the underlying principles of journalism.

Attaway-Fink's (2004) research, a national survey of executive and managing editors, focused on the reporting practices of newspapers related to market research. She found a clear sentiment on behalf of these news executives that "when making story assignments, editors should keep target audiences in mind" (p. 149). Still the audience focus remains weak at best because it is based on data gathered by market research departments, not on an authentic, deep understanding of the audience.

Understanding the Audience, Creating Experiences and Engagement

What we know is that an authentic, deep understanding of the audience is characterized by creating high-quality experiences, which collectively lead to engagement with a media product (Mersey, Malthouse, & Calder, 2010). News managers must lead their organizations to create such experiences. As summarized by Brakus, Schmitt, and Zarantonello (2009) there are a variety of experiences that consumers (and brands) can expect: the product experience, the shopping and service experience, the consumption experience, and the brand experience. Brakus et al. (2009) prize the brand experience, explaining that they "conceptualize brand experience as subjective, internal consumer responses (sensations, feelings, and cognitions) and behavioral responses evoked by brand-related stimuli that are part of a brand's design and identity, packaging, communications,

Table 6.1 Sample of Descriptions of Experiential Brands

Brand	Experiences
American Express	• It's an interactive experience • Part of luxury, sophistication, and exclusivity • Because of sponsoring activities, I feel fun, excitement, and entertainment
Apple/iPod	• I love the touch and feel of the products • I enjoy playing with all the products • I am part of a "smarter" community • This brand intrigues me • I really feel Apple products go with my way of life • I use the iPod when I am jogging, and I exercise more because of the iPod
Google	• The search is elegant; it creates a mood of playfulness and curiosity • I feel happy and proud because I am "smart" and "in-the-know" • With Google I change the way I organize and interact with information
MasterCard	• Makes me think about precious things in life • I feel more youthful than using American Express or Visa • Initially the "Priceless" campaign was emotive, but it's now simply a way of identifying the brand for me
Starbucks	• Smells nice and is visually warm • It's comfortable and puts me in a better mood • It's like being around a Barnes & Noble's crowd
W Hotel	• Being part of something fun, happening, and exciting • It was an amazing feeling to hang out in the lobby • Service is disappointing
Washington Mutual	• I have positive feelings because of their friendliness • It's a place I want to go and do not have to go • I also had a negative one-time experience

Source: Brakus et al. (2009, p. 56).

and environments" (p. 53). For each brand considered a strong experiential brand, Brakus et al. asked two raters to select associated sensory, affective, cognitive, behavioral, and social experience descriptors, which are detailed in Table 6.1.

Interestingly, even in cases where a negative experience was noted—for example, W Hotels and Washington Mutual—it became clear that strong experiential brands enjoyed different types of descriptions than weak experiential brands. "In contrast to the strong experiential brands, participants described weak experiential brands mostly in terms of price and promotions, as well as functionality and basics, even though they were explicitly primed with an experiential terminology," explained Brakus et al. (2009, p. 55).

News products must become strong experiential brands to survive, and the push for them to do so must come from news managers in order to ensure that the core principles of journalism are preserved as a part of this process. The fact is that news media companies have opportunities to create experiences but have generally failed to do so. The Media Management Center (2003) at Northwestern University worked with the Magazine Publishers of America and the American Society of Magazine Editors to study the experiences readers have with magazines. They found 39 distinct experiences associated with magazine reading—35 motivators and 4 inhibitors, which are shown in Table 6.2.

To create experiences such as those detailed in Table 6.2, news organizations must "know" their audiences at a more meaningful level than they do now. The experience of "it's for people like me," for example, requires one to know who "people like me" are exactly. In addition, news managers must determine if there are experiences unique to their topics of coverage, modes of communications, or audiences that merit attention.

Conclusion

A deep level of audience understanding on the part of news managers, and news organizations in general, is the necessary foundation for the creation of relevant products and related business models to sustain the Fourth Estate. By allowing market research departments to control the research and understanding of audience, news managers have unwisely given the reins of innovation and product development at news media companies to market researchers as opposed to experienced journalists.

In a speech on "The Age of Ideas," Kevin Roberts, CEO Worldwide of Saatchi & Saatchi, said,

> No matter what kind of business or organization you are, your first job in this narrowcast world is competing for the attention of consumers. That's the eyeball part. Then the real job begins—making connections with the hearts, minds, guts and nerve ends of consumers. The ability to create those connections, not the number of eyeballs you can access, is going to decide the media winners.
>
> (Media Management Center, 2003)

He is correct. But for the survival of the news business—and the essential journalism it provides—news media managers must take the microphone from advertisers and market researchers in front of other more vocal spokespeople. News media managers simply must take the lead,

Table 6.2 Motivators and Inhibitors of Magazine Readership

Motivators	Inhibitors
• I get value for my time and money • It makes me smarter • It's my personal timeout • I often reflect on it • The stories absorb me • I learn things here first • It's part of my routine • I find the magazine high-quality and sophisticated • I trust it • I feel good when I read it • It's relevant and useful to me • It's brief and easy for me to read • I build relationship by talking about and sharing it • I find unique and surprising things • It improves me, and helps me try new things • I save and refer to it • I keep or share articles • I think others in the household would enjoy the magazine • It's for people like me • It grabs me visually • I'm inspired • I get a sense of place • I'm touched • I feel I know the writers • I like seeing people of color in this magazine • I like its seasonality • I like some of the ads a lot • It requires me to focus • I read the ads • It reinforces my faith • It helps me look good; it's sensual, even sexy • I want more ad information • This magazine's website is important to me	• It disappoints me • This magazine irritates me • I dislike some of the ads • It leaves me feeling bad

Source: Media Management Center (2003).

and the news industry must support more research on audience, experiences, and engagement and use those findings to drive the conversation among market researchers and advertisers about how to create strong news products.

References

Althaus, S. L., & Tewksbury, D. (2000). Patterns of internet and traditional news media use in a networked community. *Political Communication*, 17(1), 21–45.

Althaus, S. L., & Tewksbury, D. (2002). Agenda setting and the "new" news: Patterns of issue importance among readers of the paper and online versions of the New York Times. *Communication Research*, 29(2), 180–207.

Ariely, D. (2010, June). Column: You are what you measure. *Harvard Business Review*. Retrieved January 14, 2013, from http://hbr.org/2010/06/column-you-are-what-you-measure/ar/1

Attaway-Fink, B. (2004). Market-driven journalism: Creating special sections to meet reader interests. *Journal of Communication Management*, 9(2), 145–154.

Baum, M. A. (2003). *Soft news goes to war: Public opinion and American foreign policy in the new media age*. Princeton, NJ: Princeton University Press.

Becker, B. W., & Connor, P. E. (1981). Personal values of the heavy user of mass media. *Journal of Advertising Research*, 21(5), 37–43.

Bennett, W. L. (2003a). *News: The politics of illusion* (fifth edn.). New York: Longman.

Bennett, W. L. (2003b). The burglar alarm that just keeps ringing: A response to Zaller. *Political Communication*, 20(2), 131–138.

Boczkowski, P. J., & Peer, L. (2011). The choice gap: The divergent online news preferences of journalists and consumers. *Journal of Communication*, 61(5), 857–876.

Brakus, J. J., Schmitt, B. H., & Zarantonello, L. (2009). Brand experience: What is it? How is it measured? Does it affect loyalty? *Journal of Marketing*, 73(3), 52–68.

Carr, J. (2009). "Letting them eat cake": Narrative templates in current affairs/news journalism. *Pacific Journalism Review*, 15(2), 54–70.

Chan, J. K., & Leung, L. (2005). Lifestyles, reliance on traditional news media and online news adoption. *New Media & Society*, 7(3), 357–382.

Chyi, H. I., & Lasorsa, D. (1999). Access, use and preferences for online newspapers. *Newspaper Research Journal*, 20(4), 2–13.

Comcast Spotlight. (2012a). CNN. Retrieved March 13, 2012, from http://www.comcastspotlight.com/network/cnn

Comcast Spotlight. (2012b). Headline News. Retrieved March 13, 2012, from http://www.comcastspotlight.com/network/headline-news-cnn

Committee of Concerned Journalists. (1997). Principles of journalism. Retrieved January 14, 2013, from http://www.journalism.org/resources/principles.

Connor, P. E., & Becker, B. W. (1975). Values and the organization: Suggestions for research. *Academy of Management Journal*, 18(3), 550–561.

Davis, J. (2000). Substance: Trumps style. *Mediaweek*, 10(21), 58–62.

Delli Carpini, M. X., & Williams, B. A. (2001). Let us infotain you: Politics in the new media environment. In W. L. Bennett & R. M. Entman (Eds.), *Mediated politics* (pp. 160–181). New York: Cambridge University Press.

Gans, H. J. (2004). *Deciding what's news: A study of CBS Evening News, NBC Nightly News, Newsweek, and Time* (25th anniversary edn.). Evanston, IL: Northwestern University Press.

Gentzkow, M., & Shapiro, J. (2010). Ideological segregation online and offline. Retrieved January 14, 2013, from http://faculty.chicagobooth.edu/jesse.shapiro/research/echo_chambers.pdf

Hamilton, J. T. (2004). *All the news that's fit to sell: How the market transforms information into news.* Princeton, NJ: Princeton University Press.

Hoffman, D. L., Kolsbeek, W. D., & Novak, T. P. (1996). Internet and web use in the US. *Communications of the ACM*, 39(12), 36–46.

Johnson, M. (2001). How do we read online? *Quill*, 89(1), 10–13.

Johnson, T. J., & Kaye, B. K. (2000). Using is believing: The influence of reliance on the credibility of online political information among politically interested internet users. *Journalism and Mass Communication Quarterly*, 77(4), 865–879.

Kovach, B. & Rosenstiel, T. (2001). *Elements of journalism: What newspeople should know and the public should expect.* New York: Three Rivers Press.

Los Angeles Times. (2011). Media Kit: Audience. *Los Angeles Times Media Group.* Retrieved November 20, 2011, from http://mediakit.latimes.com/audience/

Leung, L. (1998). Lifestyles and the use of new media technology in urban China. *Telecommunications Policy*, 22(9), 781–790.

McManus, J. H. (1994). *Market-driven journalism: Let the citizen beware?* Thousand Oaks, CA: Sage.

Media Management Center. (2003). Highlights from the Magazine Reader Experience Study Toolkit. Retrieved November 27, 2011, from http://www.mediamanagementcenter.org/research/magazinetoolkit.asp

Mersey, R. D. (2010a). *Can journalism be saved? Rediscovering America's appetite for news.* Santa Barbara, CA: Praeger.

Mersey, R. D. (2010b). The identity experience. In A. Peck & E. C. Malthouse (Eds.), *Medill on media engagement* (pp. 81–93). New York: Hampton Press.

Mersey, R. D., Malthouse, E. C., & Calder, B. J. (2010). Engagement with online media. *Journal of Media Business Studies*, 7(2), 39–56.

Mindich, D. T. Z. (2005). *Tuned out: Why Americans under 40 don't follow the news.* New York: Oxford University Press.

Patterson, T. E. (2003). The search for a standard: Markets and media. *Political Communication*, 20(2), 139–143.

Prior, M. (2007). *Post-broadcast democracy: How media choice increases inequality in political involvement and polarizes elections.* Cambridge, UK: Cambridge University Press.

Rokeach, M. (1979). *Understanding human values: Individual and societal.* New York: The Free Press.

Schudson, M. (2003). *The sociology of news.* New York: W. W. Norton.

Stone, G. (1987) *Examining newspapers: What research reveals about newspapers.* Newbury Park, CA: Sage Publications.

Tewksbury, D. (2003). What do Americans really want to know? Tracking the behavior of newsreaders on the internet. *Journal of Communication*, 53(4), 694–710.

Tewksbury, D. (2005). The seeds of audience fragmentation: Specialization in the use of online news sites. *Journal of Broadcasting & Electronic Media*, 49(3), 332–348.

Tewksbury, D., & Althaus, S. L. (2000). Differences in knowledge acquisition among readers of the paper and online version of a national newspaper. *Journalism and Mass Communication Quarterly*, 77(3), 457–479.

Thorson, E. (2008). Changing patterns of news consumption and participation: News recommendation engines. *Information, Communication & Society*, 11(4), 473–489.

The New Yorker. (2011). Media Kit (Circulation/Demographics). *Condé Nast*. Retrieved November 20, 2011, from http://www.condenastmediakit.com/nyr/circulation.cfm

Underwood, D. (1993). *When MBAs rule the newsroom: How marketers and managers are reshaping today's media*. New York: Columbia University Press.

7

RESPONDING TO SYSTEMATIC REFORM, MARKET CHANGE, AND TECHNOLOGICAL INNOVATION

China's Book Publishing Industry in Rapid Transformation

Guosong Shao, Ph.D., Yingping Wei, Jingan Yuan, Ph.D., and Chunhua Zhang, Ph.D.

China's book publishing industry has attracted much attention from the public in recent years. First, China's book publishing industry is serving the world's largest potential reader market. After Chinese citizens have reached certain affluence levels and no longer worry about such basic needs as food and clothing, they demonstrate more demand and higher requirements for cultural products including books. Second, after 30 years of reform and opening up, China not only possesses large-scale state-owned book publishing and distribution entities but also has a large number of private publication and distribution companies. Particularly the latter has shown strong creativity and supply capacity. Third, the Chinese government attaches great importance to the book publishing industry. In 2007, the publishing industry was integrated into the national "soft cultural power" strategic framework; in 2010 it was included into *China's Twelfth Five-Year Plan* as a pillar industry of national economy; and finally, due to China's special political structure, the book publishing industry in this country has some characteristics different from its counterparts in Western countries. Such characteristics have hindered the development of the industry to some extent; they deserve our careful investigation.

This chapter attempts to examine the state of China's book publishing industry. It particularly investigates how the book publishing industry deals with the changes in government regulation, the market, and information technology. The chapter is divided into four parts: the first part presents how China's book publishing industry has been heavily shaped by government policies; the second part analyzes the current status and existing problems of China's book publishing market; the third part examines the impact of information technology on and the countermeasure strategies by the book publishing industry; and the last part summarizes the main content of the chapter and also briefly discusses the future of China's book publishing industry.

Led by the Government: The Reform of China's Book Publishing System

Publishing Groups Functioning as Government Agents in Managing the Industry

Since the founding of P.R. China in 1949, the Chinese government had adopted a policy called "Zhuguan Zhuban," whereby a publishing company is managed by its regulator/administrator. The policy was arguably established to safeguard the ideology security and to ensure the healthy development of the publishing industry (Song, 2003). Guided by this policy, China gradually formed several big publishing systems. They include the publishing entities managed and administered by: the various ministries of the central government; the local press and publication regulators; the universities and the major research institutes; the national non-government organizations; and the People's Liberation Army (PLA) (Song, 2003). In other words, the book publishing industry is a product of "government-enterprise combined as one," in which the enterprise is part of the government.

In the past decade, China began to promote the reform of the publishing system, mainly separating the publishing sector from the government. For example, in 2002, the Zhonghua Book Company, the Commercial Press, and other major publishers and distribution companies formed China Publishing Group, decoupling from their previous administrator—the General Administration of Press and Publication (GAPP). In 2003, the printing enterprises owned by the GAPP formed China Printing Group Corporation, thus decoupling from its administrator in a similar way. The local press and publication administrations also actively promoted systematic reform. As of 2007, 93 percent of Chinese provinces had completed the reform of separating governments from publishing enterprises, of separating management from regulation (Feng, 2007). The governments changed their functions from running the enterprises to merely establishing regulations, from managing their subordinates to regulating the entire industry within their jurisdiction. The old administration model lasting for decades largely came to an end.

Under the new model, the agents of the governments—publishing groups—have been formed. While the governments carry on the functional changes, the publishing group formation process is nearing completion. The publishing and/or distribution groups decoupled from the governments are now administered by the governments. The publishing and/or distribution companies within the groups are no longer managed by the governments but by their parental groups. After such reform, the functions of the governments were changed to mainly stimulate the vitality of the market. To a certain extent, such changes promoted the prosperity of the book publishing industry.

The Limited Openness of Book Contents

Based on classical Marxist theory and historical experience, the Chinese government attaches great importance to the ideological security and thus carries on the reform of the book publishing industry with great caution. The publishing industry is often referred to as the "last bastion" of reform. This is especially reflected in the limited openness of book contents.

Under the *Regulations on Publishing Administration* promulgated by the GAPP, all book topics and contents that have academic value, accumulative cultural value, or practical value in terms of ideological, cultural, scientific, or artistic aspects are considered publishable; on the contrary, those that have no ideological, cultural, scientific, or artistic value, or have serious problems, or are prohibited from being published by state policy, are considered unqualified and cannot be published. The standard for error rate during the proofreading process is set to be one-ten thousandth, that is, the books with error rate above this standard should stop selling or be destroyed. There is also a grading standard, which divides books into four levels—excellent, good, qualified, and unqualified—in terms of editorial quality (Wang, 2005). In addition, no one is allowed to publish subjects that violate national or public interests (Wang, 2005). According to China's *Administrative Penalty Law*, publishers that publish unqualified or prohibited books are subject to penalties, including warnings, fines, and business suspension for rectification.

Given the ideological nature of publishing, China sets strict market access policy on book publishing. In particular, China implements a licensing system, in which an applicant must meet a set of requirements for personnel, administrative structure, and publishing scope in order to launch a publishing company. This differs from the publishing registration system prevailing in Western countries. Before the 1980s, the book publishing industry was a restricted zone for private capital; after the 1980s, in order to solve the problem of insufficient funding, the publishing industry spontaneously adopted the practices of "cooperative publishing" and "authors pay for the publishing cost" (Hao, 2008). These two practices were implicitly approved by the government. Though the government later denied the legal status of "cooperative publishing" and also restricted the scope of "authors pay for the publishing cost," these two practices have never been stopped in reality (Hao, 2008).

Since China implements the licensing mechanism in the publishing industry, private companies have actually no legitimate rights to publish. They need to buy the International Standard Book Number (ISBN) from state-owned publishers while risking being investigated. In the law enforcement practice, however, the government often "opens one eye and closes the other." As long as the private book studios do not publish illegal books, their operations are permitted, at least implicitly.

The Strategic Planning for the Book Publishing Industry

In recent years, the Chinese government actively carried on strategic planning for book publishing to further the development of the industry. Take the digital publishing industry, for example. As information technology penetrates the book publishing industry, the GAPP has promulgated a series of documents to support the digitalization of book publishing. In August 2010, for example, the GAPP issued a document named *Several Comments on Speeding up the Development of China's Digital Publishing Industry*. This document stipulated that by the end of the twelfth Five-Year Plan (2015), the output of China's digital publication would account for 25 percent of the total output of the publishing industry; there would be about 10 national digital publishing bases or national digital publishing industry parks that generated 10 billion RMB revenue each; there would be 5–8 massive-volume digital content delivery platforms that combined books, periodicals, and audio-visual electronic publications; and there would be 20 major digital publishing enterprises that were internationally competitive and generated 1 billion RMB revenue each (GAPP, 2010a). Furthermore, the document proposed that by 2020, the traditional publishers should have basically completed digital transition, and the digital products and services account for a dominant share in their total business (GAPP, 2010a). These plans received enthusiastic response from the local governments and the publishing groups. Up to now, the country has set up 9 digital publishing bases (Chen, 2011). As an effort to reinforce the implementation of these policies, the Ministry of Finance has since 2010 begun providing subsidy to the digital operation of large publishing enterprises (GAPP, 2010b).

In addition to promoting the digitalization of book publishing, the government has also actively pursued the globalization of Chinese books. In 2003, for example, the GAPP proposed the "going out" strategy for China's publishing industry. Subsequently, a number of supportive policies such as "Promoting Chinese Books to Foreign Markets" followed (Liu, 2007). In 2007, the government listed book publishing as an integral part of soft power, which has been highly valued as a strategy for the country to compete in the world (Liu, 2007). Given such large-scale government support, China's book publishing industry expects to expand to the international community at an accelerating rate.

Large but not Strong: The State of China's Book Publishing Market

With the propulsion of the reforms of economic and political systems, China's book publishing industry has been in a high growth period since the early 1980s. The most distinctive characteristics of the industry at that time were the large-scale introduction of foreign books. In particular, the rapid economic development gave birth to the introduction of a large number of foreign economics and management books; similarly, the tremendous progress in information technology was accompanied by the expansion of foreign computer science books. Wave after wave of book introduction hugely enriched China's book market, and powerfully stimulated the growth of domestic books. Due to such growth, the seller's market has turned into a buyer's market, and contemporary readers have many more options when buying books (Chen, 2006).

However, the structure of China's book production is unbalanced. This is mainly reflected in two aspects: first, textbooks account for a high proportion of all books over a long period of time, and the publishing industry has a strong dependence on the revenues generated from the production of textbooks; second, the variety of best-selling books for the general public is still low. These problems can be largely attributed to the market: historically, the public did not have a high demand for books other than textbooks and teaching aid books due to the low level of economic development, national literary progress, and cultural awareness. Commentators thus argue that, in order to improve the literacy level of the nation, the publishing industry should become less dependent on textbooks while increasing the proportion of general-interest books (Zhou, 2005).

In recent years, the proportion of general interest books has factually been growing while the proportion of textbooks has been falling. In 2009, the total number of general interest books increased by 4.53 percent, the total page numbers increased by 4.61 percent, and the total price increased by 8.94 percent; on the other hand, the total number of textbooks dropped by 5.43 percent, the total pages dropped by 3.56 percent, and the total price dropped by 0.34 percent (Yao, 2010). This structural change reflected the increase in the readers' options, and also the improvement of the national literacy level.

Another feature of China's book publishing market is that it has a low level of industry concentration. This may be because China's publishing sector is mainly set up within the administrative regions, and mergers among publishing entities often occur within the same region and are implemented through administrative orders. These factors accelerate the trend of regional segmentation of the book publishing industry. Although there have been individual cases of cross-regional mergers and acquisitions, they are not enough to become a sign of significant improvement in breaking regional barriers.

The book publishing industry is generally seen as a chain including editing, publishing, printing, and distributing businesses. In China, the competitive environment of each link in this chain is very different from each other. There is a jingle in this industry: "publishing houses sit and wait for food to come; bookstores stand and look for food; printing factories look for food on their knees." This shows that the low-tech printing market has high competition and low profits; meanwhile, publishers often have specific content resources so that the competition among them is much less intense. It is argued that this may be attributed to the different degree of openness. It is observed that after the reform, China's printing and distribution companies now face a lower market access barrier, and only the publishing area still maintains a strict market access barrier.

The Plight of the Private Book Publishing Industry

The relationship between two types of market players—private publishers and bookstores and state-owned publishing houses and bookstores—and their individual statuses have recently become the focus of public attention. Before the end of the 1970s, the state-owned publishing houses and Xinhua Bookstore distribution channels dominated the entire book publishing market. From 1998 to 2008, private and state-owned distribution companies were about equal in terms of their marketing capability while private publishing businesses grew steadily despite the huge challenge imposed by state-owned rivals. The number of private publishing studios is currently ten times higher than the number of state-owned publishers (Jiang, 2011).

In January 2010, the GAPP issued the *Guideline on Further Promoting the Development of News and Book Publishing Industry*, which listed the private book industry as a "new force of cultural production," and intentionally encouraged, supported, and guided private capital to enter the book publishing fields in various means. Therefore, the private book industry legally becomes the "advanced productive forces." In May 2010, the newly established Beijing Publishing Industry Creative Park began to provide private book publishers with free ISBNs (Ji, 2011). In December 2010, Hunan Tianzhou Science, Education and Culture Co., a private publisher, was successfully listed on the Shenzhen Stock Exchange. These examples demonstrate that private publishing has been recognized by the market.

A critical question is how influential the private publishing industry is in China. According to the statistics issued by the *China Book Business Report*, between January 1, 2009 and June 30, 2010, the top five general-interest books were produced by private enterprises; among the top 100 books, private enterprises also accounted for more than 60 percent (Hao, 2011a). According to Jiuge Distribution Company, one of the largest social science book wholesalers in China, private publishing enterprises accounted for 45 percent of all its suppliers while state-owned publishing ones accounted for the remaining 55 percent; in addition, the private sector accounted for 70 percent of the total sales revenues while state-owned publishers accounted for only 30 percent (Hao, 2011a). Only in the areas where there was a high degree of monopoly, such as primary and secondary school textbooks, did the state-owned publishers have better performance.

The 2010 Press and Publication Industry Analysis Report issued by the GAPP clearly showed that the proportion of private economy steadily improved in recent years. Specifically, the proportion of private sector among all of the 131,000 press and publishing enterprises nationwide rose from 70 percent in 2009 to 76.1 percent in 2010 (GAPP, 2011). Among printing and copying companies, the proportion of private ones in terms of total output, value added, total revenue, and total profit increased from 76.9 percent, 75.5, 76.9, and 74.8 in 2009 to 86.4 percent, 84.4, 86.1, and 84.4 in 2010, respectively (GAPP, 2011). Among distribution companies, private ones' total output, value added, operating income, and share of total profits increased by 60.6 percent, 62.9, 60.5, and 64.4 in 2009 to 61.1 percent, 63.6, 61.8, and 66.0 in 2010, respectively (GAPP, 2011).

Although the above data indicate that the private publishing economy is on the rise, its status is very fragile. After forming into groups and listing in the stock market, the state-owned publishing and distribution companies have obtained much more capital and market influence than their private rivals. The market shows a trend of "state-owned enterprises advancing while private-owned ones pull back." More importantly, practitioners at private publishing companies generally lack confidence in their future in the private sector. They often try to join a state-owned enterprise or seek an opportunity in the digital publishing business (Wu, 2011).

The private bookstores are in an even more severe situation. Because labor costs and rent costs quickly increase, private bookstore outlets and networks now show a contraction trend. This is inconsistent with the expansion trend of book publishing; it also arguably puts people's cultural consumption and the development of the book industry in an unfavorable situation. In October 2011, a well-known bookstore chain, Photosynthesis Books, met with cash flow problems, which led to the closure of some of its stores (Chong, Chen, & Zhang, 2011). This incident attracted much public attention, as shown in intensive media coverage. Some people argue that the government should also take measures to stimulate the development of the private book industry, especially providing stronger monetary policy support.

Shaped by Technology: Industrial Change Caused by Technology Innovation

The rapid development of information technology is fundamentally changing the book publishing industry's production, distribution, and consumption models. These changes are particularly reflected in the prevalence of digital publishing in the country.

According to *the 2010–2011 China Digital Publishing Annual Report* issued by China Press and Publication Research Institute, the overall revenues for the digital publishing industry are 21.3 billion RMB in 2006, 36.2 billion in 2007, 55.7 billion in 2008, 79.9 billion in 2009, and 105.2 billion in 2010 (Hao, 2011b). The revenue of 2010 is five times that of 2006. The annual growth rate reaches 49.7 percent. Of the total revenue of 105.2 billion RMB in 2010, mobile phone publishing accounts for 35.0 billion RMB, online games accounts for 32.4 billion, Internet advertising for 32.1 billion, electronic books for 2.5 billion, blogs for 10 million, online journals for 749 million RMB, online newspapers for 600 million RMB, online cartoon for 600 million, and online music for 280 million (Hao, 2011b). Based on these data, we can find that mobile phone publishing, online games, and Internet advertising account for 33.3 percent, 30.8, and 30.5 respectively of the total digital publishing revenues. It is predicted that mobile publishing, based on reading terminals such as mobile phones, may become the major form of digital publishing in the future.

It should be noted that the market leaders in digital publishing are not traditional publishers but emerging information service operators such as China Mobile Communications Group and Founder Group as well as information content providers such as Shanda Literature Company. Electronic books produced by traditional publishers only generated overall revenue of 2.48 billion RMB in 2010, which was negligible in terms of market share.

A typical example of digital publishing is the Starting Point Chinese Network, a website launched by Shanda Literature Company. The website collects excellent content generated by users and charges a fee for consuming such content. It creates values for writers and continuously extends the value chain for more market players. Specifically, the website integrates the roles of publisher, broker, and sales vendor, forming a self-contained publishing industry chain (Wei, 2007). In fact, its business model is similar to that adopted by traditional publishers. This kind of website is arguably poised to replace traditional publishing, which is facing a crisis of being marginalized. Concerning the impact on the traditional publishing industry, a Chinese publisher named Mo Zhixu pointed out in his blog post "The Last Publisher" that web contents and digital operation are beneficial to traditional publishers in the short term but will fundamentally destroy the traditional publishing industry in the medium to long term; that is because due to digital operation, traditional publishers will inevitably lose the right to review books and to grant market access so that they will inevitably lose most of the pricing right and eventually become the authors' servants–agents (Mo, 2007).

Faced with the challenges imposed by information technology, traditional publishers have leveraged their traditional resources to explore opportunities in digital publishing. The People's Military Medical Press is a successful example in this regard. After building a strong database and an advanced digital platform, the Press designed and developed many new digital products. Specifically, the Press provided five kinds of media services (i.e., book, reading card, disk, network, and database) and also combined five functions (i.e., reading, listening, watching, consulting, and carrying) into one, thus solving many of readers' old problems with medical books, such as it being hard to buy a complete set of books, hard to find accurate answers from the books, hard to understand the book contents, and inconvenient to carry the books. This is arguably a major breakthrough from the traditional medical publishing model. Currently, the Press is proposing to introduce six categories of cross-media intelligent products, including cross-media intelligent books, a cross-media intelligent network reading card, cross-media e-book CD-ROMs, composite cross-media intelligent publications, large-scale medical databases, and the *Armed Forces Digital Medical Book Series* that can be customized (Qi, 2010).

Regarding book distribution, online bookstores play an increasingly important role in the market. Online bookstores' sales have accounted for one-third of the total book market, and even up to 60–70 percent in some categories and areas (Qiu, 2011). For a period of time, the major players of the online book distribution market were Dangdang and Amazon China, both of which started from online book sales and then developed toward online department stores. In 2010, China's information technology product sales giant Jingdong Mall entered book sales. In 2011, China's large household appliance vendor Suning Electronics Company established the website Suning Yigou Book Sales Channel.

When they entered the online book sales industry, the first weapon they used was lower prices. They acted like "bad boys" who did not expect to make a profit from selling books. For Suning Electronics, its ultimate objective was to sell home appliances and general merchandise sales, and its online book store was just a tool for the company to attract public attention. With regard to Jindong Mall, its chairman Liu Qiangdong blatantly claimed on his blog that he didn't allow his online bookstore to make profits; his only object was to increase online traffic. In fact, traditional publishers are gradually losing their pricing capability while traditional bookstores are overwhelmed by the "price war" launched by online bookstores emerging in recent years.

Due to the aggressive expansion of major online bookstores and the lack of policy protection, many of the traditional private bookstores almost have no ability to fight back. By contrast, state-owned Xinhua Bookstore Company has partially completed grouplization and initial public offering (IPO). Many of its subordinate companies, such as Xinhua Wenxuan, Zhejiang Xinhua Bookstore Group, and Beijing Xinhua Distribution Group, have established online sales platform to compete with those new online bookstores. In June 2010, Xinhua Bookstore nationwide launched the "China Xinhua Bookstore Cross-Regional Collaboration Network" (the "UniNetwork"). This network was used to supervise the sales of retail outlets, make online exchange of publication information, strengthen the collaboration of logistics, and facilitate online payment (Sina, 2010). It is unclear whether the Xinhua Bookstores with strong capital and government support can compete with those emerging online bookstores. Whatever the outcome is, however, it will have a major impact on the market structure of the book publishing industry.

Conclusions

China's book publishing industry is now in a rather complicated situation: there are opportunities; there are also challenges. First, there is a gradual relaxation of government regulation and a strong national policy support for this industry. On the one hand, these measures agitate the market players, and infuse a competitive force into the industry; on the other hand, there is too much administrative interference, which has led to "no separation between administration and management." Second, the industry has a potentially huge market, but the structure of the market urgently needs adjustment. The private sector demonstrates high vitality in both the publishing and distribution markets, but its prospects remain unclear due to the long-term policy bias towards the state-owned sector and the squeeze from state-owned monopolistic groups. Third, book publishing has witnessed the penetration of information technology. This not only puts traditional publishing and distribution models into difficult situations but also brings creative changes in ideas and styles of publishing and distribution.

So far China's book publishing industry has basically completed its industrialization and commercialization processes. It is argued that the Chinese government should consider whether to carry out more or less administrative intervention, how to better macro-control the industry, and how to create a fair market environment for encouraging the inflow of private and foreign capital and for stimulating the further development of the industry. For publishing and distribution companies, the most important issues they should consider are how to fully seize the opportunities created by government policies, play their technical advantages, align with market demand, and lead the cultural fashion to achieve the "win-win" of social and economic benefits.

Perhaps the main limitation of this study is that it is largely descriptive so that some of its claims lack the support of substantive data. It describes what has happened to China's book publishing industry, but it cannot predict what will happen in the coming years. Future studies may conduct a quantitative study for overcoming these kinds of drawbacks. In addition, the present study tries to identify policy intervention, market change, and technology innovation as three determinants of China's book publishing industry. Such identification, though principally correct, fails to reveal more specific factors that are shaping the development of the industry. In this regard, future research may focus on a single book publishing or distribution company and conduct a case study for furthering our understanding of China's transitional book publishing.

References

Chen, J. (2011, July 11). Four major drawbacks of digital publishing surfaced. *Beijing Business*. Retrieved November 15, 2011 from http://media.people.com.cn/GB/40757/15119153.html

Chen, X. (2006). *On China's publishing industry*. Shanghai, China: Fudan University Press.

Chong, X., Chen, J., & Zhang, F. (2011, October 11). Beijing photosynthesis books bankrupted. *Beijing Business*. Retrieved December 10, 2011 from http://news.sohu.com/20111031/n323961137.shtml

Feng, W. (2007, October 11). The GAPP changing its functions. *China News Publishing Journal*. Retrieved December 10, 2011 from http://news.sina.com.cn/c/2007-10-11/113314064128.shtml

GAPP (2010a). *Several comments on speeding up the development of China's digital publishing industry*. Retrieved November 12, 2011 from http://www.gapp.gov.cn/cms/html/21/508/201009/702978.html

GAPP (2010b). *The application for 2010 Cultural Industry Special Funding launched*. Retrieved January 20, 2012 from http://www.gov.cn/gzdt/2010-06/05/content_1621130.htm

GAPP (2011). *The 2010 press and publication industry analysis report.* Retrieved December 10, 2011 from http://www.gapp.gov.cn/cms/html/21/367/201107/720474.html

Hao, Z. (2008). *Chinese press and publication industry's 30 years of reform and opening up.* Beijing: People's Publishing House.

Hao, Z. (2011a, April 21). The report on the development of China's private book publishing. *China Book Business Report.*

Hao, Z. (2011b, July). China Digital Publishing Annual Report 2010/2011. *Publishing World.*

Ji, S. (2011, April 16). Part of Beijing private book publishing companies obtained ISBNs. *China Book Business Report.*

Jiang, G. (2011). The imagination and reality of the cooperation between state-owned and private publishing. *Science & Technology and Publishing*, 9.

Liu, B. (2007). Striving to create a new situation for Chinese books to go out. Retrieved October 18, 2011 from http://www.gapp.gov.cn/cms/html/21/1006/200704/449425.html

Mo, Z. (2007). The last publisher. Retrieved September 29, 2011 from http://blog.tianya.cn/blogger/post_show.asp?idWriter=0&Key=0&BlogID=1005488&PostID=10608787

Sina (2010). The cross-regional collaboration network of Xinhua Bookstores to be launched. Retrieved September 15, 2011 from http://book.sina.com.cn/compose/c/2010-12-16/1634281399.shtml

Song, M. (2003). Exploring the origin and adjustment of the Zhuban Zhuguan policy of the publishing industry. *Publishing Science*, 4: 4–6.

Qi, X. (2010). The People's Military Medical Press successful realized cross-media operation. Retrieved October 28, 2011 from http://news.xinhuanet.com/book/2010-01/07/content_12769746.htm

Qiu, Y. (2011). What did online bookstore change. *China Quality Long March*, 7.

Wang, L. (2005). The rationale of regulating the changing publishing industry in China. *Publishing and Distribution Research*, 3.

Wei, Y. (2007, September). Stepping into traditional publishing: The return of content websites. *The Publisher*, 1.

Wu, L. (2011, October 18). The publishing industry ushered in the era of private operation. *The Rule of Law Weekend.* Retrieved December 2, 2011 from http://news.hexun.com/2011-10-18/134331238.html

Yao, Z. (2010, September 7). The basic situation of the news and publications industry in 2009. *China News Publishing Journal.* Retrieved December 1, 2011 from http://www.ppsc.gov.cn/tjsj/201009/t20100907_76674.html

Zhou, W. (2005). *Research on the publishing industry.* Beijing, China: China Renmin University Press.

Section III

LATIN AMERICAN AND HISPANIC MME RESEARCH

8
CONVERGENCE IN THE MEXICAN MEDIA INDUSTRY 2011

María Elena Gutiérrez-Rentería, Ph.D.[1] and Josefina Santana Villegas, Ph.D.

Introduction

As in other countries, the majority of communications firms in Mexico face challenges and opportunities due to digital convergence. These have fostered convergence among some industry sectors, as well as changes in business models, related to the implementation of strategies designed to promote an active presence on the Internet and attract audiences (Albarran, 2010, Chan-Olmsted, 2011; Grant & Wilkinson, 2009; Sullivan & Jiang, 2010). Well-considered strategies on the part of some Mexican entrepreneurs have even contributed to changing media consumption habits (Gutiérrez-Rentería, 2011b).

At the same time, Mexico has increased its offering of content and distribution channels, resulting in more attractive options in information and entertainment than in previous decades (Gutiérrez-Rentería, 2010, 2011a). From the point of view of the entrepreneur immersed in this field, the competitive environment in the industry is greater than ever. Some actors have anticipated the macro and micro economic environment in Mexican industry, as seen in market participation and business models. Others, on the contrary, have been passive, and their content offerings reflect their lack of action.

The purpose of this study is to show the principal strategic actions carried out by Mexican entrepreneurs in an environment in which digital convergence has forced them, in a certain way, to improve their offerings, and diversify their business in other sectors which converge with the telecommunications sector if they wish to stay afloat. Finally, it is of interest to identify the main characteristics related to digital convergence of the principal Mexican traditional media to attract and maintain audiences in their Web pages.

This chapter is divided into four parts. The first deals with the background of the communications industry in Mexico. The second part describes the principal players in Mexican industry and their current strategic actions related, mainly, to digital convergence and digital content distribution platforms. The third part of this chapter explains the methodology used to analyze how Mexican communications firms have used digital convergence to improve their offering and distribution of content. The fourth section shows the results of the study, followed by the conclusions.

Industry Background

The Mexican government took actions to liberalize the state audiovisual industry in the 1990s. The measures were designed to face the economic crisis as well as to confront the challenge of market globalization. In 1993 the telecommunications industry was liberalized and public television was privatized.

During this same period, institutions and legal mechanisms were put into place to regulate healthy competition among companies. The Federal Law of Economic Competition was created in 1992, and the Federal Commission of Competition began its activities in 1995. In the past decade, the telecommunications sector in Mexico has become one of the motors of society. The number of participants has increased and diversified, as have the activities that support the sector.

At present, telecommunications is one of the industries that has experienced more growth in Mexico. Sectors that have experienced greater growth are television via satellite or cable, in terms of paid subscribers, followed by mobile telephony (Comisión Federal de Telecomunicaciones, 2011).

However, fixed-line telephone services have experienced a downturn due to technological substitution and the changing profile of the user. Traditional fixed-line services are being replaced by mobile phones; dial-up connections to the Internet are being replaced by broadband, and voice over Internet services are becoming more popular (Comisión Federal de Telecomunicaciones (COFETEL), 2011). According to COFETEL there are over 97 million mobile phone subscribers in Mexico. Prices for traditional services continue to drop, thanks mostly to competition in the sector.

Media consumption habits among young people have changed (Nielsen, 2008). Currently, young people access the Internet through mobile devices, especially laptop computers and mobile phones (Milward Brown México, 2011). Access to information and entertainment through the Internet, smartphones, and interaction through social media for both producers and consumers of content, have all contributed to attracting younger audiences in the national market.

In 2010, the National Institute of Statistics and Geography (INEGI) reported that 29.8 percent of all Mexican homes had a computer; 94.7 percent of households had a television set, and 80.6 percent had fixed-line or mobile phones (Instituto Nacional de Estadística y Geografía, 2011). In 2010, there were over 12 million Internet subscribers, of whom 97 percent had broadband (Comisión Federal de Telecomunicaciones, 2011).

With regards to digital technologies that allow for industry convergence (in this case, those related to media communications), Mexican authorities have made an effort to regulate the industry while at the same time facilitating competition. An example is the Convergence Agreement published in 2006 by the Secretariat of Communications and Transportation (2006). The agreement establishes the authority and requirements for companies to offer triple play services. In the same way, COFETEL signed an agreement that sets the standard for land-based digital radio, as well as establishing policies for radio firms to make the voluntary move to digital technology (Comisión Federal de Telecomunicaciones, 2011).

With regards to advertising investment in the media in Mexico, commercial television still takes the largest slice of the advertising pie, followed by radio (García, 2012). However, the percentage of advertising in online media continues to grow significantly.

Principal Communications Firms and Strategic Actions

Telecommunications Industry

Audiovisual communications companies—radio and television—as well as those devoted since their origin to fixed-line telephony in Mexico, have taken advantage of the opportunities offered by digital convergence and industry liberalization to broaden their offerings (Gutiérrez-Rentería, 2011a). Some of the principal firms have taken advantage of their position in the domestic market to successfully penetrate the Latin American market through triple or quadruple play. Such is the case of América Móvil owned by Carlos Slim; Grupo Televisa under Emilio Azcárraga-Jean, and TV Azteca owner Ricardo Salinas Pliego. The first two of these occupy privileged positions in the domestic market.

Both América Móvil (owner of Telmex, Telmex Internacional, and Telcel) and Grupo Televisa have been able to take advantage of their privileged position and the characteristics of new technologies for industry convergence. Grupo Televisa has alliances with other Mexican firms which offer services through their cable networks throughout the country. América Móvil offer the same as Grupo Televisa in other Latin American countries, not in Mexico (América Móvil, 2010, 2011a). Other companies which participate in the stock market through the Mexican Stock

Exchange and offer the triple play are Grupo Televisa, Megacable, and Cablevisión.

At present, Grupo Televisa and TV Azteca are the two commercial television companies with coverage throughout the country and with funding through advertising. The following table shows the principal companies by number of subscribers and participation in the domestic capitals market (see Table 8.1).

The competitive environment has changed, so much so that even once fierce competitors have joined forces. Such is the case of Televisa and TV Azteca. Megacable has special agreements with cable companies belonging to Grupo Televisa. Grupo Iusacell, devoted to mobile telephony, now has shared interests with Grupo Televisa and Grupo Salinas. These companies have created alliances to compete against Carlos Slim's América Móvil, which accounts for almost 80 percent of the total revenue of companies participating in Mexico's telecommunications industry (Trejo-Pech & Gutiérrez-Rentería, 2011).

In the domestic market, Telmex, also part of América Móvil, requires government authorization to offer the triple play and to add value to a company whose revenue has been decreasing, and whose principal source of income is the mobile telephone company Telcel. América Móvil acquired 100 percent of the American company Claxson Interactive Group, devoted to the development, integration, and delivery of entertainment solutions for digital distribution platforms in Latin America (América Móvil, 2011a). Telcel is currently the leading mobile telephone services provider in Mexico in terms of subscribers.

In September, 2011, América Móvil reported 241.5 million mobile phone subscribers in Latin America, 29.3 million fixed telephone lines, 4.6 million broadband Internet accesses, and 12.5 million subscribers for pay television (América Móvil, 2011b). This information covers all the companies owned by entrepreneur Carlos Slim throughout Latin America.

The majority of the strategies applied by Mexican entrepreneurs is focused on taking advantage of digital convergence and becoming involved in triple and quadruple play services in the domestic market. Some of these companies also do business in the Latin American market.

Radio Industry

Radio in Mexico continues to be an important medium for the population. As with television, companies have a strong influence on cultural, political, and economical life in Mexico (Gutiérrez-Rentería & Santana, 2012). This sector has also benefited from digital technologies, and some companies offer radio programming on the Web.

Table 8.1 Principal Strategic Alliances of Mexican Companies in the Telecommunications Sector (2011)

Year of Creation	Company	Main Business	Strategic Alliances in Mexico	Strategic Alliances or Acquisitions Abroad
2000	América Móvil (Telmex, Telcel, Telmex International)	In Mexico: Wireless Communication, Internet, Mobile Phone, Fixed Telephone. In Latin America: Triple and Quadruple Play	Multivisión	Telcel, Comcel, Claro, Tracfone (Colombia, Brazil, United States), Claro (Argentina and Uruguay), Telmex (Colombia), Claro (Chile, Dominican Republic, Ecuador, El Salvador, Guatemala, Honduras, Nicaragua, Panamá, Perú, and Puerto Rico), Embratel and Net (Brazil), Claxson Interactive Group (United States)
1994	Axtel	Fixed Telephone, Paid Television, Internet	-	
2003	Grupo Iusacell	Mobile Phone	Grupo Salinas (TV Azteca)	-
2004	Megacable Holdings	Quadruple Play	Grupo Televisa, Telefónica	-
1973	Grupo Televisa	Multimedia, National Broadcasting, Paid Television (Satellite and Cable), Triple Play in Mexico	Megacable, Telefónica, Grupo Prisa	TV Record, Sky Brazil (Brazil), Inversiones Audiovisuales La Sexta, Telefónica Media, Telefónica (Spain), China Internacional Television Corporation (China), Univisión and Telemundo (United States), Endemol (Netherlands), BBC Worldwide (Inglaterra)
1993	TV Azteca	National Broadcasting, Internet		Azteca America, Los Angeles KAZA TV (United States)

Source: Compiled by the authors.

Table 8.2 Principal Mexican Radio Companies

	Year of Creation	Company	Main Business	Core Business
1	1965	Grupo Acir	Radio	Advertising
2	1962	Grupo Imagen Radio	Radio	Advertising
3	1930	Grupo Multimedios	Triple and Quadruple Play, Radio and Press	Advertising and Subscribers
4	1952	Grupo Radio Centro	Radio	Advertising
5	1984	Grupo Radio Digital	Radio	Advertising
6	N.D.	Grupo Radiodifusoras Capital	Radio	Advertising
7	1940	Multimedios Estrella de Oro	Radio	Advertising
8	1967	MVS Comunicaciones	Satellite Television and Radio	Advertising and Subscriber
9	1980	Promomedios	Radio	Advertising
10	1968	Radio Fórmula	Radio	Advertising
11	1940	Radiodifusoras Asociadas	Radio	Advertising
12	1930	Radiópolis	Radio	Advertising
13	1970	Radiorama	Radio	Advertising
14	1966	Somer	Radio	Advertising

Source: Compiled by the authors.

At present, there are around 1,149 commercial radio stations: 759 on AM and 390 on FM. The majority of these are affiliated with a group. Likewise, there are 365 other registered stations, the majority FM, belonging to public institutions, universities, or indigenous communities.

National companies with strong penetration in the national market are Grupo Acir, Radio Fórmula, Grupo Imagen, Grupo Radio Centro, Organización Impulsora de Radio, Grupo Radio Capital, Radiorama, Radiópolis (Grupo Televisa), MVS Comunicaciones, Grupo Monitor, Radiodifusoras Asociadas, Multimedios, Promomedios, Somer, NRM Comunicaciones, Ultratelecom, and Mac Ediciones (Gutiérrez-Rentería & Santana, 2012). Table 8.2 shows the principal radio companies in the country.

Press

The oldest newspapers in Mexico are *El Dictamen* from the state of Veracruz, which was founded in 1898, and *El Universal*, created in 1916.

Table 8.3 Largest Mexican Chain Companies Ranked by Number of Newspapers

Rank	Main Newspapers	Chain Company	Regional Market	Number of Dailies
1	Esto, Excelsior, La Prensa, El Occidental, El Sol	Organización Editorial Mexicana	Northwest, West, North Central, South Central	56
2	Reforma, El Norte, Mural, Metro, AM	Grupo Reforma	South Central, Northeast, West	12
3	Milenio	Milenio Diario	South Central, West, Northeast	7
4	Rumbo de México, Estadio, Diario de Toluca, El Corregidor	Mac Ediciones y Publicaciones	South Central	6

Source: Compiled by the authors.

The press in Mexico is regional instead of national. The principal editorial groups have local papers, which also provide national news. There are around 337 registered newspapers. The states with the greatest circulation are Distrito Federal, Nuevo León, and Jalisco.

Most newspapers are financed by advertising, principally from the government, financial institutions, automobile companies, and department stores, followed by reader subscriptions and, finally, single issue sales. There are approximately 11 free newspapers.

In Mexico, newspaper publishers are not required to issue daily circulation reports. Official information on circulation is obtained from what dailies publish in a commercial directory; this does not always coincide with actual circulation data. However, there are institutions devoted to data verification and some publishers approach them for auditing. The most important of these are the Institute of Media Verification, IMARC, and PriceWaterhouse. Table 8.3 shows the principal chain companies according to number of dailies

Companies that hold the greatest number of regional newspapers are Organización Editorial Mexicana, Grupo Reforma, Mac Ediciones y Publicaciones, and Grupo Milenio (Multimedios). Some Mexican newspapers have alliances with foreign papers, such as *El Universal* which distributes content with the *Miami Herald*, or *Grupo Reforma* which distributes content from the *New York Times* on Sundays. *The News* is published by Editorial News de México in the English language, and, at present, it is the most expensive daily newspaper in Mexico at a cost of $1.06 US (equivalent to 15 Mexican pesos).

Methodology

The purpose of this study is to identify the content offerings of industry leaders in Mexican television, radio, and Internet press, according to the different digital platforms (Fundación Telefónica, 2008). The intention is to show if traditional communications media firms have taken advantage of the opportunities offered by digital convergence to improve their content offerings. The method used for this study is qualitative, using content analysis.

The study is intended as a glance at the current situation of the Mexican telecommunications industry with regards to digital convergence, a global phenomenon which represents challenges and opportunities to media companies.

For the first stage of this analysis, a database was created including data from the two commercial television chains in the country, as well as the most important companies participating in triple and quadruple play in Mexico. The database included the most important radio groups with nationwide coverage, and economical and political influence on the country. With regards to the press, 50 newspapers were analyzed; these were selected based on their circulation stated and published in *Directorios MPM Publiciarios Tarifas y Datos Medios Impresos*. In all, 70 different media sources were analyzed based on these criteria.

Six items were selected for analysis, based on what communication companies offer their audiences through their digital platforms. It is interesting to know if, in the Mexican case, the traditional media (daily newspapers, television and radio stations) have embraced the Web as a means of expanding the reach of their publications or broadcasts (Grant & Wilkinson, 2009). Moreover, this study tries to identify if the media companies are taking the content from the traditional outlet and repeating it on the Website; or if these companies are providing new forms to present the content and promote interaction with the audience, taking advantage of digital convergence and social networks such as Facebook and Twitter. Also, the study is interested in identifying the presence of advertising on the digital platforms of the media companies (Croteau, Hoynes, & Milan, 2012). The items are:

1. Free content: open access to all digital content of the media company;

2. Paid content: access to digital content only for subscribers;
3. Advertising: presence of advertisers on the digital platform;
4. Multimedia information presentation;
5. Social networking sites like Facebook or microblogging like Twitter;
6. Apps for mobile devices.

Analyzing these companies using the same lens of digital convergence can aid in understanding the current situation of the national industry in a competitive digital environment.

Results

The research results show that approximately 80 percent of television and radio companies in the country offer updated content on their Web pages, and use social networks and microblogging to interact with their audiences, primarily through Facebook, Twitter, and YouTube. About 75 percent of the firms offer open access to all the content and only 55 percent have advertising. Multimedios and Televisa are the only companies which sell content on a single item basis.

Moreover, about 70 percent of Mexican newspaper companies offer updated content; 72 percent of these offer free access to all their content and 74 percent have some kind of advertising. Only 66 percent use social networks to interact with their audiences. Companies that stand out in this field are El Universal, Grupo Reforma, and Milenio (Multimedios).

With regards to convergence in Mexican radio and television, 67 percent of the companies offer interactivity through their digital platforms and multimedia contents. Some 76 percent are active in social networks and only 48 percent offer apps for mobile devices.

In the case of the Mexican press, 66 percent of the companies have taken advantage in some measure of digital convergence in their offerings to readers. Only 20 percent of the 50 newspapers studied offer apps for mobile devices; 42 percent offer interactive Web pages and multimedia content, and 66 percent are active on social networks. Newspaper publishers which take full advantage of digital platforms are: El Universal; companies which make up Grupo Reforma (El Norte, Reforma, and Mural); Milenio (Grupo Multimedios); Rumbo de México; El Financiero; La Jornada; and Diario de Yucatán.

Analysis of television, radio, and press in Mexico shows that 70 percent of communications companies offer updated content and free access. More than 50 percent have advertising, with the press reflecting the largest percentage in this area—more than 70 percent. A little over 10 percent sell single content items to the user (see Figure 8.1).

Finally, it can be said that 67 percent of the companies in the audiovisual industry in Mexico take advantage of digital convergence to foster

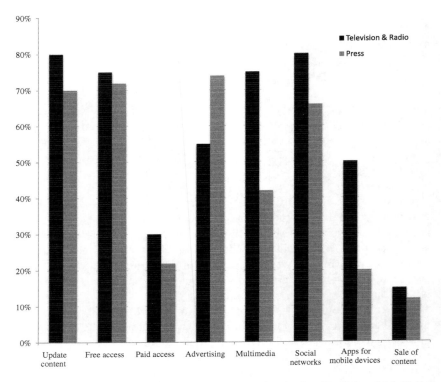

Figure 8.1 Total Percentage of Characteristics that Define Traditional Media in Mexico on the Web, 2011

Source: Self-produced.

interactivity and offer multimedia content in their Web pages. Only 48 percent offer an app to facilitate access to content from digital devices and, like newspaper publishers, they use Internet-based social networks strategically. Results obtained through this analysis confirm that digital convergence is a reality for Mexican audiovisual companies. In general, the audiovisual industry takes advantage of 60 percent of the digital technologies that facilitate convergence among industries, whereas for newspaper publishers it is only 43 percent.

Conclusions

The purpose of this research is to provide a framework for understanding the *status quo* of the convergence in the Mexican media industry. Digital technologies have to contribute to change the media landscape in this country. The digital revolution has also helped to transform the delivery of media content in Mexico. Otherwise, convergence brought competition between media and telephony firms. That is the case of América Móvil, from Carlos Slim, and Grupo Televisa, from Emilio Azcárraga-Jean.

This study shows the participation of Carlos Slim in the Latin American media industry. Telmex, which had a fixed-line public monopoly in Mexico, tried to compete against Grupo Televisa and TV Azteca in the domestic market through the offer of triple play. Both companies tried to compete against Carlos Slim through increasing the price of advertising. Otherwise, Grupo Televisa made a strategic alliance with TV Azteca. Grupo Televisa bought 50 percent of Iusacell, the mobile phone company belonging to Grupo Salinas (the owner of TV Azteca).

While digital technologies have fostered convergence among industries, in Mexico the rules of the game are not yet well established by government authorities charged with promoting a healthy and competitive national market. Through this study, it is clear that the markets for information and entertainment are more competitive when compared to previous eras. Traditional companies are also participating with digital platforms. Industry leaders in each sector present audiovisual content that reduces the gap between what used to distinguish television from radio or the press; the gap in regards to online content offerings is minimal.

On the other hand, younger audiences in Mexico have characteristics that completely distinguish them from adults. Thus, strategies designed to capture these younger markets are characterized by a high degree of fragmentation and by the production of content.

This study is intended to reflect the general state of the communications industry and of digital convergence in Mexico. It can contribute to future research that could help define greater criteria in regards to quality and sector competition.

Limitations and Future Research

The study presents an overview of how the leaders of the media industry in Mexico have taken advantage of the opportunities presented by digital technologies that foster convergence between traditional media and the telecommunications sector.

The limitations of the study are related to lack of information from the media companies in Mexico. In the literature, there are few studies about the Mexican media industry from the perspective of media economics and media management.

This study may serve to further research related to the type of digital media consumption content by the audience with the current offer from the media companies. Another aspect of interest for research would be the economic, legal, and political impacts on society resulting from the convergence of the media industry in Mexico.

Notes

1 With special thanks to Jesús Aidé Leal Soberanes, student of communications at Universidad del Occidente de Sonora, who participated in *Verano Científico 2011* at Panamericana Universidad; with support from her university and from el Instituto Delfín (http://www.programadelfin.com.mx).

References

Albarran, A. (2010). *The Media Economy*. New York: Routledge.
América Móvil (2010). *Memoria Anual*. Retrieved April 15, 2010 from http://www.americamovil.com/amx/cm/filings/reporte2010.pdf
América Móvil (2011a). *América Móvil informa al público inversionista*. Retrieved May 10, 2011 from http://www.americamovil.com/amx/cm/news/2011/2011_04_27.pdf
América Móvil (2011b). *Reporte Financiero y Operativo del Tercer Trimestre 2011*. Retrieved November 1, 2011 from http://www.americamovil.com/amx/es/cm/reports/Q/3T11_Vf.pdf
Chan-Olmsted, S. (2011). Media Branding in a Changing World: Challenges and Opportunities 2.0. *International Journal on Media Management*, 13(1), 3–19.
Comisión Federal de Telecomunicaciones [COFETEL] (2011). *Índice de Producción del Sector Telecomunicaciones*. Retrieved March 20, 2011 from: http://www.cft.gob.mx/es/Cofetel_2008/Cuarto_Trimestre_2010.
Croteau, D., Hoynes, W., & Milan, S. (2012). *Media/Society: Industries, Images, and Audiences*. fourth edition. Los Angeles: Sage.
Fundación Telefónica (2008). *La Generación Interactiva en Iberoamérica. Niños y adolescentes ante las pantallas*. Spain: Ariel.
García, J. (2012, April 30). Estudio Anual de inversión en medios 2012 *Merca2.0*, 10, 48–51.
Grant, A., & Wilkinson, J. (2009). *Understanding Media Convergence. The State of the Field*. New York: Oxford University Press.
Gutiérrez-Rentería, M. (2010). Grupo Televisa ante la convergencia digital y las nuevas tecnologías: análisis económico (2003–2009). *Revista de Comunicación*. 9, 26–41.
Gutiérrez-Rentería, M. (2011a). Análisis de los aciertos estratégicos y el impacto económico de Carlos Slim-Helú en la industria de las Telecomunicaciones. *Revista de Comunicación*. 10, 7–24.
Gutiérrez-Rentería, M. (2011b). Mexican Telecommunication Industry: Challenges and Opportunities in Digital Age. *Journal of Spanish Language Media*, 4. Retrieved April 15, 2011 from http://www.spanishmedia.unt.edu/english/downloads/journal/vol4JSLM
Gutiérrez-Rentería, M. & Santana, J. (2012). Understanding the Radio Industry in Mexico: Challenges and Opportunities. In Hendricks, J. (Ed.). *The Palgrave Handbook of International Radio*. London: Palgrave.
Instituto Nacional de Estadística y Geografía. (2011). *Usuarios de Internet en México*. Retrieved November 15, 2011 from: http://www.inegi.gob.mx/est/contenidos/espanol/temas/Sociodem/notatinf212.asp

Milward Brown México (2011). Estudio de Consumo de Medios entre los Internautas Mexicanos 2011. *The Interactive Advertising Bureau México.* Retrieved December 15, 2011 from http://www.iabmexico.com/estudios/ECM11

Medios Publicitarios Mexicanos (2011, May 1). *Tarifas y Datos Medios Impresos.* México: Directorios MPM Publicitarios.

Nielsen (2008). *Cambios del mercado mexicano 2007.* Retrieved May 13, 2008 from http://www.amai.org/datos_files/Cambios_mercado_mexicano_2007.pdf

Secretaría de Comunicaciones y Transportes [SCT] (2006). *Acuerdo de Convergencia de Servicios Fijos de Telefonía Local y Televisión y/o/ Audio Restringidos que se Proporcionan a Través de Redes Públicas Alámbricas e Inalámbricas.* Retrieved December 20, 2006 from http://www.ordenjuridico.gob.mx/Federal/PE/APF/APC/SCT/Acuerdos/2006/03102006(1).pdf

Sullivan, D. & Jiang, Y. (2010). Media Convergence and the Impact of the Internet on the M&A Activity of Large Media Companies. *Journal of Media Business Studies,* 7(4) 21–40.

Trejo-Pech, C. & Gutiérrez-Rentería, M. (2011). Systematic Risk and Organization of the Multimedia and Telecommunication Industries in México. *China-USA Business Review,* 10(11), 1097–1109.

9

A CASE STUDY ON MEDIA DIVERSIFICATION

Caracol and RCN TV Channels—Beyond the Traditional Business Model

Germán Arango-Forero

Despite their consolidation on the traditional advertising market, the Colombian television networks Caracol and RCN have developed an aggressive strategy beyond the traditional business model, that includes programming based on interactive participation of viewers, product placement, internet services, international alliances, and the extension of their brands on the close (pay) television system. This chapter summarizes some of the most important strategies applied by the networks during the first decade of the twenty-first century.

The Colombian commercial television industry has been characterized during the first decade of the twenty-first century by a duopolistic market structure led by the two most important networks, Caracol and RCN. Despite their consolidation on the national media market, the two broadcasting companies have implemented an interesting diversification on their traditional business model based on advertising.

Caracol television and RCN television were launched as the first two Colombian national private TV channels in 1998. Although Colombia is the second largest Hispanic language country after Mexico, with up to 45.5 million inhabitants by the end of 2010 (DANE, 2007), the country had only two nationwide commercial channels for over 40 years (Arango-Forero, Arango, Llaña, & Serrano, 2010, p. 64).

Before the national television commission was created in 1995, the Colombian government took total control of the television networks, enabling different channels for state-defined programming and frequencies in which program slots were leased to privately owned companies, which undertook the job of producing and programming. This was achieved through lease contracts for a defined length of time and a determined set of programming options (Arango-Forero, Gutiérrez, Forero et al., 2009, p. 68).

A CASE STUDY ON MEDIA DIVERSIFICATION

Since 1958 both Caracol and RCN acted as private producing companies and broadcasted on the public frequencies. In 1997 the two firms obtained the license to operate as exclusive private networks for ten years. In 2008 the licenses were renewed for ten more years.

It took Caracol and RCN only five years (between 1998 and 2003) to consolidate a duopoly market structure in the Colombian commercial television system, despite the presence of a third national commercial channel Canal Uno (still owned by the government and broadcasted by private producers), eight regional public channels, and one commercial local frequency (City TV) broadcasted from Bogotá, the Colombian capital.

As shown in Table 9.1, during the first decade of the twenty-first century the television advertising investment share in Colombia remained very stable and accounted for up to 50 percent, while the national television channels took the big part of the cake.

Audience ratings have also remained very stable for the Caracol and RCN networks. Considering there are only three national commercial channels, by the end of the second semester of 2011 around 89.7 percent of Colombians watched Canal RCN, while 85.0 percent watched Canal Caracol and only 12.1 percent watched Canal Uno (Asociación Colombiana para la Investigación de Medios [ACIM], 2011). By the end of 2011 RCN television reported profits of 50.813 million Colombian pesos (COP), nearly US$26 million, while Caracol reported profits of 43.369 million COP, nearly US$23 million (El Universal, 2012).

Despite the consolidation of the two networks on the commercial open Colombian television system, both companies have implemented new strategic business models looking for the diversification of their traditional sources of revenues based on advertising (commercial sections). This chapter aims to summarize the most important and profitable strategies applied by the two networks, ranging from the interactive participation of watchers to the international joint ventures and alliances that have projected Caracol and RCN beyond the Colombian borders.

Caracol, Prime Time, and Interactivity

It is 8:47 in the evening, Wednesday November 30th, 2011, at the prime time of Colombian television. Caracol channel has reached a historical peak of 52.4 percent of the Colombian audience share with the reality show called "Yo me llamo ..." (My name is ...), a contest based on imitators of famous singers. "Yo me llamo" is a live show inspired by similar TV formats like "Lluvia de estrellas," produced by RTVE in Spain and "Yo soy," produced by MEGA in Chile. For the definitive moment of the last episode the show had about 70 percent of the total audience share (Semana, 2011, p. 13).

Table 9.1 Colombia: Media Advertising Share, 2000–2010 (%)

Medium/Year	2000	2001	2002	2003	2004	2005	2006	2007	2008	2009	2010
Television	48.7	51.5	51.4	51.7	53.3	52.9	51.9	50.3	51.2	50.3	49.4
National	**45.7**	**48.9**	**48.1**	**48.6**	**50.3**	**50.0**	**48.7**	**47.0**	**47.8**	**46.7**	**45.9**
Regional/Local	3.0	2.5	3.2	3.1	2.9	2.7	3.2	3.2	3.3	3.3	3.3
Close (Pay TV)	0	0	0.1	0.1	0.1	0.1	0.1	0.1	0.1	0.3	0.3
Radio	23.1	19.9	20.5	19.6	19.1	19.1	18.8	18.8	19.6	20.7	20.9
Newspapers	21.7	22.8	22.4	22.9	21.5	20.6	21.3	23.1	20.9	20.8	20.8
Magazines	6.5	5.7	5.7	5.8	6.1	6.2	6.8	6.5	6.0	5.3	5.0
Internet	0	0	0	0	0	1.2	1.2	1.2	2.3	2.8	3.9
	100%	100%	100%	100%	100%	100%	100%	100%	100%	100%	100%

Source: Comisión Nacional de Televisión, informe sectorial de televisión 2011.

Note: The close television share refers only to the advertising investment made on the own channel broadcasted either by the satellite or the cable company operator.

A CASE STUDY ON MEDIA DIVERSIFICATION

"Yo me llamo" was launched on August 22nd, 2011. After three months of competition from Monday to Friday, 70 episodes (1 hour each) and the previous elimination of 22 finalists, Jorge Martínez, who played the role of Rafael Orozco (1954–1992), a famous Caribbean singer of the Colombian rhythm known as "vallenato," and Luis Correa, who played the role of the Spanish ballad big star Nino Bravo (1944–1973), competed in the final for a prize of 500 million Colombian pesos (COP), around US$265,000.

During the last week of the show, Martínez and Correa had defeated the other two semifinalists Laura Padilla (who imitated the Colombian pop star Shakira) and Yerick Reyes (who played the role of the Caribbean salsa star Marc Anthony).

"Yo me llamo" was hosted by the Venezuelan actor and model Ernesto Calzadilla. The members of the jury were the Colombian actress and singer Amparo Grisales, the imitator and humorist Luz Amparo Alvarez, and the musical promoter Jairo Martínez. During the first stage of the show, they were in charge of choosing the final 22 participants from thousands of contestants who were previously eliminated in Bogotá, Cali, Medellín, Barranquilla, Pereira, and Bucaramanga, the six largest cities of Colombia.

The jury also decided who the final 12 contestants were. But from that moment the live show elimination process was based only on SMS (short messages service), also known as text messages, sent by millions of enthusiastic viewers through their cell phones, supporting their favorite performers every night.

After the last performances by the two finalists the voting process was declared over at 10 p.m. The text messaging service remained available during the next 24 hours. Finally Calzadilla declared Jorge Martínez the winner with 54.83 percent of the votes versus 45.17 percent who voted for Correa. According to Semana magazine (2011, p. 13) approximately 740,000 text messages were sent by watchers during the last day of the show. Considering that the cost for each message was around US$1 (1,800 COP), revenues from these texts were around US$700,000 (1,332 million COP). In Colombia, the revenues from text messaging services are distributed among the cell phone operator (Comcel 60 percent, Movistar 50 percent, and Tigo 40 percent), the different technological platforms integrator (10 percent) and the TV channel that gets between 40 and 60 percent, depending on the cell phone operator.

But text message service was not the only economical strategy applied by Canal Caracol with "Yo me llamo" under the diversification business model. Thanks to the unprecedented success of the program, Caracol also launched a karaoke DVD with the most successful 40 tracks performed by the contestants during the show. The DVD was produced in alliance with the international entertainment company Endemol and Discos Fuentes, a national audio record company. Also, Caracol announced by the end of the year a 2012 national live tour promoting the four finalists in the largest cities of the country.

"Yo me llamo" also had an aggressive positioning strategy through Internet and social networking. During the program viewers could visit the official website of Caracol (www.caracoltv.com) and vote for the favorite songs they wanted the contestants to perform. Audience members could decide about the clothing and the look of the 12 final participants. Viewers could participate on an interactive karaoke section as well, in which they could upload their own performances and vote for the top ten features.

Caracol promoted "Yo me llamo" through social networking sites Facebook and Twitter (hashtag #yomellamo), where audiences acted as critics and claimed for the return of some participants to the show. Comments and criticisms were presented by the host during the show. According to Aníbal Fernández, the program director, the feedback through social networking made viewers feel like an important part of the show (El Universal, 2011).

Once the show ended, Caracol announced the production of a biographical novela (soap opera) inspired by the life and the career of Rafael Orozco, the famous Colombian vallenato singer (imitated by Jorge Martínez) who played most of his career for a band called *Binomio de oro* (Golden binomial). Orozco was recognized as one of the most important vallenato singers, until he was shot and killed on June 11, 1992 in the city of Barranquilla at the age of 38.

A Battle Under the Duopoly Market Structure

After two and a half years of losing the war for the prime time rating share, "Yo me llamo" finally allowed Caracol to defeat RCN in programming between September and November 2011.

In response, on September 13th RCN launched the third season of "Factor XS" (The XS Factor), a music contest reserved for kids between 8 and 15 years old. Factor XS emerged from the original X Factor created by Simon Cowell and produced in Colombia by Canal RCN. The reality show for kids became a hit for RCN during the first two seasons (2006–2007). RCN was the first channel in Latin America to launch musical live contests with the audience's participation through phone calls and a text messaging voting system with The X Factor in 2005.

Despite the success of the two first seasons, Factor XS could not threaten "Yo me llamo," the Colombian audience's preference. However, once the successful Caracol show ended, RCN retook control of the prime time share by December with its novelas and reality programming (Ibope, 2011). Factor XS finished its season on December 21st with the interactive participation of millions of viewers who voted for the winner of the program.

Since 1998, RCN and Caracol have built a strong duopoly structure on the Colombian free commercial television market. As private channels, between 1998 and 2004 they competed against the two traditional national commercial channels (Canal 1 and Canal A) frequencies owned by the government but broadcast and marketed by independent producers. In 2004 Canal A suffered a financial crisis and disappeared as a commercial channel. Since then the frequency has turned into a national public broadcasting system (PBS) called Señal Institucional.

Despite the presence of a third national commercial channel (Canal 1) and a local private channel (City TV) in Bogotá the two big networks take control of the majority of the Colombian television market. Besides commercial television, the Colombian PBS includes two national channels (Señal Colombia and Señal Institucional) and eight regional frequencies.

A New Key Rival

The Colombian television industry has been divided into two sectors: the so called open (or free) television system, that includes all the Colombian commercial and non-commercial channels, and the so called close (or pay) subscription model, provided either by satellite or cable operators. In Colombia the close (pay) television model includes a subscription system called "Televisión comunitaria" (community television). This consists of small cable television distributors, located in local communities, which include in their basic packages local, regional, national, and some international channels.

The close (pay) television system through the subscription model has become the main competitor for Caracol and RCN during the first decade of the twenty-first century. By the end of 2011, the average number of households—following the Latin American definition—with a pay television model was estimated at 44 percent. However, Colombia had the second largest pay TV market in the region with a penetration of 78 percent of households (69.5 percent in the low income bracket, 81.6 percent in the middle income bracket, and 89.2 percent in the high income bracket). For comparison, Argentina remained number one in the region with an average of 79 percent of households with pay TV (LAMAC, 2011).

According to the Latin American Multichannel Advertising Council (LAMAC), the entire pay television system accounted for 37 percent of the total Colombian audience share by the end of 2011. During the previous four years, the rate of pay TV growth has been 63 percent. Table 9.2 shows the evolution of the Colombian TV rating share from 2007 to 2010.

Table 9.2 Colombia: Television Audience Share, 2007–2010

	2007	2008	2009	2010
Pay TV	23%	29%	36%	37.8%
Caracol	33%	29%	28%	24%
RCN	33%	29%	25%	26%
Others	11%	13%	11%	12.2%

Source: Ibope MWS Colombia, 2011; LAMAC, 2011.

Note: The share of pay TV includes 69 international channels measured by Ibope.

Table 9.3 Gap between Audience Share and Advertising Investment Share in Pay TV in Latin America

Country	Pay TV Penetration	Pay TV Advertisement Investment Share	Pay TV Audience Share
Argentina	79%	27%	42%
Brazil	29%	6%	8%
Chile	56%	5%	25%
Colombia	78%	6%	38%
Mexico	41%	9%	22%

Source: LAMAC, 2011.

By 2005, the open commercial TV rating share in Colombia was 79.7 percent declining to 58.1 percent five years later. However, during the same period (2005–2010) the cumulative increase in sales grew in favor of the commercial free television from 15 percent to 53.3 percent, largely for the benefit of Caracol and RCN. But the Colombian case is not isolated in the region, because the open free commercial TV system remains very powerful in most countries in Latin America in terms of advertising investment share, as one can see in the principal economies of the region as shown in Table 9.3.

Considering the penetration of the pay TV model in Argentina and Colombia, the advertisement share still remains very low, considering the audience share size. In Colombia the penetration and impact of the pay TV model is more evident among kids and young audiences between 18 and 39 years old, while parents and older viewers remain loyal to the traditional open free TV system.

Previous research conducted by the author in 2010 confirmed the audience's fragmentation phenomenon among young people (17–24) who lived in the 10 largest urban areas. From a total of 125 channels included in the basic and premium television packages offered by Telmex (cable) and Direct TV (satellite) including local, regional, national, and international channels, there were 57 different mentions to the question about their first favorite channel; 64 for the second; 70 for the third; 76 in the case of the fourth; and 80 in the case of the fifth (Arango-Forero & González Bernal, 2011). "Although Colombian private frequencies RCN and Caracol remain among the preferences of youth, the penetration of international thematic frequencies contained on the pay television model is evident, led by Discovery, FOX, MTV, TNT and Warner" (Arango-Forero & González Bernal, 2011, p. 45).

As Arango-Forero and González Bernal (2011) state, there is an evident television oversupply and an undeniable influence of thematic and specialized international channels available for Colombian television consumption. Although Caracol and RCN are still considered familiar channels and remain on the preferences of viewers (mainly among parents, adults, and the low and middle income brackets), the two national private networks have started to specialize their content and to focus mainly on news, novelas, and reality shows like the Caracol big hit "Yo me llamo."

Sara Gutiérrez is the programming and marketing vice president of RCN Television. In an interview with the author, she argues that there is enough supply for everyone and there is not a direct competition between the international offer and the open free TV system:

> We know that we cannot compete against the rhythm, color and texture of close television formats. Open TV production is still simpler in comparison with international productions. Even formats and narratives are still different. Short-term stories (between 12 and 24 episodes) work very well in cable but in open TV the traditional 120 episodes format (like the traditional novela) still works very well and audiences enjoy them.
>
> (Gutiérrez, 2011)

RCN Moving Ahead on Business Diversification

The three national television commercial channels in Colombia (Caracol, RCN, and Canal 1) got 47.8 percent of the advertisement investment share during the first quarter of 2011. Local and regional television got only 2.7 percent, while newspapers got 23.8 percent, radio 21.9 percent, and magazines 3.5 percent (Conexionista TV, 2011b). Despite the strength of the traditional business model based on the advertising income (commercial sections), the two big networks have developed interesting and successful new sources of revenues based on diversification.

In 2001, RCN television signed a five year agreement with the US-Hispanic network Univision in order to co-produce novelas and formats with an international flavor, mainly for the Spanish language population in the United States. Thanks to the alliance, 8.86 percent of the RCN channel revenues (nearly US$8 million) came from international sales during the first year (El Tiempo, 2002).

In 2002, due to the boom of reality and musical programs, RCN introduced the first audience voting system, as well as ringtones and a news subscription service through the cell phone platform (Dinero, 2009). By December 2005, the network reported 2.5 million text messages sent by the viewers who decided the winner of the first season of the musical reality show Factor X (The X Factor). Revenues coming from SMS for the whole Colombian media industry accounted for 20,000 million Colombian pesos, nearly US$9 million that year (Dinero, 2006).

By 2008, thanks to previous successful deals with international companies, Disney Latin America (through Vista Producciones) and RCN signed a co-production agreement that started with a Spanish version of the successful TV series Desperate Housewives. The second step was the co-production of a Colombian version of the American hit Grey's Anatomy called "A corazón abierto" (El Tiempo, 2008).

The same year, RCN entered into the thematic close television system (pay TV) launching the 24-hour news system called NTN24. The project was aimed to produce news for the Hispanic population in Latin America. Broadcast from Bogotá (Colombia) the informative agenda is more global than national, supported by correspondents reporting from the principal capitals of the world. After 2 years NTN24 was positioned among the 20 most watched television channels on the pay TV system in Latin America (Portafolio, 2008).

One year later, RCN launched RCN novelas, an entertainment thematic channel devoted to novelas and broadcast through the UNE cable distributor system that holds 26 percent of the cable market share in Colombia, while Telmex remains number one in cable with 47.8 percent of the market share (Conexionista TV, 2011b, p. 13).

Gabriel Reyes, president of RCN, announced in 2008 that the main goal of the network was to become not only a big content producer for both open and close digital television, but also for the Internet platform (Dinero, 2008).

By 2010, RCN and MSN signed an agreement looking for more audiences. MSN users could find local and regional news, but also information about novelas, entertainment, and the whole RCN programming combined with services provided by Windows Live such as Hotmail (12.3 million active users) and Messenger with 9.8 million active users in Colombia (Interactic, 2010).

In 2010 RCN created a new firm, Ennovva, that aimed to explore new media strategies and alternative business opportunities. Devoted to web development projects, online marketing, mobile applications, and social media marketing, Ennovva is also charged with exploring international new business opportunities, merchandising, and the film industry through a branch named RCN Cine.

Ennovva and RCN launched a 2010 TV contest called "Rico al instante" (Instantly rich). According to the Ennovva president (Angarita, 2011),

> The first season of the program (10 episodes) was based only on text messages. Viewers who wanted to participate just needed to send a SMS with the word "Rico" to the 299 code. After that, five finalists competed for a prize of 100 million [COP], around 50,000 US dollars. Through SMS viewers voted the final winner. "Rico al instante" was a product developed mainly for interactivity and got more than 19 million messages, the highest number of votes in the Colombian television history until now.

Product placement is another alternative source of revenues that the network has started to develop according to Sara Gutiérrez, RCN programming and marketing vicepresident:

> It is a learning process. We as executives understand the potential market that has to be developed. However, from the creative side script writers and directors are still afraid about a negative influence that product placement might have on their projects. On the other hand, the product placement clients are very aggressive once they decide to sponsor a scene. They want their brand to become the most important part of the story, and that's challenging. Besides, they expect to have a given moment on air, and it is very difficult to guarantee. Our best product placement experience was the Colombian version of Desperate Housewives (*Amas de casa desesperadas*) where all writers, producers and clients were satisfied with the experience. But again, it is a potential new source of revenues that we have started to explore.
>
> (Gutiérrez, 2011)

As of 2012, RCN television distributes content to more than 100 countries and its programming is broadcast throughout open (free) and close (pay) television systems, via cable and satellite. Its international channel TV Colombia reaches 28 countries around the world reaching more than 9 million households.

According to Sara Gutiérrez, international alliances have become an important strategy developed by RCN.

> We are proud of our international alliances. Currently Televisa is our most important partner. The three most successful novelas broadcasted in the history of Televisa are Colombian original

ideas created by RCN: "Café, con aroma de mujer," "Betty la Fea" and "Hasta que la plata nos separe." We are not only exporting products but also selling ideas and production bibles and that is an interesting business diversification strategy.

(Gutiérrez, 2011)

Like Caracol, RCN also entered the merchandising space with the musical programs Factor X and Factor XS, as well as the musical novela "La Hija del Mariachi." Other successful merchandising projects were the biographical productions "Amor Sincero," a novela based on the life and career of Marbelle (Maureen Belky Ramírez Cardona), an artist devoted to the popular music genre called "tecno-carrilera," romantic ballads and pop ballads, and the recent production "El Joe, la leyenda," a novela based on the life and career of Joe Arroyo (Alvaro José Arroyo González 1955–2011), a famous salsa and Caribbean music composer and singer. RCN has explored the DVD market and the live shows promoting the talent that start their products. "We are moving forward but [have] still got a lot to learn and explore" (Gutiérrez, 2011).

Caracol: A Strategy Focused on Expansion

Caracol television started its diversification business strategy in 2000 by signing an agreement with the international television trading company TEPUY and one year later entered into a short term co-production contract with Walt Disney International through its branch Buena Vista International, as well as the Telemundo network and RTI (El Tiempo, 2001).

Expansion is the main goal of Caracol in terms of its diversification business strategy. By 2004 the TV network explored new international formats and narratives with its novelas and reality programs and the network conquered the foreign market, mainly in Mexico and the Hispanic population in the United States (Dinero, 2004).

Once the agreement with Telemundo and RTI concluded (that allowed the Colombian network to co-produce ten international novelas) Caracol looked for new windows of international distribution and in September 2005 acquired 25 percent, the maximum investment share that a foreign company can have on a channel property, of Gentv, a TV network located in south Florida. Gentv was launched on September 18, 2006, aimed to capture the Hispanic audience in Florida.

By 2008 Caracol Television SA and its affiliates Caracol America Corp. and Caracol Television Inc. became one of the five most important producers and distributors in Latin America, running business in more than 50 countries. On February 23, 2009, Caracol launched the new cable channel Caracol Novelas that combines classic and new novelas on its programming. Currently the channel is broadcast through the cable service company Telefónica.

In 2011, Caracol signed a three year co-production agreement with Sony Pictures Television International aimed to make between six and nine mega productions that will be produced with 100 percent Colombian talent.

Digital Terrestrial Television (DTT) is the next task for the two Colombian networks. Caracol and RCN started to broadcast their regular channels on HD by January 2011. However, there is still a lack of a regulatory framework for digital TV in Colombia. The networks do not know whether they could expand their brands with more channels on the free commercial air model, or if they will have to broadcast new digital frequencies on the pay TV system. However, both companies are planning to take advantage of DTT with new products. "Prime time on Caracol channel is now saturated with the most successful products like novelas, news and realities, but there are some niches to take care of like kids and sports fans," according to Caracol new platforms vicepresident Alejandro Bernal (Conexionista TV, 2011a, p. 14).

Launching thematic channels on the open (free) Colombian television system is the next task for both Caracol and RCN with the digital terrestrial television system. Both networks are planning to broadcast channels about sports, kids, news, and novelas. However, it all will depend on the amount of channels the networks can broadcast and the new regulatory conditions announced by the National Television Commission.

Conclusions

The diversification of the traditional business model has become a very important goal for Caracol and RCN regarding their strategic management. Although the two networks keep the highest Colombian advertisement investment share, both companies keep looking for new sources of revenues based on new technological sources of distribution and exhibition, as well as innovation of their traditional broadcasting system. The creation of attractive content programming aimed to support new business models has become a crucial factor for success as well.

The culture of business diversification does not stop. In January 2012, RCN announced an international alliance with News Corporation, one of the big seven media groups worldwide. RCN and News Corp launched MundoFox, a new television network that started broadcasting in the fall of 2012 and targets the Hispanic population in the United States. MundoFox competes against the big Spanish language networks Telemundo and Univisión. Fox provides sports and series, while RCN provides novelas, series, and information produced by the international NTN24 (EFE, 2012).

The diversification of the traditional broadcasting business model also has allowed RCN and Caracol to play an important role in the globalized media environment. Their international projection has consolidated important sales of scripts, formats, genres, productions, and co-productions. Besides direct sales via tangible products like DVD collections the intangibles like information and entertainment subscription services are becoming more important every year.

Although both Caracol and RCN constantly announce their new business strategies, it is complicated to get access to information related to their new income statements. Because both companies are private, the networks report annually gross income statements but do not differentiate between traditional and new sources of revenues. That situation represents a limit to this analysis that is mostly based on press reports.

The scope of their new strategies constitutes an issue for future research, as well as the evolution of the new markets emerged from new initiatives taken by the most relevant television networks in Colombia.

References

Angarita, C. (2011). Personal communication. Bogota.

Arango-Forero, G., & González Bernal, M. (2011). Young audiovisual audiences in Colombia: under the veneer of fragmentation and multiscreens. *The Journal of Spanish Language Media*, 4(4), 40–54.

Arango-Forero, G., Gutiérrez, L., Forero, A. et al. (2009). The media in Colombia. In A. Albarran (Ed.), *The Handbook of Spanish Language Media* (Vol. 1, pp. 63–76). New York: Routledge.

Arango-Forero, G., Arango, M. F., Llaña, L., & Serrano, M. C. (2010). Colombian media in the XXI century: the re-conquest by foreign investment. *Palabra Clave*, 13(1), 59–76.

Asociación Colombiana para la Investigación de Medios (ACIM). (2011). *Estudio General de Medios (EGM), tercera ola 2011*. Bogotá: ACIM.

Conexionista TV. (2011a). Caracol se prepara para competir con nuevos canales. *Conexionista TV*, 3, 14–15.

Conexionista TV. (2011b, November 2011). La tele en cifras. *Conexionista TV*, 3, 13.

DANE (Departamento Administrativo Nacional de Estadística) (2007). *Proyecciones nacionales y departamentales de población 2006–2020*.

Dinero. (2004). El cuarto de hora de Caracol. *Dinero*. Retrieved March 4, 2012 from http://www.dinero.com/actualidad/noticias/articulo/caracol-rcn-ahora-alta-definicon-telmex/113092

Dinero. (2006). Voto por teléfono: el gran negocio. *Dinero*. Retrieved March 10, 2012 from http://www.dinero.com/edicion-impresa/negocios/articulo/voto-telefono-gran-negocio/32635

Dinero. (2008). Telecomunicaciones, lo que viene. *Dinero*. Retrieved March 10, 2012 from http://www.dinero.com/caratula/edicion-impresa/articulo/telecomunicaciones-viene/59493

Dinero. (2009). Más que mensajitos. *Dinero*. Retrieved March 20, 2012 from http://www.dinero.com/edicion-impresa/mercadeo/articulo/mas-mensajitos/85841

EFE. (2012, Enero 25). FOX y RCN lanzan en EE.UU canal con contenidos en español. *El Espectador*.

El Tiempo. (2001). Disney firma acuerdo de coproducción con Caracol. *El Tiempo*. Retrieved March 20, 2012 from http://www.eltiempo.com/archivo/documento/MAM-510933

El Tiempo. (2002, September 19). Canales privados de TV hacen su agosto en el extranjero. *El Tiempo*. Retrieved March 21, 2012 from http://www.eltiempo.com/archivo/documento/MAM-1355932

El Tiempo. (2008). Greys anatomy será colombianizada. *El Tiempo*. Retrieved March 22, 2012 from http://www.eltiempo.com/archivo/documento/MAM-2890609

El Universal (2011). Yo me llamo, líder en rating del horario prime time. Retrieved March 13, 2013 from http://www.eluniversal.com.co/cartagena/gente-y-tv/'yo-me-llamo'-lider-en-rating-del-horario-prime-time-47662

El Universal (2012). Comcel reportó ganancias por $1,8 billones durante 2011. Retrieved March 6, 2012 from http://www.eluniversal.com.co/cartagena/economica/comcel-reporto-ganancias-por-18-billones-durante-2011-67603

Gutiérrez, S. (2011). Personal communication. Bogotá.

Ibope (Instituto Brasileño de Opinión Pública y Estadística). (2011). Rating de Colombia: Semana del 5 al 9 de Diciembre. Retrieved December 15, 2011 from http://colombiatv.wordpress.com/2011/12/15/rating-de-colombia-semana-del-5-al-9-de-diciembre/

Interactic. (2010). Alianza RCN y Microsoft: Convergencia de TV e Internet en portal de contenidos. *Interactic*. Retrieved March 7, 2012 from http://www.interctic.org.co/noticintel/primer-plano/1269-alianza-rcn-y-microsoft-convergencia-de-tv-e-internet-en-portal-de-contenidos

LAMAC. (2011). TV paga un medio masivo y maduro en Colombia. Retrieved March 20, 2012 from http://www.lamac.org/files/Investigaciones/Colombia/LAMAC_Colombia__Presentacin_clientes_2011.pdf

Portafolio. (2008). RCN estrena su canal de noticias 24 horas. *Portafolio*. Retrieved February 17, 2012 from www.portafolio.co/archivo/documento/MAM-3166746

Semana. (2011, December 5–12). Confidenciales. *Revista Semana*, 1544.

10

TWITTER USE AMONG ENGLISH AND SPANISH LANGUAGE TELEVISION STATIONS

A Traffic and Content Analysis of Dallas-Fort Worth Local Television Twitter Accounts

Julian Rodriguez

The competitive nature of television news has propelled broadcast journalism's adoption of online social networking services to mine audiences, cultivate relationships, and monetize followers (Ahmad, 2010; Copeland, 2011; Hermida, 2010b; Holcomb, Gross, & Mitchell, 2011; Niles, 2007). Since 2006, Twitter has provided new tools making possible the development and nurturing of ambient journalism, which enables "citizens to maintain a mental model of news and events around them" (Hermida, 2010b, p.298). Twitter, along with other social networking sites, provides users with access to information that is immediate, collaborative, referenceable, portable, free (ad supported), and customizable in an easy to digest user interface (Ahmad, 2010; Palser, 2010).

With the rise in smartphone penetration in the United States—46 percent of all mobile consumers by the fourth quarter of 2011—the opportunities to reach and cultivate new and emerging television audiences through online social media continue to grow (Holcomb et al., 2011; Nielsen, 2012a). Social networks and blogs are the top online destination, with Americans spending on social media sites 23 percent of their time spent online, and 40 percent of social media users accessing social networking sites like Facebook and Twitter from their mobile phones (Nielsen, 2011a). Among mobile phone users in the United States, Hispanics and Asian/Pacific Islanders have the highest smartphone penetration with 45 percent (23 million Hispanics), followed by African Americans with 33 percent penetration (13 million), and Whites with the lowest penetration with 27 percent (60 million) (Census, 2010a, 2010b, 2010c; Kellogg, 2011). Young Hispanics are actively adopting social networks and using them to stay in touch with family and friends (the terms Hispanic and Latino will be used interchangeably throughout this chapter). According to Lopez (2010), 23 percent of young Latinos (ages 16 to 25) say they use social networking sites on a daily basis to stay in touch with their friends; native born Latinos present the highest daily use of social networking sites with 31 percent, while 10 percent of foreign born declare that they use social media daily. Language dominance also plays an important role in social networking site use among young Latinos; 33 percent of English-dominant Latinos say they use social media daily, compared to 24 percent of those who are bilingual and 5 percent who are Spanish-dominant. With the increase of social network use in the United States, especially through mobile technologies and among Hispanics, it is critical to understand the thematic nature of messages shared by local television stations on social media to reach and engage their viewers:

RQ1: What is the thematic nature of messages shared by Dallas-Fort Worth (DFW) television stations on their Twitter feeds?

The adoption of mobile devices providing asymmetrical relationships with friends and followers in social networks has provided microblogging services like Twitter with the power to deliver messages of personal relevance in real time anywhere the data network provider has coverage (Copeland, 2011; Hermida, 2010a). As a consequence, access to portable computer mediated communication has influenced journalism's evolution towards a new information sharing model that is more participatory and collective (Boczkowski, 2004; Deuze, 2003; Domingo, Quandt, Heinonen, Paulussen, Singer, & Vujnovic, 2008). Twitter, which allows 140 character messages to be shared with followers, embraces user friendly data sharing/mining mechanisms organizing topics and issues for chronological analysis; these tools are employed by journalists around the world to gather and cross-reference information to enrich their journalistic endeavors (Ahmad, 2010; Bosch, 2010; Farhi, 2009; Hermida, 2010a; Perez-Latre, Blanco, & Sanchez, 2011). With more than 300 million users, Twitter offers unprecedented real-time access to online trending topics at the local and global level, an invaluable resource in the deadline-driven environment of journalism (Domingo et al., 2008; Copeland, 2011; Ingram, 2008; Stassen, 2010). However, the volume of tweets generated by reactions to political and socio-economic events, like the 2009 Iranian elections and the Arab Spring, have the potential to drown vital signals under the noisy unregulated discourse found on Twitter (Copeland, 2011; Hermida, 2010a). Journalists' Twitter adoption to access a high volume of online trending topics and updates has generated skepticism about crowdsourcing and the overall quality of content published by the news media industry (Deuze, 2004; Dowd, 2009; Parr, 2009; Wasserman, 2009).

The Dallas-Fort Worth (DFW) metropolitan area encapsulates key characteristics favoring media research. Home to the largest concentration of corporate headquarters in the United States and with a racially and ethnically diverse population of more than 6 million people, DFW has a total of 2.5 million TV Homes ranking it the fifth television market in the United States. Equally representative are DFW's 500,000 Hispanic TV Homes, which make DFW the fifth largest Hispanic television market in America (Census, 2012a, 2012b; Dallas Chamber, 2012; Nielsen, 2012b, 2012c). Studying the amount of daily tweets per DFW television station (Twitter traffic), calculating traffic correlations among stations, and identifying peak Twitter traffic behavior provide windows to understanding traffic dependency and Twitter topics DFW television stations consider to be of interest to their viewers:

RQ2: Is there a Twitter traffic correlation among DFW television stations?

RQ3: What topics generate the highest (peak) volume of tweets posted by DFW television stations?

As a collaborative online tool, Twitter represents a sample of collective intelligence too important to be ignored by the news media industry. In addition, Twitter attracts users "who are interested in, and engaged with, the news" and are more likely to visit a news website than the average person (Farhi, 2009, p.30). The viewer mining and cultivating advantages offered by social networking sites represent a vital asset to the operation of network television stations offering news and information content. A national Pew Research Center study on mainstream media Twitter use found that major news organizations "used Twitter to direct audiences to web content that the news organization has produced and posted online" (Holcomb et al., 2011, p.9). The study also found that 93 percent of tweets on mainstream media Twitter feeds contained links to home pages, and only 2 percent of tweets asked followers for information. The agenda shared by the news industry on Twitter and legacy media was "strikingly similar during the week in which both were studied" (Holcomb et al., 2011, p.8). During the sampled week by Holcomb et al., (2011), news media Twitter agenda had the Middle East unrest (Arab Spring) in first place (12 percent of all tweets), the economy in second (10 percent), and the Obama Administration in third place (3 percent). According to Greer and Ferguson (2011), local television stations in the United States used their Twitter sites mainly as a promotion and branding tool. Commercial local television stations "were more likely than public stations to have breaking news and tweets promoting newscasts"; nevertheless, breaking news messages remained in the minority with almost 80 percent (79.4 percent) of the stations that featured news stories on their Twitter site not featuring breaking news tweets (Greer & Ferguson, 2011, p.209). The study also found Twitter to be used primarily as an information source, not an online "tease" tool to convert followers into television newscast viewers (Greer & Ferguson, 2011). Although the Holcomb et al. (2011) and Greer and Ferguson (2011) studies on media Twitter use provide insightful information, neither study included any Spanish-language media outlets, an area of the media industry presenting high growth.

Hispanic Viewers and Spanish-Language Television Network Ratings

Nielsen estimates US Hispanic television households to be 14.1 million in 2013 (12.35 per cent of US TV HHs), up 1 percent from the 2011–2012 season. Hispanic TV households continue to show growth while Nielsen projects a 0.4 percent reduction in US TV households for the 2012–2013 season, from 114.6 million in 2012 to 114.2 million in 2013 (Nielsen, 2011b, 2012b, 2012c). Hispanic television ratings constantly challenge the "Big Four" (ABC, CBS, NBC, FOX), with Univision sitting in the number one spot among adults 18–49 during their 2011 "Premios Juventud" national broadcast (Univision, 2011). But this trend is not innate to entertainment events broadcast at the national level; it is also latent in local markets with Spanish-language television newscasts (Bark, 2010; Philpot, 2012). Dallas-Fort Worth has two local television stations producing Spanish-language newscasts: Univision23 (KUVN) and Telemundo39 (KXTX). Understanding the power of social media, these two television stations have adopted Twitter to reach their audiences: Telemundo39 adopted the microblogging site in May of 2009 and Univision23 decided to join the social network in April of 2010.

Since there is a lack of academic research on local Spanish-language television stations' adoption of Twitter, this study will analyze Dallas-Fort Worth's English- and Spanish-language television station use of Twitter to reach and cultivate viewers. Reaching and cultivating viewers on Twitter also requires stations to adopt Twitter syntax to connect and reference followers/users with one another and with online information promoted by the television station. Studying station adoption of Twitter syntax reveals levels of interactivity and enhances our understanding of television stations' social media strategies:

> RQ4: What kind and how often do DFW television stations use Twitter's syntax in their tweets (e.g., #Hashtag)?

Method

Data for the study were collected and obtained using online data mining services and a content analysis of Dallas-Fort Worth (DFW), Texas, television stations' Twitter accounts. Daily Twitter account traffic numbers were collected through TweetStats (http://www.tweetstats.com), and tweets for content analysis were obtained by visiting each individual DFW television station's Twitter account.

The study analyzes six Twitter accounts operated by six DFW television stations; four of these Twitter sites operated by English-language stations and the other two by Spanish-language stations. Dallas-Fort Worth television stations selected for the study include the big four broadcast networks (ABC8, NBC5, CBS11, FOX4) and the two main Spanish-language broadcast networks in the United States (Telemundo39, Univision23). Only the main Twitter account for each TV station was used in the study; these are accounts posted on each station's official website, do not belong to an individual, are the station's official Twitter account, and use the overall name of the station as its Twitter username (@wfaachannel8, @NBCDFW, @CBSDFW, @FOX4, @KUVNUnivision23, @TelemundoDallas). This traffic and content analysis study was specifically designed to include Spanish-language television stations to provide a dimension absent in previous studies of similar nature.

A total of 603 days of Twitter traffic information were collected to create a data set used for traffic correlation and frequency distribution analysis. *Traffic* is defined for the study as the number of tweets per day a television station generates on its own official Twitter account. Of the 603 days of information available (April 7, 2010, to November 30, 2011), 245 days were selected to be used for traffic correlation and frequency distribution analysis. The data set excludes 358 days because at two different points in time at least one television station had an inactive official Twitter account. The study considers a Twitter account to be *inactive* when the account exists in Twitter, is operated by the station, but the station does not generate tweets over periods of time longer than 30 consecutive days. For instance, in May 12, 2011, ABC8 (@wfaachannel8) generated 42 tweets, and by May 13, 2011, and for the next 54 days, there were zero tweets generated by the station. Excluding inactive accounts from the data set allows the study to measure only days when all TV stations were actively posting on their Twitter site. The 245 days included in the data set use each television Twitter account as an independent variable. The study then obtained Pearson correlations between DFW television stations' Twitter accounts, and created a frequency distribution of tweets per television station.

A separate correlation analysis was done by controlling for weekends. This means that out of 245 days, 175 were selected for the second phase of the study. The objective was to create two sets of findings to identify Twitter account behavioral differences, one including all days of the week and the other one including only weekdays. In addition, controlling for weekends allowed Telemundo39 (@TelemundoDallas) to be compared to other stations during days Telemundo39 was more likely to be active on Twitter. In the Dallas-Fort Worth market, and during the period of time studied, Telemundo39 did not have weekend newscasts; this in itself put Telemundo39 at a weekend Twitter activity disadvantage when compared to other local television stations. In addition, DFW television stations' Twitter accounts are news and information driven, and are mainly controlled by the television stations' newsrooms and content production units.

The information used for content analysis was obtained by visiting each television station Twitter site and saving all tweets available on each one of them. Twitter sites allow you to scroll down and fetch older tweets stored in the Twitter feed; saving as many tweets as possible from each television station increased the pool of information for sample selection. The study defines a *tweet* as any independent text-based message on the station's Twitter feed. Content analysis focused on a two-week period sample ranging from October 9, 2011 to October 22, 2011. The two-week period was selected based on diverse criteria; the 14-day sample shows Twitter account activity not influenced by irregular spikes in traffic, includes traffic activity by all television stations, excludes major American holidays, and includes two weekly business cycles.

The codebook created for content analysis contained a thematic category and a Twitter syntax category. The thematic category was divided into 13 different codes, and each coder assigned at least 1 thematic code to each tweet, and not more than 2 codes per tweet (1 = politics, 2 = economy, 3 = weather, 4 = sports, 5 = traffic, 6 = health, 7 = education, 8 = safety/crime, 9 = immigration, 10 = request information from followers, 11 = promotion, 12 = unable to determine message, 13 = other). Coders assigned codes in order or relevance; the first code was considered the dominant theme, and the second code, if assigned, was considered to be a secondary theme. The secondary theme, if assigned, was used for coder training purposes during coding disagreements. The thematic category identified the theme that best described the information contained in each tweet; for instance, a coder assigned code 3 (weather) to a tweet containing information regarding weather updates, alerts, national weather service notifications, forecasts, or any other weather-related information.

Since tweets studied were written in two languages, English and Spanish, all coders and the researcher were bilingual (fluent in English and Spanish). All coders were senior undergraduate students; they were trained and tested for agreement by the researcher with samples taken from English- and Spanish-language television station Twitter feeds.

After the first agreement test, coders identified cases of disagreement and discussed possible solutions to uncertainties. Some coding instructions were adjusted or further discussed to increase certainties at the time of assigning codes. Coder training continued until an agreement level of 0.70 or higher was consistently reached. Coder agreement was calculated using Cohen's Kappa, and final agreement levels ranged from 0.71 to 0.79 with an average agreement of 0.744. Although thematic coding is highly subjective and the study included 13 different thematic categories, coders were able to reach levels of agreement requiring no changes to the number of thematic codes initially included in the codebook.

The content analysis Twitter syntax category focused on recording the kind of Twitter syntax included in every tweet (e.g., @username). The Twitter syntax category was divided into five different codes, and each coder assigned as many codes as needed to each tweet without repeating the same code number (1 = Web link(s) included, 2 = #hashtag(s) included, 3 = @username(s) included, 4 = text included, 5 = ReTweet). For instance, a tweet containing text and including two #hashtags would be coded with code numbers 2 and 4. Initially, the *Twitter syntax category* was named *Linking category* in the codebook, but coders found the term *linking* confusing since code 4 (text) was not an online link; therefore, the category was renamed to reflect more accurately the purpose of the category. Samples from both English- and Spanish-language Twitter sites were used for training purposes, and the first test of agreement reached a 1.0 level (Cohen's Kappa). The high level of agreement was achieved due to the simple and objective nature of the Twitter syntax category coding.

Results

RQ2 asked if there is a Twitter traffic correlation among DFW television stations. Station Twitter traffic was operationalized by recording the number of tweets per day each station posted on its Twitter site between April 7, 2010, and November 30, 2011 (n = 603). A sample of 245 active days was selected from the totality of days recorded, and Pearson correlations obtained between all six DFW television stations' Twitter accounts based on active days only (n = 245). Several Twitter sites reached statistical significance (see Table 10.1). The highest correlations were found among Telemundo39 and FOX4 (0.429), NBC5 and FOX4 (0.412), NBC5 and ABC8 (0.503), and NBC5 and CBS11 (0.558).

A second degree of correlations between DFW television stations' Twitter sites was obtained by controlling the 245 active days for weekends (see Table 10.2). Controlling for weekends reduced the sample of active days from 245 to 175. This second data set yielded an overall lower correlation for Twitter traffic, with the exception of two cases:

Table 10.1 DFW TV Stations' Twitter Traffic Pearson Correlations for All Active Days ($n = 245$)

TV Stations	Univision23	Telemundo39	NBC5	FOX4	ABC8	CBS11
Univision23		0.216**	0.355**	0.252**	0.236**	0.259**
Telemundo39	0.216**		0.295**	0.429**	0.221**	0.183**
NBC5	0.355**	0.295**		0.412**	0.503**	0.558**
FOX4	0.252**	0.429**	0.412**		0.320**	0.115
ABC8	0.236**	0.221**	0.503**	0.320**		0.328**
CBS11	0.259**	0.183**	0.558**	0.115	0.328**	

** Correlation is significant at the 0.01 level (two-tailed).

Table 10.2 DFW TV Stations' Twitter Traffic Pearson Correlations for All Active Weekdays ($n = 175$)

TV Stations	Univision23	Telemundo39	NBC5	FOX4	ABC8	CBS11
Univision23		0.037	0.277**	-0.031	0.099	0.307**
Telemundo39	0.037		0.129	0.242**	0.039	0.173*
NBC5	0.277**	0.129		0.057	0.329**	0.606**
FOX4	-0.031	0.242**	0.057		-0.116	0.071
ABC8	0.099	0.039	0.329**	-0.116		0.208**
CBS11	0.307**	0.173*	0.606**	0.071	0.208**	

* Correlation is significant at the 0.05 level (two-tailed).
** Correlation is significant at the 0.01 level (two-tailed).

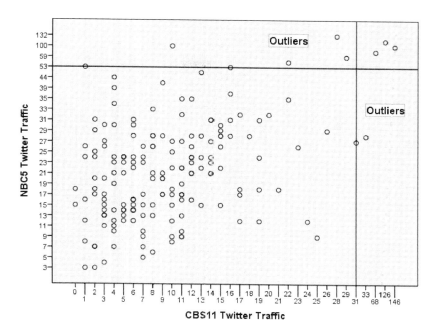

Figure 10.1 NBC5 and CBS11 Twitter Traffic Scatter Plot (All Active Weekdays) ($n = 175$)

Univision23 and CBS11 (from 0.259 to 0.307), and NBC5 and CBS11 (from 0.558 to 0.606).

Scatter plot comparisons of NBC5 and CBS11's Twitter traffic revealed that NBC5 and CBS11's correlation increases when weekends are excluded, because the number of days with zero tweets posted decrease and outlier tweets (peak traffic days) remain present (see Figure 10.1). When outliers were removed from the All Active Weekdays' data set (NBC5 traffic < 50 and CBS11 traffic < 30), correlation for NBC5 and CBS11 went down, from 0.606 to 0.256. The same can be said about Univision23 and CBS11—when outliers were removed (Univision23 traffic < 16 and CBS11 traffic < 30) similar results were observed; correlation went from 0.307 to 0.172.

Every Twitter site showed a reduction of traffic during weekends. Frequency distribution analysis showed All Active Weekdays to have a higher median than All Active Days; for instance, FOX4 had a median of 18 tweets during All Active Weekdays and a median of 16 tweets during All Active Days (Table 10.3). The absence of weekends in the data set shifts the distribution positively. Furthermore, FOX4's All Active Weekends frequency analysis has a median of only 3.5 tweets. When frequency charts for All Active Days and All Active Weekdays were created,

Table 10.3 DFW TV Stations' Twitter Traffic Frequency Distribution

	ABC8	NBC5	CBS11	FOX4	Univision23	Telemundo39
All Active Weekdays (*n* = 175)						
Mean	30.11	23.61	11.17	18.33	6.24	3.94
Median	28.00	21.00	8.00	18.00	5.00	4.00
Std. Deviation	11.921	16.663	15.595	4.271	4.775	3.238
All Active Days (*n* = 245)						
Mean	26.58	18.65	10.22	14.67	5.31	3.07
Median	25.00	17.00	7.00	16.00	4.00	2.00
Std. Deviation	12.634	16.714	15.922	6.962	4.760	3.349
All Active Weekends (*n* = 70)						
Mean	5.53	17.74	6.27	7.87	2.99	0.89
Median	5.00	16.50	4.00	3.50	2.00	0.00
Std. Deviation	2.597	9.756	8.363	16.590	3.865	2.545

ENGLISH & SPANISH TV STATION TWEETS

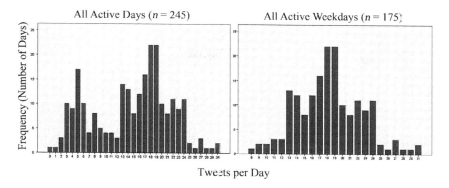

Figure 10.2 FOX4 Twitter Traffic Frequency Distribution

FOX4 Twitter traffic revealed a bimodal distribution during All Active Days (Figure 10.2).

RQ1 asked about the thematic nature of messages shared by DFW television stations on their Twitter feeds. To answer RQ1, a content analysis study was performed on a two-week period of television stations' Twitter feeds (October 9–22, 2011). The sample contained a total of 1,089 tweets distributed according to the number of tweets each television station generated during the two-week period studied. ABC8 had a total of 315 tweets, NBC5 had 248, CBS11 had 138, FOX4 had 199, Univision23 had 132, and Telemundo39 had 57. Each tweet was coded individually and was assigned at least one thematic code by bilingual coders; coders reached levels of agreement higher than 0.70 (Cohen's Kappa).

Content analysis found ABC8 as the station with the highest percentage of tweets devoted to covering politics (16.5 percent), followed by FOX4 (9 percent). The study expected to find a high percentage of tweets addressing the economic environment, but the station with the highest coverage of the economy, NBC5, dedicated only 3.6 percent of its tweets to the topic; moreover, CBS11 and Telemundo39 did not include tweets about the economy. The posting of weather-related tweets was motivated in part by Major League Baseball (MLB) games scheduled during the period studied; during the days included in the study, the Texas Rangers played most of the 2011 American League Championship Series and three games of the 2011 World Series against the St. Louis Cardinals. Coders discussed uncertainties during training; they were undecided on what code to assign when weather and sports topics were present in the same tweet. After further training and discussion, coders reached a level of agreement higher than 0.70 The study found that the two stations with the highest percentage of weather coverage also had the highest percentage of sports-related stories; CBS11 dedicated 12.3 percent and Univision23 10.6 percent of its tweets to weather. In the sports category, Univision23 committed 41.7 percent of its tweets to sports, followed by CBS11 with 38.4 percent.

Vehicular traffic, health, and education recorded low levels of inclusion across stations, with CBS11 having the highest percentage of tweets related to traffic (8 percent) and health (5.1 percent), and ABC8 leading in education coverage (3.5 percent). FOX4, Univision23, and Telemundo39 did not have traffic-related tweets, and Univision23 and Telemundo39 did not generate any tweets associated with education. Safety and/or crime-related tweets ruled the English-language television stations. FOX4 dedicated 35.2 percent of tweets to safety/crime-related topics, trailed by ABC8 (28.3 percent), NBC5 (21 percent), and CBS11 (15.2 percent). Tweets dealing with immigration issues received the least priority; 1 percent of ABC8 tweets and 0.8 percent of Univision23 tweets were related to immigration, and CBS11 and Telemundo39 did not have immigration topics in their Twitter feed (see Table 10.4).

NBC5 and Univision23 were avid users of crowdsourcing; they dedicated, respectively, 6.9 percent and 6.1 percent of their tweets to surveying their followers. Twitter feeds are also audience mining tools, and thematic code 11 measured the level of cross promotion taking place in the Twitter feed. The promotion category completely defines Telemundo39's Twitter site use as the television station assigns 75.4 percent of its tweets to cross promotion. This behavior is shared also by Univision23, which assigns the second largest percentage of its tweets (25 percent) to cross promotion. The third place in the promotion category belongs to NBC5 with 8.1 percent. The content analysis study also documented messages unable to be thematically determined by the coder; messages providing little or no context. NBC5 provided the largest percentage of tweets of such nature (12.1 percent), followed by Telemundo39 (7 percent) and Univision23 (5.3 percent). Most of the messages unable to be determined were tweets generated by the television station thanking followers or answering questions without any aggregated context.

Finally, the study added a thirteenth thematic category assigned for other topics not listed in the coding sheet. The station that allocated the leading percentage of messages under the other category was FOX4 with 25.1 percent. FOX4's high allocation was caused by the nature of its Twitter site; FOX4 described its official Twitter feed (@FOX4) as "a mix of DFW news and weird headlines" (KDFW, 2012). Out of 199 tweets coded for FOX4, 46 of them were posted as "unusual" news.

RQ4 explored Twitter's syntax use on DFW television stations' Twitter feeds. The kind and frequency of Twitter syntax use was coded by bilingual coders following a code sheet including five different codes

Table 10.4 DFW TV Stations' Tweet Thematic Content

TV Tweet Theme*		ABC8	NBC5	CBS11	FOX4	Univision23	Telemundo39
Politics	Total	52	13	6	18	1	1
	%	16.5%	5.2%	4.3%	9.0%	0.8%	1.8%
Economy	Total	6	9	0	4	2	0
	%	1.9%	3.6%	0.0%	2.0%	1.5%	0.0%
Weather	Total	9	18	17	6	14	0
	%	2.9%	7.3%	12.3%	3.0%	10.6%	0.0%
Sports	Total	59	47	53	26	55	0
	%	18.7%	19.0%	38.4%	13.1%	41.7%	0.0%
Traffic	Total	4	6	11	0	0	0
	%	1.3%	2.4%	8.0%	0.0%	0.0%	0.0%
Health	Total	15	7	7	6	2	1
	%	4.8%	2.8%	5.1%	3.0%	1.5%	1.8%
Education	Total	11	5	4	4	0	0
	%	3.5%	2.0%	2.9%	2.0%	0.0%	0.0%
Safety/Crime	Total	89	52	21	70	4	2
	%	28.3%	21.0%	15.2%	35.2%	3.0%	3.5%
Immigration	Total	3	1	0	1	1	0
	%	1.0%	0.4%	0.0%	0.5%	0.8%	0.0%
Request Info	Total	10	17	2	4	8	2
	%	3.2%	6.9%	1.4%	2.0%	6.1%	3.5%
Promotion	Total	16	20	9	4	33	43
	%	5.1%	8.1%	6.5%	2.0%	25.0%	75.4%
Undetermined	Total	7	30	2	6	7	4
	%	2.22%	12.10%	1.45%	3.02%	5.30%	7.02%
Other	Total	34	23	6	50	5	4
	%	10.8%	9.3%	4.3%	25.1%	3.8%	7.0%
n**	Total	315	248	138	199	132	57

* Only one theme assigned per TV station tweet.
** Represents total number of tweets per station found in the two-week period studied (October 9–22, 2011).

Table 10.5 DFW TV Stations' Twitter Syntax Use (October 9–22, 2011)

TV Tweet Syntax*	Web Link	#Hashtag	@Username	Text	ReTweet	n**
ABC8	91%	3%	5%	100%	4%	315
NBC5	60%	37%	29%	99%	10%	248
CBS11	41%	25%	36%	99%	9%	138
FOX4	100%	0%	0%	100%	0%	199
Univision23	83%	2%	3%	96%	0%	132
Telemundo39	42%	56%	79%	98%	21%	57

* Each tweet may contain more than one Twitter syntax category.
** Represents total number of tweets per station found in the two-week period studied.

addressing Web links, #hashtags, @usernames, text, and retweets. Coders assigned as many codes per tweet as needed without repeating the same code number. For instance, it was possible for a tweet to be coded 1, 2, 3, 4, 5; but not 1, 2, 3, 3, 3, 4, 5. The purpose was to measure if a specific Twitter syntax was used, not how many times each Twitter syntax was used per tweet. The tweets coded for Twitter syntax were the same tweets used for the thematic category; that's a total of 1,089 tweets distributed according to the number of tweets each television station generated during the two-week period studied.

Content analysis of Twitter syntax found that the two most common kinds of Twitter syntax used by DFW television stations were Web links and text. Almost every television station included text in their tweets, and FOX4 had the highest percentage use of Web links. We can relate to a high percentage use of text in tweets, but understanding Web links requires some further analysis. FOX4's tweets were generated 100 percent of the time using Twitterfeed; "Twitterfeed is a utility that allows you to feed your content (for example, blog posts or any other content that supports RSS feeds) to Twitter, Facebook, and other social platforms" (Twitterfeed, 2012). In other words, Twitterfeed allows you to push content to social networks without performing a double duty. But FOX4 was not the only station using utilities; Univision23 had its Twitter account linked to its Facebook account using a Facebook application; 83 percent of @KUVNUnivision23 tweets linked back to Univision23's Facebook page posts. Other stations shared Web links in similar ways, with differences mainly found on the utility or application adopted to feed their Twitter sites without performing double duties.

The use of retweets, #hashtags, and @username references were common practice among television stations NBC5, CBS11, and Telemundo39. The most devoted user of these Twitter syntax tools was Telemundo39 with 56 percent of tweets containing #hashtags, 79 percent containing

@username references, and 21 percent of tweets being actual retweets (see Table 10.5). Telemundo39's high adoption of Twitter syntax was consistent with the thematic content shared by the station. Its Twitter feed use for cross promotion was enriched by tweets containing all kinds of Twitter syntax tools inviting followers to follow other content associated and/or produced by the Telemundo network.

RQ3 examined the thematic nature of the highest (peak) volume of tweets generated by television stations in the DFW area. The study selected days (from February 1 to November 30, 2011) with at least one television station having Twitter traffic equal to or higher than 50 tweets for each day. A sample of 24 days was coded using the same thematic codes used to answer RQ1. Peak Twitter traffic was driven by tweets associated with weather (33.3 percent) and sports topics (33.3 percent). Weather-related tweets reported severe thunderstorms, tornado warnings, hail storms, and other National Weather Service (NWS) alerts. Tweets with sports content covered the 2011 National Football League (NFL) Super Bowl XLV at Cowboys Stadium, and the 2011 National Basketball League (NFL) finals between the Dallas Mavericks and Miami Heat. Osama Bin Laden's death on May 1st, President Barack Obama's Dallas visit on October 4th, and the removal of the Occupy Dallas Camp on November 17th, created Twitter traffic spikes of a political nature (12.5 percent). Also, 12.5 percent of spikes were driven by tweets about safety/crime topics; one spike was caused by a Waxahachie, Texas, chemical plant fire, another one by a high speed chase, and a third one by a wildfire in Possum Kingdom Lake located 75 miles west of Fort Worth, Texas. Two peak Twitter traffic days were caused by other topics; one by the death of Steve Jobs and the second one by a question posted by ABC8 on its Twitter site (@wfaachannel8) asking its Twitter followers to "R/T in three words—how would you thank a US Veteran? #vetswfaa" (WFAA, 2011). After posting the question on November 10, 2011, @wfaachannel8 posted that same day 15 tweets with @username references thanking its Twitter followers for answering the question.

Discussion

The study analyzed how television stations in the DFW, Texas, area use their official Twitter sites to communicate with their Twitter followers. What made this study unique was the inclusion of both English- and Spanish-language television stations, a characteristic rarely encountered in academic research. But this academic research deficiency is bound to change in coming years; the emergence of Spanish-language television stations and the powerful impact that these stations have on television's most sought after demographic (25–54) makes them an impossible to ignore neon-blue triceratops (Philpot, 2012). The study measured traffic correlations, thematic content of tweets, and the Twitter syntax used by each television station on its official Twitter feed.

Official television station Twitter feeds in the DFW area are news and information driven; they are controlled by the stations' newsrooms and content production units, and each station makes diverse use of its Twitter site. During the period studied (October 9–22, 2011), ABC8 was a television station sharing mainly politics, sports, and safety/crime-related stories with heavy use of Web links and textual messages; in addition, ABC8 had the highest percentage of politics-related tweets of all DFW television stations. NBC5 was well distributed among the thematic categories selected for the study, with considerable investment in covering sports and safety/crime stories, and having the highest percentage of cross promotion tweets among English-language DFW television stations. The study found that stations using Twitter feeds for cross promotion had higher adoption of Web links, #hashtags, and @username Twitter syntax. Telemundo39, for instance, presented the highest cross promotion among all stations (75.4 percent of all @TelemundoDallas tweets), and the highest overall adoption of Twitter syntax to connect followers with promoted Telemundo network products and services.

The study also found Spanish-language television stations more likely to use Twitter for cross promotion purposes than English-language stations; Univison23 occupied the second place. Still, Univision23 invested heavily in sports- and weather-related stories; in fact, Univision23 devoted the highest percentage of its tweets to sports stories (41.7 percent), higher than any other station, and was second to CBS11 on weather coverage. Among English-language stations, CBS11 devoted the highest percentage to sports stories, and also had the highest percentage among all stations in traffic coverage. CBS11 also made frequent use of Web links, #hashtags, and @username references.

There is one station that made safety/crime stories its most important topic in its Twitter site: FOX4. This station invested generously in safety/crime (35.2 percent), more than any other station, but also invested significantly in covering politics and sports. On the other hand, FOX4 devoted more than 25 percent of its tweets to cover "unusual" stories with little local relevance doubling as newscast kicker-like stories. Furthermore, FOX4 was very systematic in the use of Twitter syntax; unlike all other stations, FOX4 only used Web links and textual messages to communicate and connect with audiences. This is due to FOX4's adoption of Twitterfeed, a utility that allows you to push content to Twitter feeds, and the absence of interactivity taking place in FOX4's Twitter site (Twitterfeed, 2012).

Platforms, utilities, and applications for Twitter and other social networks continue to grow; because of this, it is of great academic interest to study local television station adoption of new and emerging online multimedia technologies. Portable devices connect content producers with their audiences, and stations with established social network platforms and social network publication standards are able to reach their audiences in real time. During the period studied in the content analysis, the DFW television stations with the largest number of Twitter interfaces adopted were CBS11 and ABC8. CBS11 used Seesmic, TweetDeck, Web access, Twitter for Mac, Tweet Button, Twitter for iPhone, and Seesmic Desktop, while ABC8 used Twitterfeed, TweetDeck, HootSuite, Web access, Twitter for Mac, and Twitter for iPhone. Of all stations, HootSuite and Twitter for iPhone were the most used mobile interfaces for Twitter, with HootSuite offering the most professional functions. These applications enabled journalists to constantly check and update their Twitter account(s), crowdsource, and connect with the collective intelligence encapsulated in the twittersphere. As telecom companies expand their data network coverage, offer greater connectivity speeds, and lower their costs, consumers will continue to adopt mobile devices with data connectivity capabilities.

Twitter traffic among television stations showed diverse level of correlations, with NBC5 and CBS11 showing the highest correlation for All Active Days (0.558). But the study found that the relationships among stations were inflated by outliers and changes in Twitter traffic behavior during All Active Weekends. These phenomena motivated a closer look at outliers' thematic nature and Twitter syntax use. The study of outliers found that DFW television stations generate the highest (peak) volume of tweets during days when hyperlocal events of great importance to the stations' coverage area take place. As a consequence, one can conclude that DFW television stations do provide prominence to local issues impacting directly their viewers and their station's interests of remaining relevant and, hopefully, profitable.

This research study offers media managers the opportunity to understand how other television stations, including Spanish-language stations, are using Twitter to connect and build relationships with their viewers. DFW television station managers can identify where their station stands compared to other local stations and if their official Twitter site truly reflects the mission and vision of the television station. The study also facilitates a deeper understanding of Twitter feeds; Twitter is not a Really Simple Syndication (RSS) feed and should not be treated as one. Twitter is not a one-way road; it requires a certain level of interaction with followers in order to successfully build trust and value. Content shared on the microblogging service represents the television station and requires the same level of professionalism invested in the air waves. Twitter account administrators and/or those responsible for tweeting need to be carefully trained. For instance, FOX4 treated its official Twitter site as an RSS feed; it had several duplicate tweets on its Twitter feed because its Twitter site

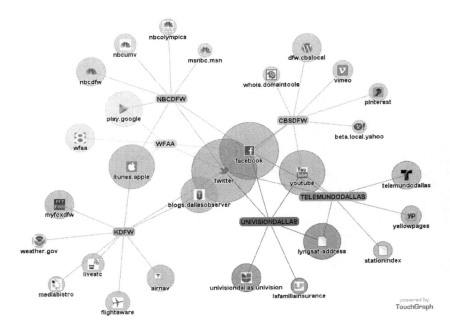

Figure 10.3 DFW Television Stations Online Networks

mirrored two categories on FOX4's official website: Local and Unusual news. This meant that every time a news story was categorized as both local and unusual, the Twitter feed duplicated the tweet on the Twitter feed.

But why should media managers invest resources on managing Twitter feeds? The answer is because local television stations, along with all other legacy media, are competing for the same growing online audience; and this growing online audience can be mined at the heart of internet usage: online social networks (see Figure 10.3) (TouchGraph, 2012).

The relationships built by television stations on social networks not only increase stations' online presence but also increase the number of webpage exposures, disseminate more efficiently newscast stories, create closer relationship with the local community, and provide faster access to their viewers in a two-way communication environment.

References

Ahmad, A. N. (2010). Is Twitter a useful tool for journalists? *Journal of Media Practice*, 11(2), 145–155.

Bark, E. (2010). *CBS11 sweeps 10 p.m. May news numbers for first time in any ratings "sweeps."* Retrieved February 1, 2012, from Uncle Barky's Bytes: http://www.unclebarky.com/dfw_files/a99371f332f5f1f4df8ed5d821dcd1b0-1599.html

Boczkowski, P. (2004). *Digitizing the News: Innovation in Online Newspapers.* Cambridge, MA: MIT Press.

Bosch, T. (2010). Digital journalism and online public spheres in South Africa. *Communication: South African Journal for Communication Theory & Research, 36*(2), 265–275.

Census. (2010a). *The Hispanic Population: 2010.* Retrieved January 27, 2012, from US Census 2010: http://www.census.gov/prod/cen2010/briefs/c2010br-04.pdf

Census. (2010b). *The Black Population: 2010.* Retrieved January 27, 2012, from US Census 2010: http://www.census.gov/prod/cen2010/briefs/c2010br-06.pdf

Census. (2010c). *The White Population: 2010.* Retrieved January 27, 2012, from US Census 2010: http://www.census.gov/prod/cen2010/briefs/c2010br-05.pdf

Census. (2012a). *State & County QuickFacts.* Retrieved March 15, 2012, from US Census Bureau: http://quickfacts.census.gov/qfd/states/48/4827000.html

Census. (2012b). *State & County QuickFacts.* Retrieved March 15, 2012, from US Census Bureau: http://quickfacts.census.gov/qfd/states/48/4819000.html

Copeland, R. (2011). Tweet all about it. *Metro* (169), 96–100.

Dallas Chamber. (2012). *DFW Facts.* Retrieved March 15, 2012, from Dallas Regional Chamber: http://www.dallaschamber.org/index.aspx?id=DFWFacts

Deuze, M. (2003). The web and its journalisms: Considering the consequences of different types of newsmedia online. *New Media & Society, 5*(2), 203–230.

Deuze, M. (2004). What is multimedia journalism 1? *Journalism Studies, 5*(2), 139–152.

Domingo, D., Quandt, T., Heinonen, A., Paulussen, S., Singer, J. B., & Vujnovic, M. (2008). Participatory journalism practices in the media and beyond. *Journalism Practice, 2*(3), 326–342.

Dowd, M. (2009). *To Tweet or Not to Tweet.* Retrieved January 27, 2012, from *New York Times*: http://www.nytimes.com/2009/04/22/opinion/22dowd.html

Farhi, P. (2009). The Twitter explosion. *American Journalism Review, 31*(3), 26–31.

Greer, C. F., & Ferguson, D. A. (2011). Using Twitter for promotion and branding: A content analysis of local television twitter sites. *Journal of Broadcasting & Electronic Media, 55*(2), 198–214.

Hermida, A. (2010a). From TV to Twitter: How ambient news became ambient journalism. *M/C Journal, 13*(2).

Hermida, A. (2010b). Twittering the news. *Journalism Practice, 4*(3), 297–308.

Holcomb, J., Gross, K., & Mitchell, A. (2011). *How Mainstream Media Outlets Use Twitter.* Retrieved February 7, 2012, from Journalism.org: http://www.journalism.org/analysis_report/how_mainstream_media_outlets_use_twitter?src=prc-headline

Ingram, M. (2008). *Yes, Twitter is a source of journalism.* Retrieved February 13, 2012, from Mathew Ingram: http://www.mathewingram.com/work/2008/11/26/yes-twitter-is-a-source-of-journalism/

KDFW. (2012). *@FOX4*. Retrieved February 23, 2012, from FOX4 Twitter: https://twitter.com/#!/FOX4

Kellogg, D. (2011). *Among Mobile Phone Users, Hispanics, Asians are Most-Likely Smartphone Owners in the US*. Retrieved January 27, 2012, from Nielsen Wire: http://blog.nielsen.com/nielsenwire/consumer/among-mobile-phone-users-hispanics-asians-are-most-likely-smartphone-owners-in-the-u-s/

Lopez, M. H. (2010). *How Young Latinos Communicate With Friends in the Digital Age*. Retrieved January 27, 2012, from Pew Research Center: Http://pewhispanic.org/files/reports/124.pdf

Nielsen. (2011a). *Social Media Report: Q3 2011*. Retrieved February 10, 2012, from Nielsen.com: http://blog.nielsen.com/nielsenwire/social/

Nielsen. (2011b). *Local Television Market Universe Estimates: Hispanic or Latino TV Homes*. Retrieved January 21, 2013, from Nielsen Wire: http://www.tvb.org/media/file/TVB_Market_Profiles_Nielsen_Hispanic_DMA_RANKS.pdf

Nielsen. (2012a). *More US Consumers Choosing Smartphones as Apple Closes the Gap on Android*. Retrieved February 13, 2012, from Nielsen Wire: http://blog.nielsen.com/nielsenwire/consumer/more-us-consumers-choosing-smartphones-as-apple-closes-the-gap-on-android/

Nielsen. (2012b). *Local Television Market Universe Estimates Comparisons of 2011–12 and 2012–13 Market Ranks*. Retrieved January 21, 2013, from Nielsen: http://www.nielsen.com/content/dam/corporate/us/en/public%20factsheets/tv/2012-2013%20DMA%20Ranks.pdf

Nielsen. (2012c). *Local Television Market Universe Estimates: Hispanic or Latino TV Homes*. Retrieved January 21, 2013, from TVB: http://www.tvb.org/media/file/TVB_Market_Profiles_Nielsen_Hispanic_DMA_Ranks2.pdf

Niles, R. (2007, July 31). *A Journalist's Guide to Crowdsourcing*. Retrieved February 15, 2012, from Online Journalism Review: http://www.ojr.org/ojr/stories/070731niles/

Palser, B. (2010). Vital but complementary. *American Journalism Review*, 32(1), 44–45.

Parr, B. (2009). *Mindblowing #IranElection Stats: 221,744 Tweets Per Hour at Peak*. Retrieved February 10, 2012, from Mashable: http://mashable.com/2009/06/17/iranelection-crisis-numbers/

Perez-Latre, F. J., Blanco, I. P., & Sanchez, C. (2011). Social networks, media and audiences: A literature review. *Comunicación y Sociedad*, 24(1), 63–74.

Philpot, R. (2012). *Local TV Ratings: KTVT Wins at 10, but KUVN Scores a Big Demographic Victory*. Retrieved March 3, 2012, from DFW.com: http://www.dfw.com/2012/03/01/585812/local-tv-ratings-ktvt-wins-at.html

Stassen, W. (2010). Your news in 140 characters: Exploring the role of social media in journalism. *Global Media Journal: African Edition*, 4(1), 1–16.

TouchGraph. (2012). *TouchGraph SEO Browser*. Retrieved March 15, 2012, from TouchGraph: http://www.touchgraph.com/seo

Twitterfeed. (2012). *We're Here to Help!* Retrieved February 10, 2012, from Twitterfeed: http://twitterfeed.com/help#faq1_1

Univision. (2011). *Univision Ranks #1 Network for the Night Among Adults 18–49 for Second Consecutive Year and Among Adults 18–34 for the Fourth Consecutive Year, Beating ABC, CBS, NBC and FOX*. Retrieved January 10, 2012, from Univision: http://corporate.univision.com/2011/

press/univision-ranks-as-1-network-for-the-night-among-adults-18–49-for-second-consecutive-year-and-among-adults-18–34-for-the-fourth-consecutive-year-beating-abc-cbs-nbc-and-fox/

Wasserman, E. (2009). *Commentary: How Twitter Poses a Threat to Newspapers*. Retrieved January 20, 2012, from McClatchy, The Miami Herald: http://www.mcclatchydc.com/2009/05/28/68915/commentary-how-twitter-poses-a.html

WFAA. (2011). *@wfaachannel8*. Retrieved December 7, 2011, from WFAA-TV Twitter: https://twitter.com/#!/wfaachannel8

11

THE STATE OF SPANISH LANGUAGE MEDIA 2012

Gabe Otteson, Jessica A. Perrilliat, and Alan B. Albarran

Spanish language media has been growing throughout much of the last decade, so it may not come as much of a surprise that an increase in the Hispanic population coincides with this growth. The 2010 US Census reveals that the Hispanic population grew by 43 percent, with Hispanics accounting for 56 percent of the population increase in the decade between 2000 and 2010. The Hispanic population is now estimated at 50.5 million, making up roughly 16 percent of the total US population (Ennis, Rios-Vargas, & Albert, 2011). Keeping these figures in mind, this chapter briefly summarizes the state of Spanish language media over the last year, focusing on radio, television, print media, the Internet, and advertising.

Radio

According to Arbitron's *Hispanic Radio Today 2010* report, radio's Hispanic reach has remained constant at 94–96 percent since Arbitron began studying Hispanic Radio in 2001 (Arbitron, 2010). Regardless of Spanish or English dominant language preference, radio reaches at least 91 percent of Hispanic men and women in all age categories under 65 (Arbitron, 2010). The Pew Research Center's report *The State of the News Media 2011* noted that Spanish language media fared better in the tough economic environment than English language media, and radio is no exception (Guskin & Mitchell, 2011). Spanish radio continued to grow, but the same difficult economic environment that hurts radio as a whole, slowed Spanish radio's growth to 0.7 percent from 2010 to 2011 (Pew Research Center, 2011).

Radio Listening Habits

Among Hispanics, men overall spent more time listening to radio than women, with the exception of teenagers. Time spent listening peaked for both genders in the 45–54 demographic. Hispanic men aged 45–54 spent on average the most time listening to radio at 18 hours 34 minutes per week. Among men the next-highest age groups were 55–64 (18 hours 26 minutes) and 35–44 (17 hours 18 minutes). These age groups also represented the highest listening for women, with ages 45–54 at 15 hours 49 minutes, 55–64 at 14 hours 50 minutes, and 35–44 at 14 hours 37 minutes. Girls and young women (12–17 and 18–24) spent more time listening to radio than their male counterparts. Girls 12–17 spent 10 hours 27 minutes (compared to boys' 8 hours 36 minutes) and young women aged 18–24 spent 13 hours 12 minutes (compared to men 12 hours 50 minutes) (Advertising Age Hispanic Fact Pack, 2011).

Spanish radio formats continued to gain ground in 2010–2011. The Mexican Regional format was the top choice among Spanish language listeners and among the top four formats overall in reaching adults aged 25–34. Arbitron's *Radio Today 2011* shows Mexican Regional was the only major format to post an increase in time spent listening year to year. Arbitron credits its Portable People Meter (PPM) measurement system in part for the increase (Arbitron, 2011a). In PPM markets, Mexican Regional outperformed its overall share and posted its highest one-year gain in five years.

The Spanish Contemporary format added to its market share for the first time since the Spring 2005 report with nearly all of its ratings data coming from PPM markets. Nearly half of the format's audience (48 percent) was between 25 and 44 years old; with 25 percent falling between 25 and 34, and 23 percent between 35 and 44. Compared to recent years, Spanish Contemporary's listener profile has shifted towards an older, more mature demographic. Spanish Contemporary stations scored highest on weekends and lowest in mornings; the opposite of radio's traditional listening structure (Arbitron, 2011a).

The Spanish Adult Hits (SAH) format posted its highest ratings to date, increasing its audience share from 0.8 percent to 1.1 percent. SAH performed 45 percent better in PPM markets than its national average, and only registered slightly lower ratings than its national average in diary-measured markets. The important 25–54 age group represented 64 percent of the format's audience composition. More than 97 percent of the Spanish Adult Hits audience is Hispanic, the highest percentage out of the formats surveyed by Arbitron in its *Radio Today 2011* report. The format also skewed heavily male and had 89 percent of its audience under the age of 65. Interestingly, the format's proportion of listening in the home was higher than any other Spanish format, and sixth highest overall (Arbitron, 2011a).

Spanish Non-Terrestrial Radio

Internet radio and satellite radio continued to broaden their appeal to Hispanic audiences in 2011. Broadcast giant Clear Channel's streaming app, iHeartRadio, has made speedy strides in popularity. Just 20 months after its initial launch, iHeartRadio had been downloaded over 1 million times via iTunes; before Blackberry and Android versions had been released (*iHeartRadio App Sees One Million iPhone Downloads; Blackberry is Next,* 2009). An October 2011 report by Triton Digital shows that while Pandora continues to draw in more total online listeners, iHeartRadio grows at about the same 10 percent rate (Triton Digital, 2011). iHeartRadio is free to download and differs from similar services like Pandora because it streams from Clear Channel radio stations nationwide (*No AM/FM receiver required,* 2008). In September 2011 Clear Channel expanded the service, offering the option of customized radio stations à la Pandora and last.fm, but the radio channels have ads and listeners cannot choose songs on demand (Best Music Apps: iHeartRadio, 2011). In the same month, Clear Channel announced an agreement with Univision to provide programming from Univision Radio (*iHeartRadio to offer Univision programming,* 2011).

Clear Channel expanded iHeartRadio's already long reach in 2010–2011 by entering into a multi-year strategic partnership with Microsoft. The deal further integrates iHeartRadio into Microsoft's XboxLive service by making iHeartRadio the only digital radio service available on XboxLive (*Clear Channel, Microsoft extend iHeartRadio/XboxLive integration,* 2011). This move could significantly impact the Hispanic market for two reasons. First, the Xbox360 ranks first among video game consoles usage (Nielsen, 2011b). Second, a 2010 survey by Univision revealed Hispanics were twice as likely as non-Hispanics to purchase video games within the next 30 days, and were 15 percent less likely to cite cost as a determining factor (Mcclellan, 2010).

Satellite radio also made strides toward reaching more Hispanic listeners. SiriusXM announced plans to roll out an expanded channel lineup, which it calls SiriusXM 2.0 (*SiriusXM introduces SiriusXM 2.0,* 2011). An integral part to this expansion is the new SiriusXM Latino lineup, which features an additional ten Spanish language music channels, as well as adding RadioFormula Mexico (24/7 news and talk from Mexico's leading broadcaster) and Playboy en Español. Upcoming additions are expected to include expanded college sports coverage on multiple Deportes en Vivo channels (as well as expanded MLB coverage), and the satellite debut of iconic talk show host Cristina Saralegui's Cristina Radio (*SiriusXM introduces SiriusXM 2.0,* 2011).

Television

Hispanic television households are also on the rise, primarily due to the growth in population. There are 13,348,190 Hispanic television households, and Nielsen has predicted the number will increase by 4.6 percent to 13,957,750 in 2012 (Nielsen, 2011b).

Among Hispanic television households in the US, there are differences according to language. Hispanic adults 18+ prefer to watch television in three ways. An estimated 16 percent of the survey participants watch television in Spanish only, 18 percent in English only, and 66 percent in both (Advertising Age Hispanic Fact Pack, 2011). Although 40 percent of Hispanics speak in Spanish and 50 percent of the Hispanic population born in the US can speak English, some choose to use Spanish as an alternative (Kahn, 2011).

The top five Hispanic local television markets remained constant in the past two years: Los Angeles (#1); New York (#2); Miami-Fort Lauderdale (#3); Houston (#4); and Dallas-Fort Worth (#5) (Advertising Age Hispanic Fact Pack, 2011). In comparing last year's numbers, there were 1,868,200 Hispanic television households and 5,659,170 total television households in Los Angeles, but this year, there was a 25,610 increase for Hispanic television households and a 7,730 increase for total television households (Advertising Age Hispanic Fact Pack, 2011). In New York, there were 1,251,460 Hispanic television households and 7,493,530 total television households, but this year, there was an increase of 24,670 in Hispanic television households and 21,800 in total television households (Advertising Age Hispanic Fact Pack, 2011). Miami-Ft. Lauderdale had 666,230 Hispanic television households and 1,538,090 total television households, but grew by 24,410 in Hispanic television households and 42,490 in total television households this year (Advertising Age Hispanic Fact Pack, 2011). For Houston, there were 561,390 Hispanic television households and 2,123,460 total television households, but this year, there was a 24,730 increase in Hispanic television households and a 53,760 increase in total television households (Advertising Age Hispanic Fact Pack, 2011). In Dallas-Fort Worth, there were 506,020 Hispanic television households and 2,544,410 total television households (Advertising Age Hispanic Fact Pack, 2011). This year there was an increase of 20,740 in Hispanic television households and 2,573,890 in total television households (Advertising Age Hispanic Fact Pack, 2011).

Spanish Language Television Networks

Spanish language television networks are also expanding. Throughout 2011 and into 2012, the Spanish language television networks have added new programming, surpassed English language television networks, and launched programming in new markets. Univision, TeleFutura, Galavisión, Telemundo, Mun2, Azteca América, Estrella TV, LATV, and V-me all had a year of growth.

Univision

Serving as one of the top five networks in the United States, regardless of language, Univision continues to be strong competition for other television networks. Among all of the Spanish language broadcast television networks, Univision is ranked #1 in the country, reaching 97 percent of all Hispanic households in the United States (Univision, 2011a). Univision owns and operates 19 full-power stations and 7 low-power stations distributed in 20 US markets as well as 3 stations, and 3 non-Univision stations in Puerto Rico (Univision, 2011b).

Univision Programming

In May 2011, Univision announced plans to expand the morning programming block for "Hoy" from three to five hours, launch four new telenovelas, and a few reality shows for finding new novela stars and child entertainers. During the first quarter of 2011, Univision beat NBC in the 18–49 demographics (Szalai, 2011).

Univision provided historic ratings for the CONCACAF Gold Cup SemiFinal in June 2011. While 10.9 million viewers watched all or part of the game, Univision reigned supreme over English language competitors as the most watched primetime network among men 18–34, regardless of language; Univision had more viewers than ABC, CBS, and FOX combined (Seidman, 2011a). With exclusive coverage of the Mexico vs. Honduras match, it was the #1 broadcast program of the day on Univision's local stations (Seidman, 2011a). Earlier that evening, 3.2 million viewers tuned in to Univision's broadcast of the USA vs. Panama match, which also broke records as the most watched non-Mexico Copa Ora match ever on any network (Seidman, 2011a).

In July 2011, Univision's digital division, Interactive Media, Inc. broadcast its eighth annual "Premios Juventud" youth awards show. With a reach of 10 million viewers, Univision became the #1 network across the nation, regardless of language, among adults 18–49, adults 18–34, men 18–49, men 18–34, women 18–49, women 18–34, kids 2–11, teens 12–17, and persons 18–34 (Seidman, 2011b).

TeleFutura

TeleFutura, Univision's sister network, comprises 18 full-power stations and 14 low-power stations distributed in 21 markets (Univision, 2011b).

In addition, The TeleFutura Television Group is distributed among 23 broadcast television affiliates and 509 cable and DBS affiliates nationwide (Univision, 2011b).

Telefutura also announced a new afternoon programming schedule in May 2011. Filled with more entertainment, TeleFutura's new programming includes "Las Nuevas Tardes de TeleFutura" which translates into "TeleFutura's New Afternoon Line-up," court room cases in "Verdicto Fina," the hit novela "Mañana es Para Siempre," and entertainment news program "La Tijera" (Gorman, 2011a). Additional program plans for 2011–2012 included the two Spanish dramas "MIA" and "La Mariposa" (Szalai, 2011).

Throughout 2011, TeleFutura continued to attract more viewers with its popular programming. Some of the higher rated programs included all of the primetime novela/series: "Reto de Mujer," "El Ultimo Matrimonio Feliz," and "Correo de Inocentes" (RBR, 2011a). TeleFutura's October airing of the "Liga Mexicana de Fútbol: San Luis vs. Cruz Azul" soccer match also produced big numbers. Within the first hour of the match, TeleFutura attracted more total viewers 2+, adults 18–49, and adults 18–34 than Telemundo's "Decisiones Extremas" (RBR, 2011a).

One of TeleFutura's biggest accomplishments for the season is its new late night show entitled "Noche De Perros," which translates as "Guys Night Out." The late night show is the very first Spanish language television show created for men (Hispanic Tips, 2011). "Noche De Perros," which premiered on October 31, 2011, began airing Monday through Friday at 11:00pm, EST. With three male hosts and three male perspectives, the show thrives on celebrity guest appearances, news, sports, and entertainment specifically for men (Hispanic Tips, 2011).

Galavisión

Galavisión, also owned by Univision, is the #1 Spanish language cable network. For the end of the 2010–2011 season, Galavisión posted record breaking ratings, with double digit growth among viewers, remaining one of the top cable networks, regardless of language (Gorman, 2011b). Its unique programming has documentary, lifestyle, comedy, and "supernatural" themes (Galavisión, 2011). Regular programming for Galavisión includes: the CONCACAF Copa Oro (Gold Cup), CONCACAF Liga Campeones (Champions League), MLS (Major League Soccer), Camino A La Copa (FIFA World Cup Qualifiers), and Primera División Mexicana de Fútbol (18 teams compete) (Galavisión, 2011). New programming for the 2011 season includes: "Un Mundo Aparte," a two year road trip documentary series; "KDABRA," the mystery series Univision considers a "Twilight meets novelas"; "Matutino Express," the new morning news show; "Los Heroes Del Norte," a story of five characters who form a band; and "Prime Gourmet," a culinary battle between two chefs (Galavisión, 2011).

During the Mexico vs. Colombia FIFA U-20 quarterfinal match on August 13, 2011, Galavisión made history. The network attracted over 1.3 million total viewers and became the fourth most-watched Spanish cable telecast ever (Seidman, 2011c). That Saturday's match attracted 2.3 million viewers who watched all or part of the game and became the #1 program among all cable networks for that day. The ratings for the first 12 games of the tournament also surpassed the 2009 tournament's ratings with a 272 percent increase of total viewers 2+, 259 percent increase of adults 18–49, 262 percent increase of adults 18–34, 254 percent increase of men 18–49, and a 255 percent increase of men 18–34 (Seidman, 2011c).

Telemundo

Telemundo, owned by Comcast, is the second largest Spanish language television network. Available in 210 markets, with a reach of 94 percent of all US Hispanic households Telemundo owns 14 stations, 46 broadcast affiliates, and more than 1,000 cable/DBS affiliates (Telemundo, 2011). Telemundo owns and operates one independent station in Puerto Rico, and exports programming to over 100 countries internationally in more than 35 languages (Telemundo, 2011). Telemundo was the fasting growing Spanish language television network among total viewers 2+ and adults 18–49 during prime time in October (RBR, 2011b). In comparison to Univision which had an 8 percent decline and Telefutura with a 37 percent decline among total viewers in prime time, Telemundo grew by 38 percent among total viewers 2+ and 30 percent among adults 18–49 (RBR, 2011b).

In April 2011, Telemundo had its best ratings ever, reaching almost 6.6 million total viewers during its broadcast of the Billboard Latin Music Awards (Business Wire, 2011a). The Billboard Latin Music Awards was #1, regardless of language, in New York and Miami among adults 18–49, adults 18–34, and total viewers in Miami (Business Wire, 2011a). The show was also a success on the web. It was the #1 trending topic worldwide on Twitter at 9:30pm, it gained more Twitter followers by +89 percent (in comparison to the day before), gained more Facebook fans by +54 percent (in comparison to the day before), and the live streaming of the show generated more than 500,000 page views (Business Wire, 2011a).

"La Reina del Sur," one of Telemundo's most watched programs, was the highest rated program in the network's entire history, attracting almost 4.2 million total viewers and over 2.8 million adults 18–49 during its May 30, 2011 finale (Villarreal, 2011). Due to its success as one of the most watched television shows, Telemundo launched its very first Emmy campaign for "La Reina del Sur" and its female lead, Kate del Castillo (Villarreal, 2011).

In October 2011, Telemundo announced that it would broadcast its very first primary Republican Presidential debate in December (EON, 2011). Held in Las Vegas, Nevada, the debate was broadcast in Spanish and is part of its news initiative, "Decision 2012," which housed all political coverage related to the 2012 election cycle (EON, 2011). Also in October, Telemundo, along with FOX, won the rights to broadcast the 2018 and 2022 World Cups (Longman, 2011). Telemundo will pay approximately $600 million to broadcast the two World Cups (in addition to FOX's $400 million). The agreements made also give Telemundo and FOX the rights to the 2015 and 2019 Women's World Cups and international tournaments (Longman, 2011). Another major announcement in October for Telemundo is its new plan to make its programs available with English and "Spanglish" subtitles in an effort to reach a more bilingual audience without alienating Spanish viewers (Chozick, 2011).

Mun2

Mun2, owned by Telemundo, is a bilingual cable network for bicultural Latinos 18–34 (Telemundo Media Kit, 2011). It reaches more than 36 million television households nationwide in the US through digital and analog cable and satellite (Telemundo Media Kit, 2011). Mun2 began its 2011 season with some "revamped" music content and programming (PR Newswire, 2011).

In January 2011, Mun2 relaunched a weekly bilingual variety show entitled "18 and Over" and made it a live music countdown television show. Within its first month "18 and Over" attracted more than 1 million viewers 2+ (PR Newswire, 2011). Mun2's regional Mexican music show, "Reventon with Yarel" attracted 52,000 people 2+ and 26,000 people 18–34 (PR Newswire, 2011). Its music block, "SMB: Salsa Merengue Bachata," has increased its fan base by +41 percent since December 2010, with 50,000 people 2+ and 24,000 people 18–34 (PR Newswire, 2011).

Azteca América

Launched in 2001 by TV Azteca (the second largest broadcast TV network in Mexico), Azteca América is a network that prides itself as being "the authentically Mexican television network for US Spanish-language viewers" (RBR, 2011c). In September, Azteca América increased coverage of US Hispanic households to 68 percent. From June 2010 until September 2011, the coverage went up over 8 percentage points (RBR,

2011c). This coverage includes full-power stations in Houston and Dallas and Comcast coverage in Philadelphia and New York (RBR, 2011c).

Estrella TV

Owned by Liberman Broadcasting, Estrella TV is found in 37 markets (Seattle Times, 2011). The network bills itself as the Spanish network that doesn't air any telenovelas (Media Moves, 2011). For the 2011–2012 Fall primetime lineup, Estrella TV announced its new dance competition show, "Mi Sueño es Bailar," which translates into "My Dream is to Dance" (Hispanic Ad, 2011). The show features celebrities partnered with professional dancers and weekly competitions, similar to the English smash "Dancing with the Stars" (Hispanic Ad, 2011). In October 2011, Mexican regional music female artist, Jenni Rivera,[1] announced her new television show on Estrella TV that dealt with social issues and included live interviews with various entertainment personalities (Latin American Herald Tribune, 2011). In May, the network had its first TV upfront in New York City, and revealed three new shows: reality show "Quiero Triunfar," investigative reporting show "El Momento con Enrique Gratas," and late night show "Esta noche con Héctor Suárez" (Media Moves, 2011).

The Spanish Language Television Market

Hispanic media alone has shown how beneficial it can be to target Hispanics. Hispanic advertising spending, Hispanic local television markets, and Spanish language television networks are constantly expanding. "Spanish-language media remain important to a changing, more acculturated, and more US-born Hispanic population in the United States" (Guskin & Mitchell, 2011).

English language media companies are also realizing this. For example, Time Warner Cable recently implemented 37 new national and international Spanish language channels to its iPad application (Business Wire, 2011b). This could be a challenge for Spanish language television owners as English language networks begin offering Spanish programming. Although Time Warner Cable's Spanish language channels are currently for iPads, it's only a matter of time before other English language networks begin offering programming catered to the Hispanic population.

Newspapers

Newspaper and print media of all languages have faced a difficult road during the recent economic recession in the United States. For the industry, 2010 represented an improvement over the previous two years; ad revenue fell roughly 6 percent, which still represented an improvement over the 26 percent fall that the industry saw in 2009 (Edmonds, Guskin, & Rosenstiel, 2011). Much like their English language counterparts, Spanish language newspapers also saw revenue and slight circulation drops. Mirroring the English newspapers, Spanish papers have been able to grow into other media forms and partnerships with companies in other media sectors (Edmonds et al., 2011). For example, ImpreMedia (a titan in Spanish print) has become more focused on being web-centric, through producing more digital content (such as videos) as well as mobile applications. In March 2010, ImpreMedia entered into a partnership with giant Univision to share content across the various platforms employed by both companies (Talan, 2010).

Revenue

The revenue picture for Spanish newspapers is looking better; the picture of how much better isn't exactly clear (Guskin & Mitchell, 2011). Kantar Media reported an increase in measured ad spending for Spanish language newspapers of 2 percent, compared to a 4.6 percent loss for overall local newspapers (Kantar Media, 2011). Another report by the Latino Print Network, which measures newspapers aimed at Hispanics in both English and Spanish, estimated a 5.6 percent drop in ad spending which still represented improvement over the prior year (Guskin & Mitchell, 2011). Local ad revenue makes up a substantially larger portion of ad revenue for Spanish newspapers than national revenue does. According to the Latino Print Network, the breakdown of advertising revenue for Hispanic newspapers in 2010 was estimated as: local—78 percent ($554 million); national—21 percent ($151 million), and Internet/Web—1 percent (7.2 million) (Whisler, 2010). From 2010 to 2011, Kantar Media reported that ad revenue growth is remaining relatively flat, with Spanish newspapers' ad revenue increasing by 1.9 percent, and overall local newspapers' revenue falling 3.9 percent (Business Wire, 2012).

The top-performing Spanish newspapers as measured by ad revenues in 2010 were (in order): Miami's *El Nuevo Herald*; New York's *El Diario/La Prensa*; Chicago's *Hoy*; Los Angeles' *La Opinion*, and El Paso/Juarez, Mexico's *El Diario*. *El Nuevo Herald* earned double the ad revenue of New York's *El Diario/La Prensa* (~$53 million and ~$25 million, respectively) but both saw losses over the previous year. The only other top five paper that saw a net decrease in ad revenue was Los Angeles' *La Opinion*, which posted a 4.9 percent decrease. Rounding out the top five, Chicago's *Hoy* saw a whopping 27.4 percent increase in ad revenue and the dual-markets of El Paso Texas and Ciudad Juarez, Mexico saw *El Diario*'s ad revenue increase by 7.7 percent (Advertising Age Hispanic Fact Pack, 2011).

Circulation

Circulation has been declining for years across nearly all languages, and the numbers didn't look much better in 2010–2011. Print circulation on the whole dropped 5 percent daily and 4.5 percent on Sunday from 2010 to 2011 (Edmonds et al., 2011), whereas Spanish circulation grew slightly, by 1.9 percent (Guskin & Mitchell, 2011). Circulation of Spanish daily newspapers suffered as well, as some of the larger newspapers posted significant circulation losses, continuing the trend from the year before. For example, ImpreMedia's *La Opinion* in Los Angeles saw a 14 percent circulation drop from the previous year; the oldest Spanish language daily paper, *El Diario/La Prensa* of New York lost 9.5 percent of its circulation; and Miami's *El Nuevo Herald* experienced a 4.5 percent drop, which represented a significant improvement from the 22 percent drop the paper experienced the year prior (Guskin & Mitchell, 2011). Some newspapers were able to post circulation gains. The free *Hoy Chicago*, owned by The Chicago Tribune, posted a 40 percent circulation gain; the expansion was attributed to the growth of Chicago's Hispanic population, particularly in the suburbs (*Hoy Chicago to increase circulation by 40%*, 2010).

Spanish weekly newspapers were a different story. Two Tribune papers in South Florida, Ft. Lauderdale's *El Sentinel* and Orlando's *El Sentinel*, saw gains in circulation. For the period ending March 2011, the Ft. Lauderdale *El Sentinel* saw its circulation increase 23 percent from the year before, while the Orlando *El Sentinel* posted a 3 percent gain (Guskin & Mitchell, 2011). Chicago's *La Raza* had the largest circulation among the Spanish weeklies, with 152,300, and is the only paper in the top five not located in the high-Hispanic populated states of California and Florida. The next highest-circulating weeklies are from California, Sacramento's *Vida en Valle* and Los Angeles' *Hoy*, which posted totals of 151,933 and 142,470 respectively. Ft. Lauderdale's *El Sentinel* saw an increase of 26 percent to 126,150 and Riverside, California's *La Prensa Riverside* circulated 107,500 copies (Guskin & Mitchell, 2011).

Magazines

Spanish magazines slightly rebounded in 2010 after taking a dive in 2009. Although a few notable Spanish magazines closed down publication in 2010, the economic impact on the industry was less significant than 2009 closures of *LATINO* and *Reader's Digest Selecciones* (Guskin & Mitchell, 2011). *Harper's Bazaar en Español* ceased regular publication in February 2010 and subsequent issues have been published sporadically (Guskin & Mitchell, 2011). *National Geographic en Español* closed in June 2010 when Televisa Publishing discontinued its US Hispanic version, but elected to continue publishing its Mexican edition (Guskin & Mitchell, 2011). Televisa also ceased publication of *Maxim en Español* in the US, but continues publication throughout Latin America (*Hispanic magazines post uneven results for 2010 but improve over 2009*, 2011). Other prominent closures in 2010 included *Cafe Magazine, Disney en Familia, Latino Future*, and *Mira!* (*Hispanic magazines post uneven results for 2010 but improve over 2009*, 2011).

Magazine Revenue

The revenue picture for Spanish language magazines has improved. Total ad revenue increased a modest 3.9 percent in 2010, to an estimated $178.8 million (*Hispanic magazines post uneven results for 2010 but improve over 2009*, 2011). *People en Español* and *Latina* are the clear leaders in ad revenue and each posted an increase in ad spending, at 4.5 percent and 9 percent, respectively (Advertising Age Hispanic Fact Pack, 2011). *Ser Padres* (the Spanish version of *Parents*) saw an increase in ad revenue in 2010 of 15 percent to approximately $15 million. Two Televisa publications round out the top five: *Vanidades* saw a rapid increase in ad revenue of 44 percent; *TV y Novelas* saw a 14 percent drop in ad revenue, due in part to Televisa reducing the frequency of its publication in 2010, and would continue to do so in 2011 (*Hispanic magazines post uneven results for 2010 but improve over 2009*, 2011).

The ad revenue picture through September 2011 (the most recent period of available data) has been even better. Spanish magazines saw total ad revenue increase by 23.8 percent, despite total ad pages remaining flat (Pelay, 2011). Several of the largest Spanish magazines saw large increases in ad spending. For example, ad revenue is up by 39.9 percent at *People en Español, Latina* saw a 12.6 percent increase, revenue at *Vanidades* went up 26 percent, and *TV y Novelas* saw revenue increase by 26 percent despite cutting back publication frequency yet again. *Siempre Mujer* had perhaps the most dramatic revenue gain, posting a 50 percent improvement (Pelay, 2011).

Internet

A recent Arbitron survey found that 45 percent of Americans over the age of 12 (across all ethnicities) consider the Internet to be the medium most essential to their lives, compared to 20 percent in 2002. Among ages 18–34, 60 percent of respondents claimed the Internet as their most essential medium (Arbitron, 2011b). It comes as no surprise, then, that the median age of heavy Internet users also skews younger than that of "traditional" radio and TV (Arbitron, 2011b). The booming (and also younger-skewing) Hispanic population in the US represents a tremendous growth opportunity for Internet media companies.

Data on Internet Adoption and Use

A 2010 Nielsen survey revealed that 72 percent of US Hispanics have a computer in their home. Of those, 89 percent have Internet access with 54 percent having high-speed or broadband access. Nearly half (49 percent) of Spanish-dominant people are on the Internet, and 40 percent of English-dominant report using some form of Spanish Internet daily (Nielsen, 2010). Despite this, the Hispanic population (18+) consume less Web content in Spanish compared to other forms of media and are more likely to consume in English (Advertising Age Hispanic Fact Pack, 2011).

While Hispanics' Internet use has grown faster than the overall population, Hispanics and other ethnic groups still lag behind Anglos in terms of overall Internet adoption. An estimated 62 percent of all Hispanics can access the Internet from home, and Hispanics are 44 percent more likely to have video and Internet enabled cell phones than the general market (Nielsen, 2011a). Approximately 65 percent of Latinos and 66 percent of African Americans went online in 2010, compared to 77 percent of Anglos. There is a sizeable gap in broadband use as well, with 45 percent of Latinos (and 52 percent of African Americans) using broadband to access the Internet, compared to 65 percent of Anglos. Cell phone adoption is slightly more even, with 76 percent of Latinos, 79 percent of African Americans, and 85 percent of Anglos owning a cell phone (Livingston, 2011). According to Livingston, these differing usage rates tie to income disparity. When income is controlled for, the differences in Internet use, home broadband access, and cell phone use between Hispanics and Anglos disappear; Hispanics and Anglos have similar usage patterns when their socio-economic situations are similar (Livingston, 2011). Hispanics and Anglos are equally likely to access the Internet and send/receive email from a cell phone, but rates of text and instant messaging are close. Despite that, Hispanics are no more likely to use the Internet from a cell phone than Anglos, they are more likely to do so *instead* of having an Internet connection at home. Only 6 percent of Hispanics report accessing the Web in this way, compared to 1 percent of Anglos (Livingston, 2011).

A Scarborough report on smartphone adoption reveals that the growth in adoption rate for Hispanics is outpacing the general population; at 380 percent compared to 256 percent, respectively (Scarborough Research, 2010). The apparent discrepancy between Hispanics' smartphone use and home Internet use raises interesting questions from content producing and advertising/marketing sides of Internet media. Will a "one-size-fits-all" marketing approach be as likely to attract Hispanics and non-Hispanics or will a targeted, medium- (or device-) specific approach be necessary? To what extent do content producers need to cater to a specific Hispanic mobile niche? Will location-based content gear more towards Hispanics? Will there continue to be a difference in Hispanics' adoption of home Internet versus adoption of mobile Internet?

Largest Web Properties among Hispanics

The Internet represents the highest percentage of Hispanics over 18 using that medium in English only, and the lowest percentage that use the Internet in Spanish only. There is a substantial discrepancy in the largest web properties among Hispanic users between Spanish primary/bilingual users and Hispanic users as a whole. Yahoo! and Microsoft sites are popular among both sets of users, with Yahoo! ranking second for Spanish primary/bilingual users and third for total users, and Microsoft ranking fourth for Spanish primary/bilingual users and first among total users. Univision properties are clearly number one with Spanish primary/bilingual users, whereas the leader among all Hispanic sites is more closely contested. Facebook ranks fourth on the total Hispanics category, but is nowhere to be found on the list for Spanish primary/bilingual users, surprising given Facebook's almost ubiquitous reach in the United States (Advertising Age Hispanic Fact Pack, 2011). Facebook's growth to near-ubiquity is evident when looking at the largest social network sites among Hispanic users. Facebook possesses a monstrous lead over MySpace in terms of number of unique visitors (a difference of over 17 million), and the site reaches over 70 percent of Hispanic Internet users, a figure that has far and away the highest Hispanic reach (the second ranked site, MySpace, reaches under 18 percent).

For Facebook and MySpace, Hispanics make up 14.5 percent and 16 percent, respectively, of their user base; figures relatively representative of the US population as a whole, with MySpace slightly over. Curiously, Windows Live Profile has an audience profile that substantially over-represents Hispanics in comparison to the general population; nearly one-third of its user base is Hispanic (Advertising Age Hispanic Fact Pack, 2011). Twitter's audience is comprised of nearly 13 percent Hispanics, but its Hispanic user base is still under-represented. LinkedIn's popularity is growing among Hispanic audiences (LinkedIn's reach has increased by nearly 2.5 percent over 2010) but its Hispanic user base is under-represented, with only 9 percent of its audience Hispanic. LinkedIn's career-based focus and traditional income (and career ladder) gap between Hispanics and Whites could be a factor in this, but a causal link has not been demonstrated.

Advertising

Ad Spending

While in 2008 the general advertising market saw a large budget decrease from the recession, from 2006 to 2010, Hispanic advertising stayed consistent at around 5–6 percent for total budget advertising (Association of Hispanic Advertising Agencies, 2011). Hispanic media advertising spending has topped all US media advertising spending for the past seven years (Advertising Age Hispanic Fact Pack, 2011). Although Hispanic media and US media advertising spending both declined in 2009, in 2010 Hispanic media advertising spending recovered by 8.4 percent, a 1.9 percent difference from all US media advertising spending (Advertising Age Hispanic Fact Pack, 2011). Hispanic media advertising spending for 2010 was $4.3 billion from the top 500 advertisers. It also recovered over $500 million and increased advertising spending by 14 percent (Association of Hispanic Advertising Agencies, 2011).

Advertising spending for different forms of Hispanic media also improved. Kantar Media reported that Spanish language newspapers increased advertising spending by 2 percent, Spanish language television by 10.7 percent, and Spanish language magazines by 5.5 percent (Kantar Media, 2011). Gross ad spending for Hispanic spot radio went up in 2010, with spending increasing 6 percent representing the fourth-highest increase after spot TV's 17.4 percent, magazines' 13.3 percent, and the Internet's 10.9 percent (Advertising Age Hispanic Fact Pack, 2011). Spanish language television advertising spending has become a support base of television programming for Hispanic viewers. Nielsen reported that overall, US television (including Spanish language programming) dominated other media forms with $33.8 billion in advertising during the first half of 2010, but Spanish language television, specifically network and cable television, saw the most growth with 24 percent and 13 percent in the first half of 2009 (Nielsen, 2011c). During 2009–2010, Spanish language cable television decreased by 1.28 percent, but Spanish language network television increased by 24.16 percent. Ad spending on Spanish Internet saw the largest increase from 2009 to 2010. Although going by the raw data, Internet spending still lags behind other forms of media (representing approximately 5 percent of total Spanish media ad spending); ad spending on Spanish Internet grew nearly 11 percent, outpacing print (with the sole exception of Spanish magazines), radio, and television (Advertising Age Hispanic Fact Pack, 2011). From 2010 until March 2011, Hispanic media advertising spending has seen a 0.8 percent increase in Spanish language television, a 22.3 percent increase for

Spanish language magazines, and a decrease in Spanish language newspapers by 7.4 percent (Otlacan, 2011).

Top Advertisers

The US Hispanic population accounted for 56 percent of net population growth from 2000 to 2010 and is expected to represent 100 percent of population growth between ages 13–49 (Nielsen, 2011a). Although the US Hispanic population continues to expand, some advertisers still do not target Hispanic media. Nielsen reported in 2010 that only 75 percent of the top 200 advertisers spent money on Spanish language television, and the ones that did only spent about 8 percent of their total ad budget (Nielsen, 2011a).

Among the top advertisers for Hispanic media reported by Advertising Age, 38 of the 50 increased advertising spending in 2010 (Advertising Age Hispanic Fact Pack, 2011). During the first quarter of 2011, the top five advertisers for Hispanic media were Procter & Gamble (#1), AT&T (#2), DirecTV (#3), McDonald's Corporation (#4), and DeutscheTelekom (#5) (Nielsen, 2011d).

Advertising Agencies

Hispanic advertising agencies are "more alive than ever" according to the co-founder of the original Interactive Advertising Bureau (IAB) Hispanic Committee, Liz Blacker (Blacker, 2011). Agencies with a committed multicultural strategy and employees who are bilingual and know how to connect with consumers, have a large advantage (Blacker, 2011). In 2010, 39 out of the top 50 US Hispanic agencies increased revenues (Advertising Age Hispanic Fact Pack, 2011). One of the top Hispanic digital advertising agencies in the US, LatinMedios.com, was recognized by Inc. Magazine as number 709 on its "exclusive ranking of the nation's fastest-growing private companies" (PR Newswire, 2010). In October 2011, Media Life Magazine reported that while English language magazines have seen advertising page gains slow down, Hispanic magazines are fine (Vasquez, 2011). Ad pages for all consumer magazines have declined by 1.3 percent, but Hispanic magazines have increased by 0.6 percent in advertising pages and 23.8 percent in total advertising dollars (Vasquez, 2011).

General market agencies are also beginning to develop multicultural strategies. PepsiCo, once one of the top 10 Hispanic advertisers in the US, has over the years declined in ranking (Wentz, 2011). In 2004, it was the sixth largest Hispanic advertiser (Wentz, 2011). In 2006, it dropped to #17. During 2007, PepsiCo was #27, and didn't make Advertising Age's

Top 50 Hispanic Advertisers list at all in 2010. PepsiCo then decided to make changes in the multicultural department (Wentz, 2011).

Conclusions

The Hispanic population in the US is booming, and shows no signs of slowing down. In light of the 2010 Census results, the future looks promising for Spanish language media. Spanish radio has done a masterful job adapting to serve a growing audience. Spanish radio is more popular today than it has ever been, the Spanish television networks are beginning to seriously challenge the Big Four, and both are embracing digital delivery systems (i.e., iHeartRadio, streaming video, etc.). Internet use among Hispanics is also on the rise, and ad spending across all Spanish media is increasing. Even in the hard-hit print media, Spanish publications appear to be in a more favorable position than their English counterparts. Spanish media's future is surely bright, but this optimism about Spanish media's glowing future must be tempered with the realization that second-further generation Latinos are more likely to be bilingual or English-dominant. The continuing growth of Spanish media and its interplay with English media are certainly worth keeping an eye on for the foreseeable future.

Notes

1 Rivera died in a plane crash in Mexico on December 2012.

References

Advertising Age Hispanic Fact Pack. (2011). Ad Age Data Center.
Arbitron (2010). *Hispanic radio today 2010: How America listens to radio.* Retrieved October 11, 2011 from http://www.arbitron.com/downloads/hisp_radio_today_10.pdf
Arbitron (2011a). *Radio today 2011: How America listens to radio.* Retrieved October 11, 2011 from http://arbitron.com/downloads/Radio_Today_2011.pdf
Arbitron (2011b). *The infinite dial: Navigating digital platforms presentation companion.* Retrieved October 16, 2011 from http://www.arbitron.com/downloads/infinite_dial_2011_execsummary.pdf
Association of Hispanic Advertising Agencies (2011). *Advertising 2011 budget alignment.* Retrieved November 10, 2011 from http://ahaa.org/downloads/pdf/AHAA_Advertising_Study_2011.pdf
Best music apps: iHeartRadio (2011). Retrieved October 30, 2011 from http://www.fiercemobilecontent.com/special-reports/what-are-best-music-apps-2011/best-music-apps-iheartradio
Blacker, L. (2011). AHAA insight: Hispanic agencies more alive than ever. Retrieved November 18, 2011 from http://www.iab.net/iablog/2011/11/ahaa-insight-hispanic-agencies.html

Business Wire (2011a). Telemundo's 2011 billboard Latin music awards presented by state farm delivers best ratings ever in 13-year history reaching nearly 6.6. million total viewers. Retrieved October 27, 2011 from http://www.businesswire.com/news/home/20110429006077/en/Telemundo%E2%80%99s-2011-Billboard-Latin-Music-Awards-Presented

Business Wire (2011b). Time Warner Cable adds 37 Spanish-language channels to its iPad app programming lineup Retrieved November 7, 2011 from http://fixed-mobile-convergence.tmcnet.com/news/2011/11/03/5905675.htm

Business Wire (2012). Kantar Media reports US advertising expenditures increased 0.8% in 2011. Retrieved March 31, 2012 from http://www.marketwatch.com/story/kantar-media-reports-us-advertising-expenditures-increased-08-percent-in-2011-2012-03-12

Census (2010). *Overview of race and Hispanic origin 2010*. Retrieved September 20, 2011 from http://www.census.gov/prod/cen2010/briefs/c2010br-02.pdf

Chozick, A. (2011). Telemundo blends English into a mostly Spanish lineup. Retrieved October 27, 2011 from http://www.nytimes.com/2011/10/26/business/media/telemundo-seeks-spanglish-speakers-in-aim-for-new-viewers.html?pagewanted=all

Clear Channel, Microsoft extend iHeartRadio/Xbox integration (2011). Retrieved October 14, 2011 from http://www.allaccess.com/net-news/archive/story/97312/clear-channel-microsoft-extend-iheartradio-xbox-in

Edmonds, R., Guskin, E., & Rosenstiel, T. ; Pew Research Center. (2011). The state of the news media 2011: Newspapers: Missed the 2010 media rally. Retrieved November 1, 2011 from http://stateofthemedia.org/2011/newspapers-essay/

Ennis, S.R., Rios-Vargas, M., & Albert, N.G. (2011). The Hispanic population: 2010. *2010 Census Briefs*. Retrieved November 5, 2011 from http://www.census.gov/prod/cen2010/briefs/c2010br-04.pdf

EON (2011). Telemundo to host its first-ever primary Republican presidential debate in December. Retrieved October 27, 2011 from http://eon.businesswire.com/news/eon/20111013006619/en

Galavisión (2011). Galavisión network. Retrieved October 25, 2011 from http://corporate.univision.com/media-brands/galavision-network/

Gorman, B. (2011a). TeleFutura announces new afternoons with "las nuevas tardes de telefutura" and "mañana es para siempre." Retrieved October 20, 2011 from http://tvbythenumbers.zap2it.com/2011/01/20/telefutura-announces-new-afternoons-with-%e2%80%9clas-nuevas-tardes-de-telefutura%e2%80%9d-%e2%80%9cmanana-es-para-siempre%e2%80%9d/79532/

Gorman, B. (2011b). Galavisión delivers best season ever with double digit growth. Retrieved October 27, 2011 from http://tvbythenumbers.zap2it.com/2011/09/28/galavision-delivers-best-season-ever-with-double-digit-growth/105369/

Guskin, E. & Mitchell, A. (2011). The state of the news media 2011: Hispanic media: Faring better than mainstream media. Retrieved October 26, 2011 from http://stateofthemedia.org/2011/hispanic-media-fairing-better-than-the-mainstream-media/

Hispanic Ad (2011). Estrella TV debuts primetime dance competition show. Retrieved October 31, 2011 from http://hispanicad.com/cgi-bin/news/newsarticle.cgi?article_id=32804

Hispanic magazines post uneven results for 2010 but improve over 2009. (2011, January 11). Retrieved November 16, 2011 from http://blog.media-economics.com/2011/01/19/hispanic-magazines-post-uneven-results-for-2010-but-improve-over-2009/

Hispanic Tips (2011). TeleFutura lets the dogs out with the new late-night show "noche de perros." Retrieved October 25, 2011 from http://www.hispanictips.com/2011/10/19/telefutura-lets-the-dogs-out-with-the-new-late-night-show-%e2%80%9cnoche-de-perros%e2%80%9d/

Hoy Chicago to increase circulation by 40%. (2010, September 17). Retrieved November 8, 2011 from http://www.portada-online.com/article.aspx?aid=3764

iHeartRadio app sees one million iPhone downloads; Blackberry is next. (2009, March 16). Retrieved November 5, 2011 from http://www.clearchannel.com/Radio/PressRelease.aspx?PressReleaseID=2378

iHeartRadio to offer Univision programming. (2011, September 27). Retrieved November 15, 2011 from http://www.allaccess.com/net-news/archive/story/96952/iheartradio-to-offer-univision-programming

Kantar Media (2011). Kantar Media reports US advertising expenditures increased 6.5 percent in 2010. Retrieved November 5, 2011 from http://kantarmediana.com/intelligence/press/us-advertising-expenditures-increased-65-percent-2010

Khan, S. (2011). Hispanic heritage month: Spanish language media gaining ground. Retrieved October 13, 2011 from http://www.ny1.com/content/special_reports/hispanic_heritage_2011/148620/hispanic-heritage-month--spanish-language-media-gaining-ground?ap=1&MP4

Latin American Herald Tribune (2011). Singer Jenni Rivera to have TV program. Retrieved October 31, 2011 from http://laht.com/article.asp?ArticleId=428552&CategoryId=13003

Livingston, G. (2011). *Latinos and digital technology, 2010.* Retrieved November 20, 2011 from http://pewhispanic.org/reports/report.php?ReportID=134

Longman, J. (2011). Fox and Telemundo win US rights to world cups. Retrieved October 27, 2011 from http://www.nytimes.com/2011/10/22/sports/soccer/fox-and-telemundo-win-us-rights-to-2018-and-2022-world-cups.html

Mcclellan, S. (2010). Univision teams up with CBS' Gamespot. Retrieved October 31, 2011 from http://www.adweek.com/news/television/univision-teams-cbs-gamespot-101975

Media Moves (2011). Estrella TV upfront. Retrieved October 31, 2011 from http://www.mediamoves.com/2011/05/estrella-tv-upfront.html

Nielsen (2010). A snapshot of Hispanic media usage in the US. Retrieved October 17, 2011 from http://www.nielsen.com/content/dam/corporate/us/en/reports-downloads/Nielsen-Snapshot-of-Hispanic-Media-Usage-US.pdf

Nielsen (2011a). What you think you know vs. what you need to know about US Hispanics and media. Retrieved November 14, 2011 from http://blog.nielsen.com/nielsenwire/media_entertainment/what-you-think-you-know-vs-what-you-need-to-know-about-u-s-hispanics-and-media/

Nielsen (2011b). Number of ethnic TV households grows: Asian TV households up nearly 10 percent. Retrieved October 13, 2011 from http://blog.nielsen.

com/nielsenwire/media_entertainment/number-of-ethnic-tv-households-grows-asian-tv-households-up-nearly-10-percent/

Nielsen (2011c). Global ad spending shows signs of growth. Retrieved November 14, 2011 from http://blog.nielsen.com/nielsenwire/global/global-ad-spending-shows-signs-of-growth/

Nielsen (2011d). State of the media: Trends in advertising spend and effectiveness. Retrieved November 14, 2011 from http://www.nielsen.com/content/dam/corporate/us/en/reports-downloads/2011-Reports/TrendsAdSpendanEffectiveness_Spreads.pdf

No AM/FM receiver required: Clear Channel brings top radio stations to Apple iPhone, iPod touch. (2008). Retrieved October 19, 2011 from http://macdailynews.com/2008/10/13/clear_channel_brings_top_radio_stations_to_apple_iphone_ipod_touch/

Otlacan, O. (2011). Kantar media reports US advertising expenditures increased 4.4% in the first quarter of 2011. Retrieved November 10, 2011 from http://www.adoperationsonline.com/2011/07/05/kantar-media-reports-us-advertising-expenditures-increased-4-4-in-the-first-quarter-of-2011/

Pelay, C. (2011, October 24). Hispanic magazine top 10 tables for January-September 2011: Ad spending up by 23.8% this year. Retrieved November 15, 2011 from http://blog.media-economics.com/category/hispanic/hispanic-magazines/

Pew Research Center. (2011). *Hispanic radio update.* Retrieved October 25, 2011 from http://stateofthemedia.org/2011/african-american/glossary/#hispanic-radio-update

PR Newswire (2010). LatinoMedios.com, a leading Hispanic digital advertising agency, made this year's inc. 500|5000 list. Retrieved November 22, 2011 from http://www.prnewswire.com/news-releases/latinmedioscom-a-leading-hispanic-digital-advertising-agency-made-this-years-inc-5005000-list-101846103.html

PR Newswire (2011). Mun2 kicks off 2011 with innovative and exclusive multi-platform music programming. Retrieved November 1, 2011 from http://www.prnewswire.com/news-releases/mun2-kicks-off-2011-with-innovative-and-exclusive-multi-platform-music-programming-115178704.html

RBR (2011a). Week 4: TeleFutura's primetime novella-series line-up delivered. Retrieved October 20, 2011 from http://www.rbr.com/tv-cable/tv-cable_ratings/week-4-telefutura-s-primetime-novella-series-line-up-delivered.html

RBR (2011b). Growth month for Telemundo. Retrieved November 3, 2011 from http://www.rbr.com/tv-cable/tv-cable_ratings/growth-month-for-telemundo.html

RBR (2011c). Azteca América up to 68% coverage of US Hispanic households. Retrieved September 29, 2011 from http://www.rbr.com/tv-cable/azteca-america-up-to-68-coverage-of-us-hispanic-households.html

Scarborough Research (2010). Hispanics are important mobile marketing targets. Retrieved November 21, 2011 http://scarborough.com/press_releases/Scarborough-Hispanics-Mobile-Marketing-Targets.pdf

Seattle Times (2011). Estrella TV signs deal with KBCB in Bellingham. Retrieved October 31, 2011 from http://seattletimes.nwsource.com/html/television/2015984707_estrellatv.html

Seidman, R. (2011a). Univision delivers historic ratings with CONCACAF gold cup semifinal reaching 10.9 million viewers. Retrieved September 29, 2011 from http://tvbythenumbers.zap2it.com/2011/06/24/univision-delivers-historic-ratings-with-concacaf-gold-cup-semifinal-reaching-10-9-million-viewers/96505/

Seidman, R. (2011b). Univision's "premios juventud" youth awards are #1 on broadcast with adults 18–49 and 18–34. Retrieved October 4, 2011 from http://tvbythenumbers.zap2it.com/2011/07/22/univisions-premios-juventud-youth-awards-are-1-on-broadcast-with-adults-18-49-and-18-34/98711/

Seidman, R. (2011c). Galavisión delivers fourth highest ratings in history of Spanish-language cable television with Mexico vs. Colombia FIFA u 20 match. Retrieved October 25, 2011 from http://tvbythenumbers.zap2it.com/2011/08/16/galavision-delivers-fourth-highest-ratings-in-history-of-spanish-language-cable-television-with-mexico-vs-colombia-fifa-u-20-match/100590/

SiriusXM introduces SiriusXM 2.0 with new music, sports, and entertainment channels, including SiriusXM Latino (2011). Retrieved October 30, 2011 from http://investor.sirius.com/releasedetail.cfm?ReleaseID=615472

Szalai, G. (2011). Univision books more televisa and original content. Retrieved October 20, 2011 from http://www.hollywoodreporter.com/news/univision-books-more-televisa-original-189935

Talan, M. (2010). Univision Interactive Media and ImpreMedia announce content exchange partnership. Retrieved November 21, 2011 from http://corporate.univision.com/2010/press/univision-interactive-media-and-impremedia-announce-content-exchange-partnership/

Telemundo (2011). Telemundo legal corporate English. Retrieved October 27, 2011 from http://msnlatino.telemundo.com/legal_corporate_english

Telemundo Media Kit (2011). Mun2. Retrieved November 1, 2011 from http://telemundomediakit.com/mun2/

Triton Digital (2011). Triton Digital releases September internet audio top 20 rankers. Retrieved November 6, 2011 from http://www.tritondigital.com/Media/Default/Rankers/september-ranker-2011.pdf

Univision (2011a). Interactive media. Retrieved December 1, 2011 from http://corporate.univision.com/portfolio/interactive-media/

Univision (2011b). Univision interactive media national. Retrieved December 1, 2011 from http://corporate.univision.com/media-brands/univision-interactive-media/

Vasquez, D. (2011). Who's not hurting: Hispanic magazines. Retrieved November 22, 2011 from http://www.medialifemagazine.com/artman2/publish/Magazines_22/Who-s-not-hurting-Hispanic-magazines.asp

Villarreal, Y. (2011). "La reina del sur" pursues primetime Emmy consideration. Retrieved October 27, 2011 from http://articles.latimes.com/2011/jun/20/entertainment/la-et-kate-del-castillo-20110620

Wentz, L. (2011). PepsiCo makes Hispanic move to alma DDB, LatinWorks from dieste. Retrieved November 22, 2011 from http://adage.com/article/hispanic-marketing/pepsico-makes-hispanic-move-alma-ddb-latinworks/229723/

Whisler, K. (2010). *The state of Hispanic print 2010*. Carlsbad, CA; Latino Print Network.

Section IV

MEDIA MANAGEMENT ISSUES FOR NEW MEDIA/ TRANSMEDIA

12

TELEVISION INDUSTRY'S ADOPTION OF THE INTERNET

Diffusion of an Inefficient Innovation

Harsh Taneja and Heather Young

The adoption of the Internet by the television industry has been a considerably turbulent and drawn-out process. The Internet problematized television as a product and threatened the industry's longstanding business models, resulting in pervasive uncertainty about its adoption. For the first time, television networks had to adapt their offerings to an entirely new platform with capabilities much different from those of traditional platforms, yet maintain their relationships with support industries. Their ongoing struggle with how to profit from making content available online warrants an inquiry into the challenges and opportunities the television industry faced throughout the process of adopting the Internet.

This study seeks to identify the factors, players, and events responsible for shaping the strategies used by television networks to adopt the Internet by performing a historical textual analysis of the television industry trade publication, *Broadcasting & Cable* (*B&C*) from 2001 to 2009. We develop a theoretical framework that explains how innovations are adopted in uncertain and complex situations. We then review specific developments and broad trends reported by *B&C* to apply our framework to the interorganizational field in which the television industry operates, in order to explain why television networks continue to struggle with adopting the Internet.

Scholars have studied the television industry's response to the Internet for nearly two decades. However, the scope of this research has served to describe the artifact itself (i.e., the network website) at a specific point in time rather than the evolutionary process of Internet adoption. Early studies examined the use of television network websites in business strategies and found that networks imposed traditional business models onto the Internet. Initially, network websites emphasized providing news and information, catering to audiences rather than advertisers (Chan-Olmsted

& Park, 2000), and were primarily used to promote television programming (Ha, 2002). Station managers perceived websites as tools for bolstering audience relations rather than outlets which might generate revenue through online advertisements (Chan-Olmsted & Ha, 2003).

Television networks by and large failed to take advantage of the Internet's interactive capabilities. As Siapera states, "innovative attributes [of the Internet] ... [were] all subsumed under, and incorporated into, existing relationships" (Siapera, 2004, p. 170). Thus, early network websites did not have interactive features and contained mainly repurposed on-air content (Chan-Olmsted & Jung, 2001); even when networks began to recognize the value of interactivity, most websites remained sources for information (Chan-Olmsted & Park, 2000; Ha, 2002; Kiernan & Levy, 1999). While high website traffic did not translate to higher ratings (Ha & Chan-Olmsted, 2001), interactive features increased the amount of time spent on a site, resulting in an increase in a network's overall brand equity (Ha & Chan-Olmsted, 2001). Cable network websites were more likely to have interactive features (Ha, 2002), which were thought to appeal to their specialized audiences (Chan-Olmsted & Jung, 2001). In some cases, networks formed partnerships with technology companies to capitalize on opportunities for brand extension and interactivity offered by the Web (Chan-Olmsted & Jung, 2001).

The focus on branding, advertising, and interactivity in prior literature has obscured additional factors that explain the online strategy of television networks. Scholars in television studies (e.g., Boddy, 2004; Caldwell, 2009; Holt & Perren, 2009; Lotz, 2007; Spigel & Olsson, 2004) have shown that many exogenous factors—in particular the complex relationships between television networks and their support industries such as studios, advertisers, and measurement services—influenced how television networks utilized the Internet. Despite their expanded focus, these studies, too, took a cross-sectional view and focused either on the impact of the Internet on the current practices or future developments in the television industry and offer little explanation of how the current state came to be.

Lacking is a longitudinal inquiry into the evolution of the relationship between the television industry and the Internet with the goal of understanding the factors that affected the process of adoption. Also, to provide a comprehensive explanation a study should not be restricted to analyzing television networks' websites. Instead the inquiry should be at the level of the interorganizational field, a term Leblebici, Salancik, Copay, and King (1991) defined as a historically specific pattern of transactions composed of actors (usually organizations) who transact directly through exchange or indirectly through competition. More specifically, in order to explain all factors that influenced the television industry's process of Internet adoption, a study should go beyond looking at television networks' websites and examine how transactions between television's support industries impacted their online strategies. "Support industries" as used so far and in the remainder of this study, refers to players that directly or indirectly impact the working of television networks. These include advertisers, advertising agencies, audience measurement companies, cable and satellite distributors, production houses and studios as well as online platform providers. In this study we address both these issues by drawing on theories that motivate a longitudinal inquiry using the television industry trade press, a data source that speaks to the inter-organizational field, not just television networks.

Conceptual Framework

As a new medium, the Internet offered an alternative distribution platform that had to be adopted by television networks, yet reconciled with traditional modes of delivery. The overarching question, which guides our inquiry, is how various factors, events, and players influenced the process of Internet adoption by television networks. In this section, we develop a framework to motivate this inquiry by applying theoretical mechanisms in diffusion of innovations and institutional change to the television industry to pose specific research questions for this study.

Disruptive Innovation: Uncertainty and Complexity

An innovation is "an idea, practice, or object that is perceived as new by an individual or other unit of adoption" (Rogers, 1995. p. 11). In the context of this study, the innovation is the use of the Internet by television companies as a promotional tool or distribution platform (i.e., innovation as "practice"). Innovations can be incremental (minor improvements to products or services), radical (offering a highly novel product or service), or disruptive (rewriting the rules of the game) (Tidd, 2001). New technologies are a source of environmental variation, and cause ferment among adopting organizations (Tushman & Anderson, 1986). In addition to the challenges posed by technology itself, two environmental contingencies, uncertainty and complexity, further affect firms' ability to evaluate innovations (Tidd, 2001). *Uncertainty* comes from the rate of change of technologies and market characteristics. *Complexity* is a function of interdependence between organizations at both the technological and process levels. The higher the interdependence within the field, the more difficult it becomes for organizations to innovate (Tidd, 2001).

We regard the use of the Internet as a delivery platform to be a disruptive innovation for television networks, as it was a new technology that inspired uncertainty and problematized the complexity of the industry. Due to the experiential nature of media products, networks could not predict how consumers would react to content on the new platform prior to making content available online. Moreover, networks had to consider the impact that adopting the Internet would have on their relationships with support industries.

Diffusion of Innovations as Fashions and Fads

The dominant perspective on diffusion of innovations considers adoption to be driven by independent, rational choices that promise to enhance technical efficiency for the adopting unit (Rogers, 1995). However, this perspective is unable to explain adoption of inefficient or disruptive innovations which, according to Abrahamson, are adopted by organizations due to "outside influence" ("fashions" set by influential organizations outside the industry) and an "imitation focus" (in which fashionable practices become "fads" through widespread imitation) (Abrahamson, 1991). From the fashion perspective, an organization's decision to adopt an innovation is influenced by an organization outside its core group, usually a "fashion setting organization" such as a consulting firm or technology company. From the fad perspective, organizations imitate competitors either to avoid giving a competitor the competitive advantage or simply to gain legitimacy (DiMaggio & Powell, 1983). These mechanisms drive innovations to be adopted regardless of their technical inefficiencies.

However, it is not always possible to attribute the diffusion process to one of these perspectives alone, and often a combination of the fad and fashion perspectives explains diffusion of innovations. Diffusion of innovations within creative industries in particular is often attributed to fads and fashions (Caves, 2000; Hirsch, 1972). Given the uncertainty that adoption of the Internet presented to television networks, we employ a fashions and fads perspective to explain the adoption of the Internet by the television industry, especially as we know in retrospect that the Internet was not adopted as an efficient choice.

Institutional Change in Organizational Fields

Organizational inertia discourages longstanding organizations from adopting new technologies, as they perceive new technologies as a threat which will hurt existing practices and current business models (Cooper & Schendel, 1976; Cooper & Smith, 1992). Past studies have demonstrated these tendencies specifically in media industries; take for instance the resistance of broadcast networks to new audience measurement technologies (Barnes & Thomson, 1994) and newspapers' responses to online publishing (Boczkowski, 2004). Thus, although institutional leadership can foster a culture of innovation (Van de Ven, 1986), organizations in mature institutional fields tend to become isomorphic in their practices and mimic one another (DiMaggio & Powell, 1983). Dominant players in such fields do not willingly change their practices. Instead, innovations are introduced by "fringe players" which Leblebici et al. (1991) define as the "the newer and/or less powerful participants [within an interorganizational field], for whom experimentation is less costly in final outcomes and who are less likely to be sanctioned by more central players" (p. 358). If successful, these practices become new institutional conventions once they attract the attention of dominant players (Leblebici et al., 1991).

In the case of the television industry, in order to incorporate the Internet as a delivery platform, television networks had to begin interacting with information technology companies working amidst or at the periphery of the Web, including Web portals, search engines, and other Internet technology providers (which we simplify hereafter as "Internet companies"), which meant the interorganizational field of the television industry expanded to include new players. In this chapter we consider television networks to be the dominant players and Internet companies to be the fringe players. It may have been the case that these fringe players introduced some of the practices that television companies adopted with regard to using the Internet.

Research Questions

In this chapter, we seek to understand why the Internet was viewed as a source of uncertainty and complexity, and how the television industry responded to these uncertainties. We are also interested in exploring the mechanisms by which innovative practices diffused within this complex interorganizational field, as well as the players who influenced the adoption of these innovations. Based on the literature, we pose three research questions as follows:

RQ1: What factors contributed to uncertainty in the television industry about adopting the Internet as a delivery platform and how did the television industry respond?

RQ2: What fashions and fads impelled the television industry to adopt the Internet?

RQ3: Which players were responsible for introducing which innovative practices online that were subsequently adopted by the television industry at large?

Data and Method

To develop an understanding of the evolution of the process of Internet adoption by the industry, we draw on television industry trade press.

Caldwell (2009, p. 203) characterizes industry trade press as a form of inter-group communication he terms "semi-embedded deep texts," which "function to bring the generalizing discussions of the nature and meaning of [media] production from one corporate media company or craft group to another." Because these semi-embedded deep texts "succeed only if they are persuasive in maintaining or forging new relationships" between players in the organizational field, they are an ideal source of insight about the perception and response of the television industry writ large to the Internet. *Broadcasting & Cable* (*B&C*), a weekly launched in 1930, is the premier trade publication of the television industry. It covers news affecting the industry including conference proceedings, personnel changes, website launches, corporate restructuring, programming trends, and opinions of industry leaders and consultants. It also provides information about developments in support industries and regulatory changes that have consequences for the television industry. *B&C* is a reliable and stable source of industry information required for longitudinal analysis.

We used digitized archives of *B&C* to gather all articles published from 2001 to 2009 containing the word "Internet" in the title or body of text, publication defined keywords, or subject codes. We began our search for articles starting 2001 so as to include the period immediately following the stock market crash of 2000–2001. The search returned approximately 3,500 articles in all. Experimentation with other keywords like "Web," "site," and "online" did not return significantly different results. We were interested in articles of two kinds: articles about television networks' presence on the Internet (e.g., websites, program types, modes of delivery) and articles about the broader context in which Internet adoption occurred (e.g., distribution practices, corporate partnerships, revenue, technology, metrics, advertising). Articles about the FCC and other regulatory issues were excluded as they were beyond the scope of this inquiry. Based on our focus of research, we selected 258 articles to be included in our detailed analysis. We read and summarized each article and classified them thematically according to the following topics which emerged throughout the course of our analysis: organizational and website strategy, technology, revenue, and innovative practices. A fifth category was used to capture articles that spoke to broader questions in the study but did not fall under a particular category. Following this process of classification and analysis, we examined themes chronologically with an eye toward broad trends of which individual events were representative.

Internet Adoption by Television Networks

Based on our analysis, we classified the period of 2001–2009 into three phases (named after representative articles published during the phase), which are tied to key turning points in television networks' online strategies. Though the Internet was pervasive by 2000, television networks halted their initial online strategies in 2001 and started from scratch following the stock market crash, making this a sensible point at which to begin our inquiry. Phase One, from 2001–2004, was one of skeptical experimentation in which networks were wary of the Internet, had justifiable doubts about its staying power, and lacked a unified strategy to incorporate the new technology into their offering. By 2004, it was clear that the Internet remained an important technology despite initial turbulence, and networks began to recognize the unique advantages of the Internet in terms of facilitating interactivity and targeting niche audiences. Phase Two, comprised of years 2005 and 2006, was one of rapid Internet adoption by networks. In 2005, more than half of the online population had access to broadband Internet resulting in an explosion of content online by 2006. This phase also sparked interest in the social features of the Internet. Phase Three began in 2007 and was typified by industry reconciliation of the fervor in 2005–2006 with the reality of issues such as distribution, monetization, and technical quality. Below we describe in detail the trends occurring within each phase by identifying the online strategies followed by television networks. Tables 12.1, 12.2, and 12.3 correspond to the phases and contain more granular details of specific *events* that inform the trends we report.

Phase One: "Tata TV Portals"

A 2001 *B&C* article titled "Tata TV Portals" aptly summarizes back-pedaling by the television industry following the stock market crash in 2000–2001. In the late 1990s, television networks had mimicked Internet innovators like Yahoo! and America Online by creating all-purpose portals which they positioned as alternative networks. These portals ultimately failed, and by 2001, networks began to reduce investments in online ventures. Some shut down websites while others tried to align them more closely with on-air offerings. Networks were uncertain whether websites should serve as a reference for information about on-air programs or function as distribution outlets. Moreover, they were unsure whether content available online should be unique or repurposed from television. In addition to these challenges, the practical fact that broadband access among the general population was limited during this time and streaming technologies expensive for broadcasters to deploy further inhibited experimentation with distribution. In 2003, some networks began streaming content that was unavailable on broadcast networks yet was appealing to a niche audience, such as college sports to a nationwide audience of alumni, archived episodes of soap operas which typically aired only once, and short newscasts which could be viewed in the workplace throughout

Table 12.1 Phase One: "Tata TV Portals"

	2001	2002	2003	2004
Organizational/ Website Strategy	• Site closings, staff layoffs at broadcast companies; more strategic site development due to budget cuts • News Corp. dissolved News Digital Media subsidiary	• AOL's promotion of PBS proved successful in driving traffic to PBS website	• Increased interest in streaming (especially in cases where targeting was important or broadcasting was not feasible): • SoapCity.com • Broadcasters' news sites • Entertainment Tonight and Yahoo! partnered to create branded website to mutual benefit	• CBS partnered with AOL and The FeedRoom in order to stream NCAA basketball online • 2004 Summer Olympics were broadcast by NBC, who used Web to distribute info about broadcast content and schedule • College Sports TV (CSTV) offered streaming games online • Netflix partnered with TiVo to offer movie downloads • SBC and Microsoft partner to offer IPTV
Technology	• Awareness of trend toward consumer media multitasking		• TiVo and other PVR technologies were introduced	
Revenue Models		• Commercial power of TV/Internet relationship was recognized by shopping networks HSN and QVC • Internet advertising revenues declined	• Increase in Internet advertising sparked renewed interest; a variety of innovative tactics for monetizing network sites emerged (e.g., interactive and targeted advertising, subscription models, cross-promotion)	

Innovators	• RealNetworks made deal with MLB and NBA to offer subscription service which proves popular	• RealNetworks expanded subscription offering	• ABCNews.com, Yahoo! Platinum were launched as subscription services • IBS and WorldNow competed for deals with broadcasters to host streaming content	• WorldNow business continued to grow to over 100 broadcast affiliates
Other Significant Developments		• Interactivity in reality programming: *American Idol*		• Instant messaging was incorporated into *Who Wants to be a Millionaire*

Source: Prepared by the authors using articles from *Broadcasting & Cable*.

Table 12.2 Phase Two: "Now Streaming"

	2005	2006
Organizational Website Strategy	• Digitization of content led to a shift in focus from platforms to distribution methods • USA Network previewed programs online to generate buzz; other networks offered extras • BBC offered clips for download • ABC strengthened infrastructure for streaming news—planned to hire more staff, make distribution deals, upgrade technologies • Networks acquired additional platforms • ESPN, CSTV offered content across multiple platforms • Personalization, interactivity, and unique content for Web • MTV, CNN • Program specific microsites (e.g., Seinfeld) • New/improved websites/services • CBS • CNN Video on Demand	• Acquisitions facilitated enhanced targeting • NBC acquired women-centered iVillage • Telemundo launched site targeting Hispanics • Networks made attempts to enhance engagement with consumers • Disney Playhouse offers subscription service which allowed customization of interactive content to skill level of child • Sci-Fi Network created fan wiki • Websites used as test market • Fox linked to RottenTomatoes and MySpace for cross-promotional possibilities • Changes to distribution • Networks offered content online (Discovery, ABC—free content, NBC—launched video portal) • CBS distributes content through Google Video Store • Networks offered content across multiple platforms • Fox sites underwent widespread redesign • Concern that multiple distribution platforms were diluting the brand prompted ABC to create team of digital experts • *American Idol* site traffic increased three-fold over 2005

Technology	• Broadband access reached tipping point (i.e., over 50% of the population had access) • Networks engaged in talks about convergence, TV everywhere (e.g., Warner)	• Attempts at streaming through mobile devices • Rapid increase in TV website revenue • More convergence devices emerged

Revenue Models	• Further increases in Internet advertising revenue; networks remained skeptical
	• Subscription models remained popular
	  • ESPN, CSTV, CNN Pipeline
		• Heavy focus on distribution across multiple outlets
		  • Revenue sharing with Yahoo! TV, Google TV
		  • iTunes
		• Rapid increase in advertising revenue
		• Advertisers demand better measurement online
		• Networks recognized new marketing opportunities afforded by Internet

Innovators	• Associated Press allowed smaller stations to stream video through their site • AOL launched portal for streaming video	• Yahoo! launched video search • Brightcove offered video distribution platform for networks • AP Online Video Network, created by MSN and AP, allowed local affiliates to stream video clips on their sites • AOL launched video streaming site, In2TV • Clear Channel Television partnered with ClipSyndicate • Google acquired YouTube
Other Significant Developments	• Surge in availability of content online	• Interest in social features of the Internet emerged • Trend toward "lifestyle" media—personalized and on demand • Programs are developed out of Internet concepts • Networks paid increasing attention to online buzz

Source: Prepared by the authors using articles from *Broadcasting & Cable*.

Table 12.3 Phase Three: "The Genie Is Out of the Bottle"

	2007	2008	2009

Organizational/ Website Strategy	• Attempts made to use the Internet to complement rather than compete with traditional offering
	  • TMZ.com launched TMZ on TV, which provided viewers with content not available online
	• New websites/players for streaming video launched
	  • Fox, ABC, A&E
	• Site redesigns
	  • Hallmark, Lifetime, Court TV, NBC
	  • Warner launched T-works, an online virtual world, and MomLogic.com
	• Desire to integrate YouTube into business
	  • YouTube channels—Hearst Argyle
	  • Live Webcasts—FOX and MLB
	  • Acquisitions—Sony acquired Grouper, second largest video sharing website, to create a streaming network
	• Alternative distribution channels; launch of Hulu with content from NBC, ABC, and FOX
		• Widespread site redesigns took place in order to make sites more attractive and improve usability in an effort to grow audiences with an eye toward monetization
		• Local stations overhauled staff to grow online revenue by hiring people with Web experience; stations reconceptualized websites as "media hubs" rather than TV outlet websites
		• National Geographic launched broadband video site to compete with Discovery
		• CBS acquired CNet Networks, Inc. to become one of top ten Internet companies
			• Interest in the concept of "viral" and attempts to harness this phenomenon
			  • FOX created new brand for promoting viral videos
			  • Weekly program that shows viral videos
			• Networks bought popular online shows from producers—some programs proved successful on Spike TV, Comedy Central; other networks experienced failure (e.g., NBC)
			• Networks encouraged user generated content on station website (e.g., Hearst Argyle)
			• Network news operations looked to Internet to compete with cable news
			• Rival firms entered into partnerships to monetize the online space and also hedge against recession
			• Networks incorporated online comments and tweets into TV shows
			  • NBC Access Hollywood, CBS Insider, WB Extra

Technology	• Attempts at integrating offerings across devices • Newer software and design upgrades • Technology vendors improved infrastructure for streaming resulting in improved streaming quality • Telestream, Akamai, Limelight Networks • NewTek offered networks a portable production truck that facilitated webcasting—used by FOX, MTV	• Further integration of television and Internet through set top devices and television sets themselves • Netflix, Sony • Recognition that seamless integration and viewing content on a television is key • Tech companies made improvements to players to enhance quality of online video	• Quality of streaming content reached broadcast quality • Online video had mass rather than niche audience • FCC pushed for set top boxes to be the device that facilitated convergence between TV and Internet
Revenue Models	• Increase in free content, especially full length episodes • NBC/iTunes deal called off as NBC demands double price per episode • Engagement thought to be the new metric to monetize audiences • Hulu launched with advertising supported model • Revenues from webisodes remained elusive	• Network AMC partnered with Nielsen to offer measurement based on viewer identity/preferences • Television attempted to unseat advantages of Internet by incorporating purchasing data into targeted advertising	• Internet viewed as tool for pretesting programs/market research through the "focus group" quality of social media • Twitter was widely used as marketing tool by television industry • Though this was sometimes detrimental due to false information • Late Night with Jimmy Fallon integrates with Twitter • Recession caused decline in advertising revenue • Immense worry about lack of a model for online revenue expressed at Industry conference • Network news websites worried about monetization • Decision that content will have to move behind paywalls; subscription will drive future

Table 12.3 (cont.)

	2007	2008	2009
Innovators	• Networks incorporated innovative promotional efforts • Facebook deal with Comcast to promote its VOD site, Fancast • Second Life—NBC, CBS, MTV experiment with fantasy games • MySpace used by CW and other networks follow suit (Fad) • Video aggregator site Hulu launched in March 2007 • YouTube launched channels for networks	• Competing video aggregator FanCast was launched in January by Comcast • TitanTV, which previously offered digital TV guides, expanded to offer "website programming" and advertising solutions to broadcasters • Entertainment Tonight struck deal with Microsoft to make content available online through MSN	• Hulu became top destination for online video content • CBS was lone holdout, faced pressure to innovate or give in
Other Significant Developments	• Writer's Guild of America strike led to new types of independently produced content • Joss Whedon's "Dr. Horrible's Sing-Along-Blog" • Producers created "webisodes" and experimented with new formats rather than new platforms (inspired in part by YouTube and popularity of user generated content) • Disney's "Prom Queen"	• NBC attempted to adapt "Quarterlife," a web series, to broadcast television; it flopped and was transitioned to Bravo	• Programs attempted to engage audiences by offering interactive elements online • Extra, The Doctors • ET offered mobile application

Source: Prepared by the authors using articles from *Broadcasting & Cable.*

the day where broadband Internet access was more common. While networks did not yet fully capitalize on the interactive capabilities of the Internet, early attempts at incorporating interactivity into programming were made during this period.

A decline in advertising revenue in 2001–2002 produced general skepticism about the role of advertising online which resulted in subscription based models, for which streaming technology was provided by software companies. As online advertising revenues picked up again in 2003, networks showed renewed interest in advertiser supported models for streaming content while some networks partnered with Web companies to launch subscription only services aimed at affluent audiences who had broadband Internet access and could afford to pay for content. Other technology companies provided streaming platforms to accommodate both subscription and advertising-driven revenue models and offered targeted advertising spots and product placements. Set top boxes such as TiVo and attempts by telecom companies to launch IPTV services made streaming online content on television screens a possibility, which contributed to confusion about whether convergence would ultimately take place on the computer or the television. Phase One was the period in which the television industry cautiously waited for the Internet to be readopted by advertisers and for broadband access to grow among consumers. By 2004, networks were convinced by positive trends in both of these measures to reinvest in the medium.

Phase Two: "Now Streaming"

A weekly feature titled "Now Streaming," which listed video content recently made available online appeared in *B&C* late in 2005 and was present until the end of 2006, when the sheer volume of content online made it impossible to list in the weekly magazine. By 2005 over 50 percent of consumers had broadband access and most networks were creating content in digital formats. These factors drove most networks to undergo efforts to stream content and, by the end of 2005, most networks had made content available online. Given that everyone was "Now Streaming," the industry's dilemma in this phase was *what, when,* and *where* to stream—a departure from Phase One in which the dilemma was *whether* to stream. Broadcast and cable networks strengthened both technological and organizational infrastructures in order to enable online content delivery. New websites which capitalized on the increased bandwidth of broadband were launched to distribute content and some networks acquired existing Web properties to target specialized demographics such as women, teens, children, and Hispanics; groups that were rarely targeted through streaming in previous years. Networks experimented with unique online content such as short clips, celebrity interviews, and behind-the-scenes videos. Other networks created dedicate microsites to engage users, where they could interact with storyworlds and characters online. Some networks even premiered shows online before they went on-air, using the Web as a test ground for market research. Smaller stations without the resources to stream content online used third party software created by Internet companies to keep their websites competitive.

By 2006, availability of television content online was ubiquitous and, to grow online audiences, networks partnered with Internet companies who developed distribution platforms to aggregate video. Although the bulk of this content was advertiser supported, subscription models did not completely fade away. In particular, content was made available on mobile devices where viewing was charged on a per episode basis. Although still small, advertising revenues from commercials embedded in online episodes grew substantially from 2005 to 2006. Yet the distribution of content without the necessary metrics to ascertain the value of online audiences quickly became problematic for advertisers, producers, and stations; broadcast affiliates and studios demanded shares of online revenues citing potential cannibalization of offline audiences. The technological focus of the industry was to provide access on multiple platforms (i.e., Internet, mobile, and television) rather than seek convergence on a single device. Phase Two consisted of a frenetic surge in free content online, the implications of which were felt by the industry in subsequent years as our description of Phase Three demonstrates.

Phase Three: "The Genie is Out of the Bottle"

The adage about the "genie"—in this case, free content—is emblematic of Phase Three, which began in 2007, and this sentiment is echoed throughout *B&C* during this time. If the previous phase witnessed networks making copious amounts of content available online for free, Phase Three saw the networks struggle to deal with the consequences of these decisions. Consumers had grown accustomed to watching content online for free, yet no reliable metrics existed to monetize audiences through advertiser supported revenue models. Moreover, networks feared that further growth in online audiences would further cannibalize audiences for broadcast content, thus diminishing overall revenue. However, since content had already been made available for free, networks' focus shifted to growing both online and on-air traffic through cross-promotional campaigns. During this time, video aggregators grew in popularity as audiences sought a single source for a range of media content. Networks continued to redesign their own websites, primarily to facilitate search. Many networks acquired online outlets in hopes of reaching newer audiences, while others launched channels on YouTube, which was previously perceived as a threat. A growth in social networking websites sparked increased interest in utilizing social features of the net to drive on-air traffic. In 2007, networks promoted themselves using social networking sites such as Facebook and Second Life; by 2009, Twitter emerged as a potent marketing and audience research tool.

The Writers Guild of America strike in 2007 left many writers with free time they used to experiment with new program formats, which led to the further integration of online video with traditional forms of programming. Several of these series became popular enough to attract the interest of networks that purchased the content to be adapted to television, but very few programs made the transition successfully. Networks also integrated online formats into on-air programs by showing viral videos during programs which featured online content. The popularity of social media led networks to bring tweets and online comments into on-air television programs. It became increasingly clear that although viewers were turning to the Web for programming, growth in the sales of high definition television sets ensured time spent viewing television remained consistent, which indicated that the two mediums complemented rather than competed with one another. With the aid of Internet companies, networks were able to achieve broadcast-quality streaming which made online content more attractive and facilitated cross-platform viewing. Although audiences for online video grew substantially, appropriate metrics for monetizing them remained elusive. Alternative measures to exposure such as engagement and the inclusion of enhanced demographic and behavioral data allowed for increased targeting of advertising messages. The lack of a currency for trading online audiences especially hurt the industry during the financial crisis and resulting recession and by 2009 commentators speculated that content would ultimately have to move behind pay walls.

Factors Affecting Internet Adoption

In this section, we draw on overall trends identified above detailed in the tables, to answer the three research questions in order.

Factors Causing Uncertainty

Widespread uncertainty about the implications of the Internet on the products and practices of the television industry contributed to the lengthy and turbulent nature of the adoption process. The commercialization of the Internet attracted the attention of advertisers, and therefore of television networks. Yet networks, although keen to adopt the Internet, were uncertain how to incorporate it into existing business models. At the most basic level, networks had to determine whether the Internet would function to promote and complement on-air offerings, or act as an alternative channel. Creative products are experience goods, the value of which is known to consumers only after consumption (Caves, 2000). This is true of television content both offline and online, so networks were forced to adopt the Internet despite uncertainty about future consumer behavior online. When networks began streaming full episodes online in addition to positioning websites as information sources, they wondered whether this strategy would cannibalize on-air audiences. Adding to the weightiness of this decision was the complexity of the interorganizational field and the need to manage the impact of making content available online on studios, affiliates, and syndication partners, all of whom wanted to reap the potential benefits of the Internet, yet viewed it as a threat to traditional business models.

Networks adopted the Internet without any plan for monetizing online audiences. This uncertainty confronted networks following the stock market crash when advertising revenues online plummeted. Even in later years when online advertising grew and networks opted for an advertiser supported model over a subscription based model, the television industry remained uncertain about how to monetize audiences online because traditional measures of exposure were hard to replicate on the Internet and existing online metrics based on impressions, clicks, and leads were unsuitable for monetizing online videos. Late in 2009 an article titled, "We Need an Online Model, and Fast" confirmed that the Industry remained uncertain years later about monetizing online content as a panel of industry executives "acknowledged the need to work quickly to identify new economic models" (Sooner or Later, All of You Will Pay, 2009).

Viewing technologies, the notion of convergence, and the question of the relationship between online and on-air viewing were all sources of uncertainty in the television industry. In Phase One, the Internet was considered a complement to the television, but in Phase Two, networks perceived online viewing would cannibalize offline audiences and revenues. By Phase Three, the two mediums again were thought to complement each other and networks focused on facilitating a seamless viewing experience through set top boxes that received both Internet and television. Constant changes to technologies and their configurations have problematized what solutions the television industry has been able to conjure.

Fads and Fashions

Given the prevailing uncertainty about adopting the Internet, television networks looked to successful players in the online space for evidence of effective strategies. Owing to their fundamental dependence on advertisers, networks were influenced most by fashion setting organizations (usually Internet companies) that successfully attracted online advertising, such as Google, Amazon, and MySpace. Other networks subsequently imitated these strategies triggering a fad throughout the industry. The role of fashions and fads in influencing Internet adoption by the television industry is evident from the introduction of the Internet. In the late 1990s, television networks including CNN, CBS, Fox, and Disney had modeled themselves after portals like Yahoo! and Ask.com, positioning websites as alternative networks whose production processes ran parallel to those of traditional television stations. Yet television portals were abandoned following the stock market crash and were criticized by one analyst for being "ill-conceived, non-visionary, overpriced when being acquired, unremarkable, unclear, reactionary and badly executed" (Shaw, 2001).

The decision by networks to imitate one another in Phase Two by creating broadband websites and streaming full episodes online for free is another instance of innovation based on a fad. Initially, a handful of networks offered content geared toward specialized audiences who had broadband access and an appetite for unique content traditionally unavailable on-air. However, within a year, all manner of content was made available for free online across broadcast and cable networks. Similarly in Phase Three, competing networks' decisions to make their content available on aggregator Hulu, which used an advertiser supported revenue model, are illustrative of diffusion under conditions of uncertainty when innovations are adopted due to prevailing fashions and fads and not necessarily because they are efficient choices. Most of the time, networks also imitated each other in the nature of content they made available on their websites. In Phase One, networks' websites failed to take advantage of interactive capabilities and functioned as information providers. Interest in interactive features was triggered by the success of *American Idol*, which provided viewers with opportunities to engage with the program by voting for their favorite contestant. However, in Phase Two, most networks viewed websites as content hubs, where viewers could stream full episodes. In Phase Three, the growth of social networking websites and other user generated platforms made most networks again view websites primarily as drivers of traffic both on-air and on other online platforms, and many websites were again redesigned. The fashion setters in this phase were social media websites like Facebook, Twitter, and YouTube. In each phase, the successful companies (fashion setters) and trends in online adoption by other networks (fads) shaped the strategies of television networks.

Innovative Players

Television networks themselves had little to no expertise with the Internet, which hindered their ability to exploit the Internet's unique capabilities (i.e., targeting audiences and opportunity for two-way communication) or foresee important developments in Web based technologies. In order to adopt the Internet, the television industry needed the technical support and expertise of Internet companies that networks sought by engaging these companies in partnerships. Networks forged partnerships with Internet companies for four purposes: developing streaming technologies; creating online advertising formats, developing convergence devices, and facilitating distribution of content online. These partnerships initially formed at the fringes of the television industry, yet the necessity of such partnerships meant that Internet companies would become an integral part of the interorganizational field. Owing to television networks' dependence on them, practices initiated by these players were influential in shaping the Internet adoption by television networks.

Of course, networks did not initially have the capability to stream content online, which required them to turn to software companies like RealNetworks, WorldNow, and IBS, which provided networks with the necessary technology. Even in the later phases as streaming became prevalent, smaller stations that did not have their own broadband capabilities used platforms developed by Associated Press and Microsoft to stream content on their own sites. Yet the dependence of networks upon Internet companies did not end there; networks were also unequipped to drive traffic to their online content. After networks uploaded content online (Phase Two), they relied on distribution platforms created by AOL, Yahoo!, and other Internet giants to make their content widely accessible. Video aggregator Hulu, which emerged as the dominant destination for commercially produced online videos, although owned in part by networks, was independently managed by a private equity firm. Google's acquisition of YouTube and its subsequent popularity forced television networks to create channels on the service despite considering it a competitor. YouTube continued to be advertiser supported, and this arrangement remained the dominant model for the monetization of online videos. Firms like Microsoft, Netflix, and other technology providers introduced solutions and devices that facilitated convergence between television and the Internet. In sum, these instances indicate that Internet companies became more central than television networks in guiding how advertisers and consumers interacted with online content, including that produced by television networks. Eroded from their erstwhile position of centrality in this advertiser–consumer relationship, television networks were unsuccessful in reconciling their traditional business models with this new mode of delivery.

Conclusion

Throughout the period of this inquiry, the television industry struggled to capitalize on the Internet; though the Internet captured both audience attention and advertiser interest, television networks remained uncertain about online consumer behavior and business models. Therefore, television networks' online strategies have been heavily influenced by Internet companies, which successfully attracted online advertising dollars. This explains why networks rushed to create portals in the late 1990s, were relatively inactive in the early 2000s, created online broadband channels in 2005–2006, and from 2007–2009 again considered websites to be complements rather than act as substitutes for on-air programming. Moreover, networks had little expertise in adapting their offerings to the Internet and therefore relied on partnerships with Internet companies to implement their online strategies, and the latter guided how advertisers used the Internet. This explains why the television industry was unsuccessful in imposing traditional business models on the Internet and continues to struggle for a new online model.

Like all studies, ours too has its limitations. We rely exclusively on one data source, i.e., *Broadcasting & Cable*. Although quite a representative and reliable trade publication, it is quite possible that our interpretations were guided by the tone of the publication, especially the predictive tone of opinion pieces that appeared at the beginning of each year during our period of inquiry. Future inquiries would then do well to incorporate other sources, such as alternative trade publications or even interview industry executives. These would lend greater validity to our findings.

Despite this limitation, this study thus makes several important contributions. The longitudinal inquiry conducted here establishes that Internet adoption by the television industry was driven by a combination of certain fashions and fads from the beginning due to the complexity of the field, organizational inertia, and uncertainty about the technical efficiency of the innovation. This historical perspective facilitates a more holistic understanding of online strategies *presently* being pursued by television networks. Additionally, the impact of the transactions between various constituents of the industry on the process of Internet adoption highlights the need for scholarship on media industries to move away from "making 'industry' one thing, a monolith, rather than acknowledging that 'the' industry is comprised of numerous, sometimes conflicted and competing socio-professional communities, held together in a loose and mutating alliance by 'willed affinity'" (Caldwell, 2009, p. 200).

References

Abrahamson, E. (1991). Managerial fads and fashions: The diffusion and rejection of innovations. *Academy of Management Review*, 16(3), 586–612.

Barnes, B., & Thomson, L. (1994). Power to the people (meter): Audience measurement technology and media specialization. In J. S. Ettema & D. C. Whitney

(Eds.), *Audiencemaking: How the media create the audience* (pp. 75–94). Thousand Oaks, CA: Sage.

Boczkowski, P. (2004). *Digitizing the news: Innovation in online newspapers.* Cambridge, MA: The MIT Press.

Boddy, W. (2004). *New media and popular imagination: Launching radio, television, and digital media in the United States.* Oxford: Oxford University Press.

Caldwell, J. (2009). Cultures of production: Studying industry's deep texts, reflexive rituals, and managed self-disclosures. In J. Holt & A. Perren (Eds.), *Media industries: History, theory, and method.* Oxford: Blackwell Publishing.

Caves, R. E. (2000). *Creative industries: Contracts between art and commerce.* Cambridge, MA: London: Harvard University Press.

Chan-Olmsted, S., & Ha, L. (2003). Internet business models for broadcasters: How television stations perceive and integrate the Internet. *Journal of Broadcasting & Electronic Media,* 47(4), 597–616.

Chan-Olmsted, S., & Jung, J. (2001). Strategizing the net business: How the US television networks diversify, brand, and compete in the age of the Internet. *International Journal on Media Management,* 3(4), 213–225.

Chan-Olmsted, S., & Park, J. (2000). From on-air to online world: Examining the content and structures of broadcast TV stations' web sites. *Journalism and Mass Communication Quarterly,* 77(2), 321–339.

Cooper, A., & Schendel, D. (1976). Strategic responses to technological threats. *Business Horizons,* 19(1), 61–69.

Cooper, A., & Smith, C. (1992). How established firms respond to threatening technologies. *The Executive,* 6(2), 55–70.

DiMaggio, P., & Powell, W. (1983). The iron cage revisited: Institutional isomorphism and collective rationality in organizational fields. *American Sociological Review,* 48(2), 147–160.

Ha, L. (2002). Enhanced television strategy models: A study of TV web sites. *Internet Research,* 12(3), 235–247.

Ha, L., & Chan-Olmsted, S. (2001). Enhanced TV as brand extension: TV viewers' perception of enhanced TV features and TV commerce on broadcast networks' web sites. *International Journal on Media Management,* 3(4), 202–213.

Hirsch, P. M. (1972). Processing fads and fashions: An organization-set analysis of cultural industry systems. *The American Journal of Sociology,* 77(4), 639–659.

Holt, J., & Perren, A. (2009). *Media industries: History, theory, and method.* Oxford: Blackwell Publishing.

Kiernan, V., & Levy, M. (1999). Competition among broadcast-related web sites. *Journal of Broadcasting & Electronic Media,* 43(2), 271–279.

Leblebici, H., Salancik, G., Copay, A., & King, T. (1991). Institutional change and the transformation of interorganizational fields: An organizational history of the US radio broadcasting industry. *Administrative Science Quarterly,* 36(3), 333–363.

Lotz, A. (2007). *The television will be revolutionized.* New York: NYU Press.

Rogers, E. (1995). *Diffusion of innovations* (fourth edn.). New York: Free Press.

Shaw, R. (2001). Ta ta, TV portals. [Article]. *Broadcasting & Cable,* 131(17), 39.

Siapera, E. (2004). From couch potatoes to cybernauts? The expanding notion of the audience on TV channels' websites. *New Media & Society*, 6(2), 155–172.

Sooner or Later, All of You Will Pay. (2009). [Proceeding]. *Broadcasting & Cable*, 139(40), 3–3.

Spigel, L., & Olsson, J. (2004). *Television after TV: Essays on a medium in transition*. Durham: Duke University Press.

Tidd, J. (2001). Innovation management in context: Environment, organization and performance. *International Journal of Management Reviews*, 3(3), 169–183.

Tushman, M., & Anderson, P. (1986). Technological discontinuities and organizational environments. *Administrative Science Quarterly*, 31(3), 439–465.

Van de Ven, A. (1986). Central problems in the management of innovation. *Management Science*, 32(5), 590–607.

13

THE TRANSMEDIA EXPERIENCE IN LOCAL TV NEWS

Examining Parasocial Interaction in Viral Viewership and the Online Social Distribution of News

Joy Chavez Mapaye, Ph.D.

Before the advent of digital and social media, most would argue that talent was king on local television (Allen, 2001; Eastman, 2000). Local TV stations guarded popular anchors and reporters. Personalities dominated the local TV airwaves and, ultimately, the ratings. News managers and news consultants knew the formula was simple: the more likeable the personality, the more likeable the station, the more likely viewers would tune in and bring needed advertising revenue with them. Personality and the viability of the station have always been linked.

This linkage is a core principle behind branding. Bellamy and Traudt (2000) maintained that strong brand identity is vital to producing audiences, expanding markets, and opening new markets. They defined branding as a way to make a product "stand out" from competitors. For television, Freeman (1999) explained, this means creating a distinct personality from other channels of programming. This distinction or strong brand image has a greater likelihood of becoming part of an individual or family's routine—a phenomenon called "channel repertoire" (Ferguson, 1992; Heeter & Greenberg, 1988). Research has shown that despite the unending number of channel choices, viewers tend to follow a routine and limit their choice to select channels. Bellamy and Traudt emphasized that differentiation is vital in establishing this type of loyalty. Anchors and other news personalities help to provide this difference.

Some scholars argue it is also this difference that will help people cross media platforms. Jenkins (2006) maintains that people are more likely to pursue a transmedia experience if there is an emotional attachment, something Jenkins' research refers to as "affective economics." Jenkins found evidence of affective ties in entertainment television. In local television news, Levy (1979) found evidence of this emotional bond in the form of parasocial interaction.

The notion of parasocial interaction (PSI) establishes that emotional bonds can exist between audience members and mediated personalities. A parasocial relationship is one-sided and not reciprocal (Horton & Wohl, 1956). It is the audience member, not the mediated performer, who forms the relationship through continual encounters over time. In some cases, this bond could be even more important than the television content itself (Giles, 2002; Perse, 1990).

In 1999, Hoerner adapted the PSI scale to examine interaction between Web visitors and Web sites. Rather than actual persons as the basis for parasocial interaction, Hoerner maintained that the persona of the Web site itself could be the foundation of a parasocial relationship. However, while Hoerner helped move the study of parasocial interaction to the Internet, no studies have yet applied Web PSI to that of local TV news Web sites. Further, despite the range of activity regarding TV PSI in the late 1980s and early 1990s, very little movement has taken place in terms of developing the TV PSI construct. This is especially true in terms of its applicability to the local news context and how parasocial interaction affects the loyalty and commitment of online viewers. In addition to these theoretical limitations, the conceptualization of the television news audience has not been fully developed in parasocial research. Past studies in parasocial interaction have failed to recognize the capabilities of audience members to do promotional work on behalf of local news stations. In a digital and social media age, these capabilities can no longer be ignored in the management and marketing of local TV news. As such, this study attempts to address all of these issues surrounding parasocial interaction by assessing the importance of parasocial interaction on local TV news Web site visitors' loyalty and commitment to the TV station's news programs, station Web site, and station brand.

Background and Context

TV News Changes

In the late 1990s and early 2000s, social media emerged as a new and different way to engage the TV news audience. Social media is defined as public or semi-public Web-based services that allow people to view and share connections and commentary online (Boyd & Ellison, 2007). The early 2000s saw an explosion in social media sites (Boyd & Ellison, 2007). Friendster came out in 2002, followed by MySpace in 2003, Facebook in 2004, and YouTube in 2005. In many ways, YouTube revolutionized video sharing. Prior to YouTube, it was difficult for ordinary people to disseminate video content to a potential audience of millions. Many other social networking sites also developed at this time, including Twitter in 2006, foursquare in 2009, and Pinterest in 2010. Television news took notice and with good reason. From 2005 to 2009, the share of adult Internet users using social network sites more than quadrupled from 8 percent to 35 percent and the number of users is projected to continue to increase exponentially (Lenhart, 2009).

The 2010 Pew report described today's new multi-platform media environment as portable, personalized, and participatory (Purcell, Rainie, Mitchell, Rosenstiel, & Olmstead, 2010). Approximately 37 percent of Internet users help create news content, comment about news, or disseminate news through social media sites such as Facebook or Twitter. Of those who get news online, 75 percent get news through e-mails that have been forwarded or posts on social network sites and 52 percent share news links through e-mail or networks. News is now social and participatory.

Viral Viewers: Audience as Promotion

Indeed, the new media environment has allowed TV viewers and online news users to be part of the news promotion process. Whereas distinctions previously existed between audience and promotion, today the audience itself functions as promotion. Rather than simply promoting to an audience, the audience can help promote the television news content to others.

In some ways, this has always been the case. Marketing practitioners and scholars are quick to point out that word-of-mouth communication (WOM) has been around for a while (O'Leary & Sheehan, 2008). Yet, as Cheong and Morrison (2008) observed, more research remains to be done on the influence of what they call a "revolution" in electronic WOM and user-generated content. Many consider viral marketing to be part of this revolution. Viral marketing is defined as a phenomenon that facilitates or encourages people to pass along a marketing message or a particular brand's story though "word-of-mouse" (Scott, 2010). It is the idea that information and content can spread quickly from one person to the next via the Internet. This content can now also include videos. TV news content today can be passed on from one person to an entire network of people fairly easily. The content is often "contagious" or viral, spreading quickly. In many cases, television today is not just viewed, but reviewed, customized, and then passed on. Today's social and digital media landscape has enabled the emergence of a new type of local and national television news audience: the viral viewer.

This study characterizes viral viewers as engaged and committed segments of the television audience. These viewers are not only loyal; they work to promote television brands and products. In the case of local television news, they can help promote news stories and function as fans, perhaps motivated in part by parasocial interaction or affective ties to the station's news personalities or news site. This research seeks to determine to what extent these viral viewers exist on local television news Web sites and to examine the formation of the online local television news audience's loyalty and commitment to the station news brand.

Literature Review

TV and Branding

Despite the amount of applied research generated regarding local television news and branding, academic research on the topic has been scarce. While branding is deeply entrenched in marketing literature, its application to the media industry and television is still developing (Chan-Olmsted & Kim, 2001). Although some published studies have been closely related (Aaker, 1996; Keller, 1998; Owen, 1993; Ryan, 1999), few academic studies have examined media branding in television.

Bellamy and Traudt (2000) sought to address this gap with their study on television branding as promotion. The authors called attention to the importance of branding in television by stating, "It is perhaps the only means of gaining a place in a television viewer's channel repertoire" (p. 157). The concept of channel repertoire essentially ties into the idea of brand loyalty. Bellamy and Traudt identified viewer satisfaction, viewer loyalty, and personality as particularly relevant to television. However, while these attributes are all important, Hughes (2008) argued the most essential aspect of brands in the current marketing environment has not yet been studied: whether or not customers are willing to evangelize the product.

Hughes maintained that in order to measure evangelization only two questions are needed for any survey: (1) How did you hear about us? (2) Would you go out of your way to recommend our product to a friend? (p. 218) The first question tracks marketing effectiveness and WOM. The second question provides the degree of evangelization the consumer is willing to provide.

To some extent, the idea of evangelization is rooted in the concept of opinion leaders. The idea first emerged during the 1940s presidential election. Later, Katz and Lazarsfeld (1955) showed the applicability of interpersonal influence in other contexts (food, fashion, entertainment, etc.). Levy (1979) demonstrated that this influence also was relevant to TV news, where individuals engaged in surveillance of news topics in order to tell others about news. In marketing, Feick and Price's (1987) concept of market mavens also articulated the need to examine opinion leaders and interpersonal influence on brands.

For the television brand, the product can be both on-air and online. Ha and Chan-Olmsted (2004) established Web sites as extensions of the television brand and helped determine predictors of loyalty. Based on a random sample, standard multiple regression determined five features most likely to predict loyalty for cable television sites: (1) news/weather updates; (2) background for news; (3) information about stars/gossip; (4) episode synopsis; and (5) sweepstakes. Additionally, the study discovered the three most important sources of knowledge about the networks' Web sites were through cross promotion on television, search engines, and WOM. However, fully examining cross promotion was difficult in that a large number of respondents were non-television Web site visitors. Nevertheless, Ha and Chan-Olmsted helped ascertain predictors of loyalty for potential members of the online television audience.

Building on the idea of improving loyalty, Gupta and Kim (2007) explored ways to increase engagement and develop commitment in virtual communities. Data for the study were collected from a Web site for two weeks. Gupta and Kim found that the balanced effects of cognition (usefulness and quality) and affect (pleasure and arousal) were important factors to consider in the formation of commitment. Commitment is defined as the "member's helping behavior and active participation in the virtual community" (p. 30). The researchers maintained that understanding the mechanism by which this commitment is formed is essential.

Transmedia Storytelling and Affective Economics

For media companies, programs on different media platforms help to extend the company or show brand (Eastman, 2000). Through synergy, media companies attempt to provide different points of entry for the audience. Often, the transmedia experience or transmedia storytelling is used to bring an audience from one medium to another. Jenkins defines transmedia storytelling as multiple texts of the narrative, a story not contained within a single medium.

Caldwell (2003) argues these strategies attempt to build a relationship as well as an emotional bond with the audience. Through individualization and immersion of media content, members of the audience become invested in story, and ultimately, the brand. As Caldwell explains, effective branding "is frequently praised for having created psychological and empathic relationships with consumers" (p. 138).

Jenkins suggested that a perspective grounded in affective economics was better suited to explain television audience and promotion in today's participatory culture. Affective economics takes into account the multiple platforms and applications that comprise digital and social media. This approach is based on feelings and uses emotional capital to harness audience activity to help with television promotion. Jenkins (2006) noted that many have called affective economics "the solution to a perceived crisis in American broadcasting—a crisis brought about by shifts in media technology that are granting viewers much greater control over the flow of media into their homes" (p. 54).

While somewhat critical of the profit motive behind promotion and marketing efforts, Jenkins (2006) reconciled that the old television model of audience flow appeared inadequate in the new digital environment. Jenkins noted that audience measurement was often "clumsy" and that the "impression" or ratings method of measuring an audience does not provide much information. Impressions simply count who is there. Expressions, however, are affect-based and provide quality evaluation of a broadcast product. This evaluation includes attentiveness to programming and long-term investment in the television brand.

In order to assess whether affect brought TV viewers across platforms, Jenkins conducted an online survey of *American Idol* viewers. The survey was posted on the official FOX Web site. Results of the survey indicated most fans discovered the show through WOM. Some found the show through channel surfing and began watching because of program awareness through promotions. An emotional connection developed with show contestants as viewers got to know contestants' backgrounds and aspirations.

TV and Parasocial Interaction

The notion of an emotional connection with television personae began in the 1950s, when Horton and Wohl (1956) published their seminal work on parasocial interaction, in the journal *Psychiatry*. The authors were interested in what they described as observations of intimacy from a distance or the illusion of face-to-face relationships with mediated performers.

However, while the concept of parasocial interaction was groundbreaking, it didn't gain significant attention until the advent of uses and gratifications research in the 1970s (Spigel & Olsson, 2004). Years after, Levy (1979) attempted to test parasocial interaction and investigate the concept as it applied to television news. The data provided evidence for parasocial interaction. Levy noted that members of the news audience created affective ties with newscasters; these ties were further strengthened over shared experiences. These experiences included important news stories or the "happy talk" banter among newscasters. Viewers with higher levels of parasocial behavior increased their exposure to the newscasts, hoping to have more opportunities to "interact" with the news personae.

Several years later, Rubin, Perse, and Powell (1985) created a 20-item PSI scale. In 1987, Rubin and Perse modified the original 20-item parasocial interaction scale to 10 items. Since then, the 10-item scale has been used to study a range of questions concerning TV viewing motivation (Conway & Rubin, 1991), satisfaction with soap operas (Perse & Rubin, 1988), local TV news involvement (Perse, 1990), and others.

For the online platform, Hoerner (1999) was the first to adapt the PSI scale. Hoerner sought to examine the interaction between Web visitors and the Web site as a persona. The study argued that the definition of persona as outlined by Horton and Wohl (1956) has changed and that the "literal, mediated personality of the newscast or soap opera is gone" (p. 146). Instead, Hoerner maintained that Web sites can be free of an actual persona and can function as the persona itself. In other words, it is possible for visitors to Web sites to form parasocial relationships with the site alone. Hoerner maintained Web sites could have personality.

Using Rubin et al.'s (1985) original 20-item TV PSI scale, Hoerner developed a 15-item scale, modifying items to reflect online users' Web browsing activity. Research participants from a university sample were used to test the new Web PSI scale. The 15-item scale was reduced to 10 items after factor analysis revealed some statements did not contribute to parasocial interaction.

Hypotheses

Given the review of literature, this study proposes four hypotheses. The hypotheses seek to reexamine findings and relationships from previous studies and place them in the new context of local TV news, using a purposive online audience sample. Key constructs for this study include: TV PSI (Rubin, 1994; Rubin & Perse, 1987a, 1987b); Web PSI (Hoerner, 1999); loyalty (Ha & Chan-Olmsted, 2004); and commitment (Gupta & Kim, 2007). All Cronbach alpha values were at 0.8 or above, which is considered preferable in social science studies (Field, 2005). Past studies have found all scales used for this study to be reliable and valid. While the TV PSI, Web PSI, and loyalty constructs remain relatively unchanged from the cited studies, the commitment construct has been modified to incorporate items that assess digital evangelization or willingness to help promote television content on air and online through "viral" means. Gupta and Kim's (2007) original commitment construct did not incorporate the element of evangelization, otherwise known as word-of-mouth (WOM) or participants' willingness to help make content "viral" online. As WOM is critical to branding, inclusion of this component to the commitment construct will be beneficial and complementary to the loyalty construct used by Ha and Chan-Olmsted (2004). Underlying this modified commitment construct is the notion of affective economics theorized by Jenkins (2006) and Hughes' (2008) concept of evangelization.

While the hypotheses for these earlier studies helped to establish key relationships, these relationships have not been examined within the local TV news environment. This study hopes to assess whether these relationships exist within this framework. For the first two hypotheses, Gupta and Kim (2007) established that cognition variables (usefulness and quality) are positively related to commitment toward the site. While this relationship has not been established for the loyalty construct, or the relationship with local TV news stations, the literature, particularly Ha and Chan-Olmsted (2004), indicates the relationships could be applicable to local TV news stations and their Web sites. For the last two hypotheses, Rubin and Perse (1987a, 1987b) and Hoerner (1999) have shown these affective relationships as predictors of loyalty and repeat viewing and visiting. These constructs have not yet been applied to the commitment scale. However, the literature indicates these positive relationships could exist. Once these relationships are assessed, standard multiple regression is proposed similar to Ha and Chan-Olmsted to determine the best predictor of loyalty and commitment.

> H1: Perceived station usefulness and quality is positively related to loyalty and commitment toward the station and site.
>
> H2: Perceived site usefulness and quality is positively related to loyalty and commitment toward the station and site.
>
> H3: Perceived relationships, in the form of TV PSI, are positively related to loyalty and commitment toward the station and site.
>
> H4: Perceived relationships, in the form of Web PSI, are positively related to loyalty and commitment toward the station and site.

Method

Web site visitors to six local TV stations in the Pacific Northwest were invited to participate in the online survey posted on each station's Web site. The survey participants represented the online local TV news audience for one station in Alaska (KTUU), one in Washington (KHQ), and four in Oregon (KEZI, KOBI, KDRV, and KOHD). Given the purposive sample, the overall response rate could not be calculated. However, the validity of the sample was assessed through comparative means. Comparisons with previous studies show the sample exhibits a similar profile to that of Internet users in past studies (King, 1998; "The State of the News Media," 2010). To further assess validity, responses were compared using statistical tests. These responses showed there were no statistically significant differences between early responders and late responders of the survey, therefore strengthening validity arguments.

Recruitment contact protocols followed the procedures outlined in Dillman's (2007) Tailored Design Method (TDM). Following a pilot test, the survey was administered the last two weeks of October 2009 and the first two weeks of November 2009. As an incentive to participate, respondents were offered a chance to win a $150 gift certificate from Amazon.com.

Four hypotheses summed up the core relationships this study sought to examine. In order to answer the hypotheses, correlation analysis was used. First, the research used a Pearson product–moment correlation coefficient to investigate the strength of the relationship between two variables for each of the hypotheses. Only variables found to have significant relationships from the correlation analysis were used for multiple regression. Multiple regression is an extension of correlation. The technique is used not only to explore relationships, but also to examine the predictive ability of independent variables on one continuous dependent variable (Aaker, Kumar, & Day, 2007). In the case of this study, standard multiple regression was used to determine the best predictor of loyalty and commitment.

Results

Respondent Profile

In total, 327 respondents started the survey. Responses from the six stations involved in the study were as follows: KHQ (N = 107), KTUU (N = 111), KEZI (N = 69), KOBI (N = 18), KDRV (N = 11), and KOHD (N = 11). Overall, 277 surveys were valid for analysis. Approximately 62.6 percent of respondents were women, 37.4 percent were men. The majority of respondents (76 percent) were White/Anglo, while 10.3 percent identified themselves American Indian/Native American/Alaska Native; a little more than 5 percent total were Black/African American or Hispanic/Latino. Those who consider themselves Asian/Pacific Islander, mixed race/ethnicity, or preferred not to answer made up 8 percent of total respondents. The mean age for respondents was 45, with the minimum age at 18, the maximum at 77 years old. Most respondents had some college education (44.3 percent) or their bachelor's degree (23.3 percent).

Respondent Media Use Profile

The majority of respondents visited the local TV news site where they found the survey because of habit (53.3 percent), a story during the station's newscast (12.5 percent), a promotion during the newscast or commercial break (6.3 percent), a blog article or link (5.2 percent), or a combination of both on-air and online means (10.5 percent). Most respondents visited the site often, visiting several times a week (30 percent), once a day (17.1 percent), or several times a day (18.8 percent).

A majority of respondents (91.6 percent) watch local television news and specifically watch the on-air newscasts affiliated with the TV news site (90.5 percent). Those who watch the on-air newscasts affiliated with the site watch often: several times a week (28.4 percent); once a day (31.5 percent); or several times a day (25.9 percent). Most respondents watch these newscasts during their regularly scheduled time (81 percent), use a combination of watching live newscasts, on the Internet or recorded by DVR (9.5 percent), or the Internet alone to watch newscasts (5.6 percent). As a whole, respondents felt the TV station associated with the Web site was different from other TV stations in the area. A 1 indicated strong disagreement; a 5 pointed to strong agreement that the station was indeed different. The idea of station difference resonated with respondents (M = 3.73, SD = 1.11). As for satisfaction with news from the local station (1 indicated not at all satisfied, 5 meant extremely satisfied), respondents tended to be quite satisfied (M = 4.22, SD = 0.854), with very little variability in the assessment of this satisfaction.

In addition to these questions, respondents were asked about their relationship with their favorite newscaster. Ninety percent of respondents did not personally know their favorite newscaster, 80 percent had never met their favorite newscaster in person, and 92 percent had never attempted to contact their favorite newscaster. Of those who had attempted to contact their favorite newscaster, most used e-mail, while one mentioned using the phone. Another respondent reported using Facebook to initiate contact. Online, 81 percent had not read their favorite newscaster's biography on the Web site, while 15 percent reported reading newscaster biographies. The rest reported the newscaster did not have a biography on the Web site. In order, the five highest rated items on the TV PSI scale were: I see my favorite newscaster as a natural, down-to-earth person; if there were a story about my favorite newscaster in the newspaper, magazine, or online, I would read it; I look forward to watching my favorite newscaster on the news; when my favorite newscaster reports a story, he or she seems to understand the kinds of things I want to know; my favorite newscaster makes me feel comfortable, as if I am with a good friend.

Hypothesis 1

Hypothesis 1 predicted that perceived usefulness and quality of the TV news Web site is positively related to loyalty and commitment toward the station and site. The results indicate there is a positive correlation between the variables of site usefulness and quality and loyalty (r = 0.470, p = 0.001), with moderate levels of site usefulness and quality associated with loyalty. Usefulness and quality helps to explain nearly 22 percent of the variance in respondents' scores on the loyalty scale. Results also showed that site usefulness and quality is positively correlated with commitment (r = 0.438, p = 0.001), with moderate levels of usefulness and quality associated with commitment. Site usefulness and quality helps to explain approximately 18 percent of the variance in respondents' scores on the commitment scale.

Hypothesis 2

Hypothesis 2 predicted that perceived usefulness and quality of the TV station's local news programming is positively related to loyalty and commitment toward the station and site. The results show there is a positive correlation between the variables of usefulness and quality of local news and loyalty (r = 0.444, p = 0.001), with moderate levels of usefulness and quality of local news associated with loyalty. Usefulness and quality of local news helps to explain nearly 19 percent of the variance in respondents' scores on the loyalty scale. Results also showed that usefulness and quality of local news is positively correlated with commitment (r = 0.433, p = 0.001), with moderate levels of usefulness and quality of local news associated with commitment. Usefulness and quality of local news helps to explain approximately 18 percent of the variance in respondents' scores on the commitment scale.

Hypothesis 3

Hypothesis 3 predicted that perceived relationships, in the form of TV parasocial interaction, is positively related to loyalty and commitment toward the station and site. The results indicate there is a positive correlation between the variables of TV parasocial interaction and loyalty (r = 0.397, p = 0.001), with moderate levels of parasocial interaction associated with loyalty. TV parasocial interaction helps to explain nearly 16 percent of the variance in respondents' scores on the loyalty scale. Results also showed that TV parasocial interaction is positively correlated with commitment (r = 0.417, p = 0.001), with moderate levels of parasocial interaction associated with commitment. TV parasocial interaction helps to explain approximately 17 percent of the variance in respondents' scores on the commitment scale.

Hypothesis 4

Hypothesis 4 predicted that perceived relationships, in the form of Web parasocial interaction, is positively related to loyalty and commitment toward the station and site. The results show there is a positive correlation between the variables of Web parasocial interaction and loyalty ($r = 0.517$, $p = 0.001$), with moderately high levels of parasocial interaction associated with loyalty. Web parasocial interaction helps to explain nearly 26 percent of the variance in respondents' scores on the loyalty scale. Results also showed that Web parasocial interaction is positively correlated with commitment ($r = 0.574$, $p = 0.001$), with high levels of parasocial interaction associated with commitment. Web parasocial interaction helps to explain approximately 32 percent of the variance in respondents' scores on the commitment scale.

Correlation analysis determined relationships existed with the four variables of site usefulness and quality, station usefulness and quality, TV parasocial interaction, and Web parasocial interaction when correlated with loyalty and commitment. Once these relationships were established, standard multiple regression was used to conclude which of the four variables was the best predictor of both loyalty and commitment.

The results of the first model indicated the four predictors explained 37 percent of the variance in loyalty ($R^2 = 0.366$, $F_{(4,193)} = 27.88$, $p = 0.001$). Web parasocial interaction significantly predicted loyalty ($\beta = 0.30$, $p = 0.001$), as did station usefulness and quality ($\beta = 0.226$, $p = 0.001$), and TV parasocial interaction ($\beta = 0.180$, $p = 0.005$). However, site usefulness and quality ($\beta = 0.078$, $p = 0.386$ n.s.) did not contribute significantly to the regression model.

The results of the second model indicated the four predictors explained 41 percent of the variance in commitment ($R^2 = 0.413$, $F_{(4,188)} = 33.07$, $p = 0.001$). It was found that Web parasocial interaction significantly predicted commitment ($\beta = 0.477$, $p = 0.001$), as did station usefulness and quality ($\beta = 0.228$, $p = 0.001$), and TV parasocial interaction ($\beta = 0.183$, $p = 0.004$). However, site usefulness and quality ($\beta = -0.082$, $p = 0.351$ n.s.) did not contribute significantly to the regression model.

The four hypotheses accurately predicted positive relationships with station usefulness and quality, site usefulness and quality, TV parasocial interaction, and Web parasocial interaction with loyalty and commitment. Both regression models showed that out of these variables, Web parasocial interaction, station usefulness and quality, and TV parasocial interaction all serve as statistically significant predictors of loyalty and commitment. In addition, Web parasocial interaction exhibited the largest beta coefficient when compared to the contribution of other variables.

Discussion

Implications for Theory

This research helped to bridge three important gaps in local television news scholarship. First, the study brought parasocial interaction into the digital age by applying both the TV and Web parasocial constructs to local TV news. Second, the study sought to re-conceptualize the online local TV news audience as both capable of functioning as audience members and as active promoters of TV content, establishing the notion of viral viewers. The modification of Gupta and Kim's (2007) commitment construct helped to further develop this concept. Third, this research addressed the need to integrate and update the academic literature on branding and local TV news to address the transmedia environment of today's digital media ecosystem.

Correlation analysis for the study's hypotheses showed support for the propositions predicting positive relationships with loyalty and commitment and the variables of station usefulness and quality, site usefulness and quality, TV PSI, and Web PSI. However, the regression models showed not all these variables had significant contributions. As a predictor of loyalty and commitment, the regression models point to Web PSI as the strongest indicator. Respondents who had higher Web PSI scores were more likely to be loyal ($\beta = 0.30$, $p = 0.001$) or committed ($\beta = 0.477$, $p = 0.001$) to the news station and site. Those with higher TV PSI scores were also likely to be loyal ($\beta = 0.180$, $p = 0.005$) or committed ($\beta = 0.183$, $p = 0.004$), but not as strongly as Web PSI. The data also showed that station usefulness and quality, not site usefulness and quality contributed significantly to the regression models. These results suggest that persona is critical to branding. The stronger an online viewer's relationship and emotional connection with the station Web site, the more likely the viewer will be loyal and committed. In addition, while television news personalities also help to foster loyalty and commitment, the usefulness and quality of a station's newscasts matters more. The usefulness and quality of the station site, however, comes second to the site's personality and does not help predict loyalty and commitment outcomes.

News Anchors/Personalities

Indeed, the results from statistical tests involving TV PSI show that news anchors and news personalities matter to viewers' loyalty and commitment. The power of this affective tie is evident in other higher-rated scale items: viewers were willing to cross platforms to learn more about their favorite newscaster. In addition, respondents also looked forward to their interactions via the newscasts. However, while viewers were willing to cross platforms for their favorite newscaster, respondents' media use show respondents might not be ready to take the TV parasocial relationship to the next level. The majority of respondents had not read their favorite newscaster's biography, blog, or contributed comments to the newscaster's blog.

While seemingly contradictory, Giles (2002) argued the phenomenon of parasocial interaction is fairly complex, with varying degrees of PSI based on different media figures. Rather than examine PSI in isolation, Giles maintained that PSI should be considered in the matrix of usual social activity. In other words, most respondents appeared content with their current newscaster relationship via television newscasts. Once respondents feel the need to elevate this relationship, they will take action to do so by going online or accessing other media in order to fulfill their parasocial relationship needs. The bottom line, however, is that news personalities remain important to viewers and the station.

News Web Sites

The results from statistical tests involving Web PSI showed that a Web site's persona or design matters to viewers' loyalty and commitment. This study showed strong evidence that Web persona was relevant to site design. What requires more study, however, was whether this persona was intrinsic to the site alone or whether the persona was transferred from the station's newscasters. Given that the Web PSI items came before the TV PSI items and newscaster questions, this study leans toward the conclusion that scores were based on site persona alone, divorced from the station's newscasters. News managers should also take note that most respondents visited the site often, visiting several times a week (30 percent), once a day (17.1 percent), or several times a day (18.3 percent). Respondents also rated several features found on local TV news Web sites. Of the features, the majority selected "always" for local news, breaking news, and weather. Lastly, respondents believed a Web site should also be useful with current issues and events, followed by easy to use. In both design and practice, respondents wanted the site updated often and news items of interest easily found.

Promotion/Audience

The results showed that cross promotion was essential to local television news Web site traffic. While the data indicated most respondents came to the site out of habit, a good number of respondents (17 percent) visited the site because of promotion on the station's newscast or during a commercial break. Furthermore, the commitment construct demonstrated that the online TV news audience was willing to promote the station and its news content if given the opportunity and the right content to do so.

However, while the audience is committed to spreading television news content, part of that commitment is stipulated on the notion that the news stories are "interesting." Stations must continue to produce good content in order to make use of viral viewers. As Mantrala, Naik, Sridhar, and Thorson (2007) pointed out, good content is at the core of news products. The respondent comment below exhibits this need for quality and usefulness, intertwined with parasocial interaction. The comment also displays willingness to pass the news content to others via social networks reinforcing today's new multi-platform media environment as portable, personalized, and participatory (Purcell et al., 2010):

> Tonight I wanted to know more about the breaking news of the command post for the H1N1. I have the swine flu and can't leave my house until I am not running a fever. The 11 p.m. news is not on here yet, I will check in the morning as I wanted to Facebook the article to my friends ... I do love channel 12 as they don't forget us in Grants Pass. I like all the newscasters so picking one is too hard.

Limitations and Future Research

This study is unique in that it brought TV PSI research to the digital age and placed Web PSI research in the local television news context. The introduction of the viral viewers' concept further enhances research on audience and promotion. These contributions, however, also come with some limitations.

To begin, the tests used to assess relationships were correlation and multiple regression analysis. Neither approaches claim definitive cause and effect relationships. These relationships can only be established through experiments. The strength of relationships, however, was established.

Another limitation of this study was the nonrandom sample. Because of this, caution should be taken when projecting results to a population other than the one surveyed. However, given that the original studies on TV and Web PSI both involved convenience samples from university classrooms, this research actually provides fresh insight into both constructs in that the research's purposive sample involved real-world respondents from the population of interest. As Ha and Chan-Olmsted (2004) found, even a random sample can make analysis difficult if the sample does not possess the specific qualities sought for the study.

Even with these limitations, however, the research's respondent profile was relatively similar compared to previous studies (King, 1998; "The State of the News Media," 2010). T-tests were also used to examine key variables for differences between early and late respondents. No differences were found. Radhakrishna and Doamekpor (2008) maintained that when t-tests showed no difference between early respondents and late respondents, it is possible to generalize the findings to the population. While this approach is cautioned (Dillman, 2007), the tests did help establish some measure of validity. According to Wimmer and Dominick (2006) validity is always a matter of degree; no study is completely valid or invalid. Most studies end up in the middle. It is believed this study found that middle ground By focusing on exploring the strength of relationships rather than demographic data, this research achieved its purpose.

It is hoped that this is just the beginning for research in this area. Future research should consider some of the limitations above as well as various methods. A quantitative content analysis of parasocial interaction on local TV news Web sites would complement results from this study. This content analysis could even include an examination of different factors that contribute to "viral worthy" news stories. Lastly, the affective nature of Web sites also holds great potential. This study found that Web PSI was the strongest contribution to loyalty and commitment. A study of a Web site's affective elements could uncover important insights regarding design.

Conclusion

This is the first research of its kind to fully embrace the digital local television news environment and fundamental changes in audience. By incorporating branding, television, and affect, this study brought parasocial interaction to a new level of understanding and provided insight regarding the audience's role in today's transmedia ecosystem.

First, this research illuminates the continued importance of parasocial relationships in local television news. Far from eliminating longtime anchors, news managers should assess the overall value of a news personality to the station. This evaluation should include a news talent's role in cross promotion to online, mobile, and social media platforms.

Second, parasocial relationships are also important in Web design. Designing a site with a welcoming persona helps establish relationships with the online audience. Design should also incorporate elements that facilitate ease of use and foster online communities. In addition, Web site content should be frequently updated and news items easily found.

Third, news managers should keep a close watch on news content and quality, while attempting to produce news stories with viral potential. Rather than focusing on news production that begins and ends with "on air" content to an audience, news managers should cultivate a mindset where the audience also functions as promotion.

As with all brands, loyalty and commitment take time to cultivate. This study shows that developing an audience is not achieved by marketing/

branding alone. While parasocial relationships help bring the audience to newscasts or to the Web site, the audience will only come back so long as they receive value for their time.

This research concludes that good content and good talent in local television news are ultimately contagious. Building on these fundamentals and with the help of viral viewers, local television's continued transition to the transmedia environment and digital news age is one that warrants both scholars and practitioners watch closely and stay tuned.

References

Aaker, D. A. (1996). *Building strong brands*. New York: Free Press.

Aaker, D. A., Kumar, V., & Day, G. S. (2007). *Marketing research* (ninth edn.). Hoboken, NJ: John Wiley & Sons, Inc.

Allen, C. M. (2001). *News is people: The rise of local TV news and the fall of news from New York*. Ames, IA: Iowa State University Press.

Bellamy, R. V., & Traudt, P. J. (2000). Television branding as promotion. In S. T. Eastman (Ed.), *Research in media promotion* (pp. 127–159). Mahwah, NJ: Lawrence Erlbaum Associates, Inc.

Boyd, D. M., & Ellison, N. B. (2007). Social network sites: Definition, history, and scholarship. *Journal of Computer-Mediated Communication*, 13(1), article 11. Retrieved February 10, 2010, from http://jcmc.indiana.edu/vol13/issue1/boyd.ellison.html

Caldwell, J. T. (2003). Second-shift media aesthetics: Programming, interactivity, and user flows. In A. Everett & J. T. Caldwell (Eds.), *New media: Theories and practices of digitexuality* (pp. 127–144). New York: Routledge, Taylor and Francis Books, Inc.

Conway, J. C., & Rubin, A. M. (1991). Psychological predictors of television viewing motivation. *Communication Research*, 18, 443–463.

Chan-Olmsted, S. M., & Kim, Y. (2001). Perceptions of branding among television station managers: An exploratory analysis. *Journal of Broadcasting and Electronic Media*, 45(1), 75–91.

Cheong, H. J., & Morrison, M. A. (2008). Consumers' reliance on product information and recommendations found in UGC. *Journal of Interactive Advertising*, 8(2), 1–29. Retrieved May 3, 2010, from http://proxy.consortiumlibrary.org/login?url=http://search.ebscohost.com.proxy.consortiumlibrary.org/login.aspx?direct=true&db=buh&AN=31929438&site=ehost-live

Dillman, D. A. (2007). *Mail and internet surveys: The tailored design method* (second edn.). Hoboken, NJ: John Wiley & Sons, Inc.

Eastman, S. T. (Ed.). (2000). *Research in media promotion*. Mahwah, NJ: Lawrence Erlbaum Associates, Inc.

Feick, L. F., & Price, L. L. (1987). The market maven: A diffuser of marketplace information. *Journal of Marketing*, 51(1), 83–97.

Ferguson, D. A. (1992). Channel repertoire in the presence of remote control devices, VCRS and cable television. *Journal of Broadcasting and Electronic Media*, 38, 83–91.

Field, A. (2005). *Discovering statistics using SPSS* (second edn.). Thousand Oaks, CA: Sage Publications.

Freeman, L. (1999, June 7). On TV, image is everything. *Electronic Media*, 18.

Giles, D. (2002, August). Parasocial interaction: A review of the literature and a model for future research. *Media Psychology*, 4(3), 279–305.

Gupta, S., & Kim, H. (2007, January). Developing the commitment to virtual community: The balanced effects of cognition and affect. *Information Resources Management Journal*, 20(1), 28–45.

Ha, L., & Chan-Olmsted, S. M. (2004). Cross media use in electronic media: The role of cable television Web sites in cable television network branding and viewership. *Journal of Broadcasting and Electronic Media*, 48(4), 620–645.

Heeter, C., & Greenberg, B. S. (1988). *Cableviewing*. Norwood, N.J: Ablex.

Hoerner, J. (1999). Scaling the Web: A parasocial interaction scale for World Wide Web sites. In D. W. Schumann & E. Thorson (Eds.), *Advertising and the World Wide Web* (pp. 135–147). Mahwah, NJ: Lawrence Erlbaum Associates.

Horton, D., & Wohl, R. R. (1955). Mass communication and para-social interaction. *Psychiatry*, 19, 215–229.

Hughes, M. (2008). *Buzzmarketing: Get people to talk about your stuff*. New York: The Penguin Group.

Jenkins, H. (2006). *Convergence culture: Where old and new media collide*. New York: New York University Press.

Katz, E., & Lazarsfeld, P. F. (1955). *Personal influence: The part played by people in the flow of mass communications*. Glencoe, IL: Free Press.

Keller, K. (1998). *Strategic management: Building, measuring, and managing brand equity*. New Jersey: Prentice Hall.

Key news audiences now blend online and traditional sources. (2008). *Pew Research Center*. Retrieved November 1, 2008, from http://people-press.org/report/444/news-media

King, R. E. (1998). *The uses and gratifications of the World Wide Web: An audience analysis for local television news broadcasters (Doctoral dissertation)*. The University of Tennessee, Knoxville, TN.

Lenhart, A. (2009). Adults and social network Websites. *Pew Research Center's Internet & American Life Project*. Retrieved March 1, 2010, from http://www.pewinternet.org/Reports/2009/Adults-and-Social-Network-Websites.aspx

Levy, M. R. (1979). Watching TV news as para-social interaction. *Journal of Broadcasting*, 23, 69–80.

Mantrala, M., Naik, P., Sridhar, S., & Thorson, E. (2007, April). Uphill or downhill? Locating the firm on a profit function. *Journal of Marketing*, 71(2), 26–44. Retrieved March 20, 2009, doi:10.1509/jmkg.71.2.26

O'Leary, S., & Sheehan, K. (2008). *Building a buzz to beat the big boys: Word-of-mouth marketing for small businesses*. Westport, CT: Greenwood Publishing Group, Inc.

Owen, S. (1993). The Landor imagepower survey: A global assessment of brand strength. In D. A. Aaker & A. L. Biel (Eds.), *Brand equity and advertising: Advertising's role in building strong brands* (pp. 11–32). Hillsdale, NJ: Lawrence Erlbaum Associates.

Perse, E. M. (1990). Media involvement and local news effects. *Journal of Broadcasting and Electronic Media*, 34, 17–36.

Perse, E. M., & Rubin, A. M. (1988). Audience activity and satisfaction with favorite television soap opera. *Journalism Quarterly*, 65, 368–375.

Purcell, K., Rainie, L., Mitchell, A., Rosenstiel, T., & Olmstead, K. (2010). Understanding the participatory news consumer. *Pew Research Center's Internet & American Life Project*. Retrieved March 1, 2010, from http://pewinternet.org/Reports/2010/Online-News.aspx.

Radhakrishna, R., & Doamekpor, P. (2008). Strategies for generalizing findings in survey research. *Extension Journal, Inc.*, 46(2).

Rubin, A. M. (1994). Parasocial interaction scale. In R. B. Rubin, P. Palmgreen, & H. E. Sypher (Eds.), *Communication research measures: A sourcebook* (pp. 273–277). New York: Guilford.

Rubin, A. M., & Perse, E. M. (1987a). Audience activity and soap opera involvement: A uses and effects investigation. *Human Communication Research*, 14(2), 246–268.

Rubin, A. M., & Perse, E. M. (1987b). Audience activity and television news gratifications. *Communication Research*, 14(1), 58–84.

Rubin, A. M., Perse, E. M., & Powell, R. A. (1985). Loneliness, parasocial interaction, and local television news viewing. *Human Communication Research*, 12, 155–180.

Ryan, L. (1999, June 14). Experts say be bold, but be careful. *Electronic Media*, 36, 38.

Scott, D. M. (2010). *The new rules of marketing and PR: How to use social media, blogs, news releases, online video, and viral marketing to reach buyers directly* (second edn.). Hoboken, NJ: John Wiley & Sons, Inc.

Spigel, L., & Olsson, J. (Eds.). (2004). *Television after TV: Essays on a medium in transition*. Durham, NC: Duke University Press.

The state of the news media: An annual report on American journalism. (2010). *PEW Project for Excellence in Journalism*. Retrieved March 15, 2010, from http://www.stateofthemedia.org/2010/overview_intro.php

Wimmer, R. D., & Dominick, J. R. (2006). *Mass media research: An introduction* (eighth edn.). Belmont, CA: Thomson Wadsworth.

14

MANAGING AND FINANCING SMALL-BUDGET TRANSMEDIA PRODUCTION
The Case of Norwegian Recycling

Craig A. Stark, Ph.D.

While much of the research in convergent and transmedia production has focused on defining the concepts of each form, discussing the content produced for each, and examining how they are changing traditional storytelling methods (Grant & Wilkerson, 2009; Jenkins, 2006, 2010; Morreale, 2010; Stark, 2011), one area not often considered has been how convergent media and transmedia producers have financed and managed their productions and operations. While profitability and return on investment are often considered to be the primary measures of the success of transmedia projects, it is possible to produce transmedia content on a small-budget scale with a focus on creativity and audience satisfaction. This chapter examines the financial and management aspects of Norwegian Recycling, a producer of transmedia content that operates on a small-scale basis without an emphasis on profit maximization. This chapter also examines the concepts of transmedia and convergent media, to provide a better understanding of how content for each form can be produced. Considering the characteristics and concepts of transmedia and convergent media as well as the production motives of Norwegian Recycling provides an opportunity to learn how transmedia content can be successfully produced on an individual basis with no profit motive.

Background of Norwegian Recycling

Norwegian Recycling is an online project that is known for repurposing popular music into new and different songs. Frans Peter Bull, the creator and owner of Norwegian Recycling, was inspired after hearing the mashup "Boulevard of Broken Songs" by Party Ben via a peer-to-peer network in 2005:

> It was not the first mashup I had heard, but it was the first one that really pushed the boundaries of what I thought was possible in terms of mixing, and it blew me away. It had such an impact that I had to try to make a couple myself. The goal was to make a mashup that gives the same wow-experience as the one I had experienced. An undescribable [sic] feeling I had never felt listening to a "normal" song.
>
> (F.P. Bull, personal communication, July 10, 2011)

Since 2007, Bull has created enough material to fill five full-length albums (*Albums–Norwegian Recycling*, 2012) that are distributed through a variety of online platforms, including Facebook, YouTube, Last FM, and a home website. Users may post comments, make suggestions, listen to (and view) content, download content, and contribute to help cover production and hosting costs. Many of Norwegian Recycling's listeners are familiar with the original songs used to create the repurposed content. Familiarity with this music makes Norwegian Recycling's efforts to connect with listeners easier, leading to greater popularity and more inspiration for Bull to continue his work.

Bull can be considered a "Receiver-Sender," because he creates a "recursive loop" of communication through the use of music originally produced by others ("receiving"); he then repurposes the music into new and different content and disseminates it ("sending"). This alters the linear mode of communication used by traditional mass media systems, and initiates the creation of convergent media content by allowing input and interactivity between Bull and his listeners and viewers (Wilkinson, McClung, & Sherring, 2009). Norwegian Recycling is in the "adolescent" stage of online development, in that "the creator has established a routine and goals for the site [and] the site has established itself to hold an 'amateur' status and may remain in this phase indefinitely" (Wilkinson et al., 2009, p. 73).

In order to better gauge the convergent media efforts of Norwegian Recycling, it helps to consider the characteristics of convergent media and transmedia. Doing so provides a better understanding of Bull's efforts in the convergent media universe and shows how his work should be considered as an example of transmedia production content. Considering the characteristics of convergent media and transmedia also creates a better understanding of how these types of production can be further studied from managerial and economic perspectives.

Characteristics of Convergent Media

Wilkinson (2009) defines convergent media as "attempts to capture the process by which traditional content creators adapt to an on-demand society where the consumer wields control" (p. 98). For Burnett and Marshall (2003), convergent media encompasses the "blending of the media, telecommunications, and computer industries, and the coming together of all forms of mediated communication in digital form" (p. 1), while Quinn (2005) presents five forms of convergence (ownership; tactical; structural; information-gathering; storytelling) that categorize the concept into more workable parts (pp. 4–6). While these definitions accurately describe the structural and organizational characteristics of convergent media, they tend to emphasize the mechanical, systemic definitions that focus more on technical and marketing concerns and not on the process of content creation and consumption. Jenkins' (2006) conceptualization of convergent media is beneficial because it focuses more on content and audience reception, and is thus more applicable for the intent of this chapter. For Jenkins, convergent media relies on three primary characteristics. First, it requires the distribution of content across a variety of media platforms, which can include online and wireless media, theatrical releases, broadcasting, and print. The ease of distribution across platforms is facilitated through the conglomeration of ownership and the creation of partnerships between various media outlets. Second, in order to ensure a story's continuity, convergent media requires collaboration between the writers and the producers who work in these various platforms. This is a critical component for convergent media. For example, if the creators of a video game that accompanies the release of a motion picture provide content that conflicts with the plot, settings, or characters of the film, then audiences may become confused or frustrated. In order to avoid this, collaboration between the various platform producers must exist. Finally, convergent media relies on the collective knowledge of its audiences. Audiences do not necessarily have to be experts when it comes to knowing content, characters, storylines, or settings, but they must have at least some basic level of understanding about them (Jenkins, 2006).

A recent example of a convergent media experience is the film *Captain America: The First Avenger*, which was released in theaters in 2011. Audiences could experience the film not only by going to the theater, but also through various online, broadcasting, and print media outlets. The fact that the Walt Disney Corporation either owned these outlets, or partnered with other corporations that did, helped facilitate greater audience interest and involvement. Additionally, producers of the film's website, soundtrack, and video game provided content to audiences that reinforced the plot, settings, and characters of the film, which helped maintain the story's continuity. Finally, the audience's general familiarity and common knowledge of the characters in the film led to the creation of a convergent media experience. Audience members who were not familiar with Captain America prior to seeing the film could use a variety of media outlets (film website, video game, soundtrack, or comic books) to learn more about the character. *Captain America: The First Avenger* can be considered a convergent media experience because it used an array of distribution platforms, collaboration between producers, and the collective knowledge of the audience. These components all comprise the core of convergent media and they are increasingly relied upon as the form continues to develop in the twenty-first century.

Norwegian Recycling also qualifies as a convergent media experience; it distributes content via a wide array of media platforms (home website and social media outlets), its inspiration and creation came from a collaborative experience (hearing Party Ben via a peer-to-peer network), and it relies on and engages with the collective knowledge of its audience (listeners are familiar with much of the original music used in Bull's creations). Additionally, Norwegian Recycling demonstrates that convergent media can be produced by a single person and does not necessarily need a team of producers and collaborators.

Since Norwegian Recycling passes the "litmus test" of qualifying as a convergent media experience, the next step is to consider whether it qualifies as a provider of transmedia content.

Characteristics of Transmedia

While the concept of convergent media may seem familiar and easily understood, the concept of transmedia is still relatively new, and has thus been fairly difficult to define. Transmedia is a *form* of convergent media that emerges from the three characteristics previously mentioned. Jenkins also describes transmedia as a process "where integral elements of a fiction get dispersed systematically across multiple delivery channels for the purpose of creating a unified and coordinated entertainment experience. Ideally, each medium makes its own unique contribution to the unfolding of the story" (Jenkins, 2010, p. 944). In other words, in order to create a transmedia experience, each piece of content distributed via separate platforms must add to the overall story arc and not detract from it.

There are two other aspects that should be considered to help clarify the concept of transmedia. First, transmedia production requires the borrowing and using of material, content, and themes that have already been produced in other works of art. Usually this previously created material has been produced and distributed via large-scale media sources and has been successful standing on its own in the mainstream consciousness, which makes it well known and familiar.

At this point it is a good idea to briefly consider Jenkins' distinction between "adaptation" and "extension." Adaptation occurs when an original narrative is reproduced into a different medium with minimal changes in plot, characters, and settings. Extension, on the other hand, "expands our understanding of the original by introducing new elements into the fiction" (Jenkins, 2010, p. 945). These new elements can include changes in setting, character perspectives and appearance, enhancing or adding to a franchise's timeline, and more. A frequent example of adaptation is when popular novels are produced into feature films, such as with the *Harry Potter* series and numerous other franchises. An example of extension would be Marvel Comics' recent *Illuminati* series, which added "untold" stories to several popular superhero storylines, running parallel to classic storylines of the past (Bendis, Reed, & Cheung, 2008). Obviously there are many examples of adaptations and extensions, and oftentimes the lines between the two can be blurred (is J.J. Adams' version of *Star Trek* [2009] an adaptation because it re-tells the story of how Kirk and Spock first met, or is it an extension because it introduces new character relationships and begins with the Vulcan home world destroyed?). These concerns notwithstanding, transmedia tends to rely more on extension, because it does not need to replicate or "update" the original material, as one might see in an adaptation. Transmedia content invariably extends from the original content in the form of a different and unique creation, even if it is produced using the same medium.

The second characteristic that should be considered along with Jenkins' definition of transmedia relies heavily on the first and is generally more difficult to achieve. It is not enough to just combine or repurpose old material into something new and distribute it via multiple platforms; the transmedia product must also create its own unique and significant *experience* for the audience. Audiences need to not only recognize the original material in the repurposed work, but through that recognition they must also have a unique, significant, possibly even visceral reaction to it. This reaction is what separates transmedia content from adaptations and other forms of combined material such as remixes, relaunches, and reboots.

For Jenkins, *The Matrix* story series is a prime example of a transmedia experience that emerged from a convergent media project. *The Matrix* was a successful convergent media experience due to the collaboration between its various producers, and the agreement to distribute material across assorted media formats including films, comic books, video games, and animated shorts. Additionally, the collective knowledge of the audience in regard to the technological, religious, and philosophical metaphors and imagery that shaped the storylines and characters helped create an incredibly successful convergent media experience (Jenkins, 2006).

The Matrix stands out as a transmedia experience as the main storyline was enhanced and reinforced among the various media formats. Just as important, however, was the way in which the borrowed content was repurposed into material that ultimately connected with audiences in a significant and unique way. For example, the films relied on familiar religious and philosophical allusions to connect with audiences, which ranged from the display of biblical citations on license plates to representations of Buddhist and Christian actions by several of the main characters (Jenkins, 2006). Separately (and in their original forms), these connotations can stand on their own and in some cases have provided satisfactory experiences for their audiences for thousands of years. When these separate pieces were combined in *The Matrix*, however, the result was a unique (some might say, "mind-blowing") experience for audiences that were both familiar and unfamiliar with the material. For Jenkins (2006), this created a successful transmedia experience where "the whole is worth more than the sum of the parts" (p. 102).

A producer's ability to take "original" material in this sense and combine and repurpose it into new material that is unique and exciting to audiences is the true mark of a transmedia experience and separates it from other forms of convergent media. It is important to remember, however, that transmedia relies on the primary characteristics of convergent media. Without the core convergent media traits of collaboration, multiple distribution platforms, and collective knowledge, transmedia cannot exist.

As with any new form of media content, time and further research will change the parameters of defining transmedia. For now, combining Jenkins' process of transmedia with the assorted systemic definitions of convergent media and the additional characteristics previously discussed provides as clear a picture as possible about how transmedia can be defined and produced.

How Six Songs Collide

An example of Norwegian Recycling's transmedia production efforts is a compilation titled *How Six Songs Collide*, which repurposes six popular songs ("I'm Yours" by Jason Mraz; "Collide" by Howie Day; "Superman" by Five for Fighting; "Always Getting Over You" by Angela Ammons; "All That I Need" by Boyzone; and "Here Without You" by Three Doors Down) into one.[1] Bull has also repurposed the individual music videos from each of these songs to accompany this work. The popularity of this particular video is evident; as of April 2012 the video had been viewed almost 2 million times on YouTube (*Norwegian Recycling—How Six Songs Collide*, 2007).

Pop music fans recognize the six songs that make up this compilation and consciously they may recognize that each song provides its own separate experience and response. Judging by comments posted on the song's YouTube page, however, listeners are also discovering new experiences with the combined song that are unique and significant from the original songs:

- This is my favorite Norwegian Recycling mashup. This was the first song I heard way back when you only had one album out. Honestly I sometimes even accidentally mess up lyrics and songs when I'm singing along to some of the songs used in the mashup because they go along so well together. I just had to come back and say thanks for making such a beautiful mix.
- You know I never thought I'd say that I enjoy a Boyzone song but I really like their part in this song, this is probably the best mix up of songs I have ever heard.
- Music like this needs to happen more often in this world.
- Loveee [sic] this ... but now I cant [sic] listen to any of thesse [sic] songs alone without waiting for the others to come in ...

(Norwegian Recycling—How Six Songs Collide, 2007)

A more recent example that demonstrates the continued popularity of Bull's work is a compilation titled *Don't Stop Believin'*, which was released in 2011 and repurposes "Don't Stop Believin'" by Journey, "Waka Waka (Time for Africa)" by Shakira, "Till the World Ends" by Britney Spears, "Dancing on My Own" by Robyn, "Just the Way You Are" by Bruno Mars, and "Seek Romance" by Tim Berg.[2] The accompanying video for the song was posted on YouTube in August of 2011, and had tallied over 94,000 views as of April 2012. Similar to *How Six Songs Collide*, comments posted by viewers on the YouTube page show that they are also finding unique experiences with this song:

- I love how all your newer mashups make the lyrics flow together. Even with songs you would never put together in normal circumstances. It really shows your talent.
- I like it! Prefer it when you make me like songs I don't normally like.
- Yay, Robyn! Was my first thought. Really nice though. I like how instead of just mashing songs together in a row like many others you've actually been making songs from verses to chorus as of lately, great work!

(Norwegian Recycling—Don't Stop Believin', 2011)

With Norwegian Recycling, Bull has created a transmedia experience that not only repurposes material produced by others and stands successfully on its own, but also creates unique experiences for many listeners and viewers. The new material is a unique product that can create an entirely different reaction when compared to the original content. Much like *The Matrix*, Norwegian Recycling has created content where the whole is worth more than the sum of the parts.

Management and Financial Characteristics of Norwegian Recycling

As previously mentioned, much of the research focusing on transmedia has so far centered on how a finished product is created, how it is distributed, storytelling, characteristics of transmedia, and the content itself (Jenkins, 2006, 2010; Morreale, 2010; Stark, 2011). While this information helps us learn more about the general traits of transmedia it misses an area of concern that looks at how transmedia projects are funded and managed. Under this economic lens Norwegian Recycling provides an example of a small-budget, individually managed outfit that successfully produces transmedia content.

Bull created Norwegian Recycling in 2007, and has been its sole owner, operator, and producer. He does not have an administrative staff or technical support staff, and he relies on volunteers only for help with web page coding and design. Bull views himself first and foremost as an artist, and uses Norwegian Recycling simply as an outlet for expression. He did not start Norwegian Recycling to make a profit and has no plans to add personnel or expand production. Bull's biggest management challenge so far has been complying with US copyright regulations that involve original content and its producers. One thing that has helped Bull avoid major trouble with artists and music labels is that he distributes his material via free (or low cost) peer-to-peer and social sharing services such as Facebook, YouTube, Last FM, and Torrent. While Bull has never been directly accused of, or threatened with, copyright violations, he has had at least one video disabled by YouTube because it contained a song used without approval from the Warner Music Group.[3] As of this writing, no one has ordered him to remove any content or demanded reparations of any kind (F.P. Bull, personal communication, November 27, 2011).

Norwegian Recycling has practically no expenses, mainly because Bull uses open hosting services to distribute his content. Norwegian Recycling does have its own website, and Bull pays standard annual hosting fees for it. Bull's production equipment is relatively inexpensive and easy to maintain. He uses a Windows laptop with an M-Audio card, using Sony Acid Pro 7 for audio editing and Sony Vegas 10 for video editing. There are no studios or production equipment in the traditional, large-scale sense, and according to Bull, "Norwegian Recycling is located where my laptop is located" (F.P. Bull, personal communication, November 27, 2011).

While Bull's expenses may be low, so is his revenue. He raises money for Norwegian Recycling through a simple donation button on his website, which pulls in around $100 a year. Any income is used to help pay the costs associated with hosting fees and equipment maintenance. Bull believes charging listeners for his work would be "highly unethical," and he has no intention of ever doing so (F.P. Bull, personal communication, November 27, 2011).

Bull has a "day job" and admits that he had to save for "a long time" to afford the original home page site registration fees, and for help with a good site design. He also believes that Norwegian Recycling will never be profitable, but that doesn't concern him. When asked about any possible future challenges Norwegian Recycling may face as a small-budget producer of transmedia content, Bull doesn't mention money, and sounds more like a hobbyist than a producer: "It would be wrong to talk about challenges, when the only thing that technology gives us are more opportunities [sic]. So my challenge would be to utilize these new innovations and integrate them into my current style" (F.P. Bull, personal communication, November 27, 2011).

Bull uses Norwegian Recycling primarily as an outlet for artistic expression, and he creates content for his enjoyment and for the enjoyment of others. Since Norwegian Recycling is "run on the side" and has practically no overhead or distribution costs, Bull feels free to focus on honing his skills to produce more material for his fans to enjoy. While Bull's rationale may be somewhat unique in today's media world, Wilkinson et al. (2009) verify this perspective, claiming small-scale, personal productions and operations are often maintained through "factors other than revenue dependency and branding ... The focus for these labors of love is the content or service provided" (p. 75), and not commercial success or profit maximization.

While big-studio, big-budget transmedia franchises have entertained fans for years, the intent of these productions has always been maximizing profit. Although a return on investment is desirable and understandable, producers of transmedia content should consider that the appearance of "cashing in" could backfire. The recent efforts by producers of the TV program *Gossip Girl* to brand the program and its characters through a variety of social media outlets including Facebook and Second Life highlight this concern (Stein, 2009). The purpose was not necessarily to expand character development or create storyline extension (although it was portrayed as such), but to ultimately create buzz about fashion and lifestyle trends that were regularly displayed in the program. Although this strategy may help expand a franchise's brand and give the producers greater exposure, it could also give the appearance of trying to make a quick buck and thus violating fans' trust in the program.

Conclusion

Further research into the management and financing of small-budget transmedia production is clearly necessary, because the example of Norwegian Recycling only begins to scratch the surface. Frankly, more examples of small operations are needed. Additionally, there are several significant questions and concerns that go beyond the scope of this chapter and should be considered. What constitutes "small production" versus "big production" in regard to transmedia? Is there a point where "small" becomes "big"? If so, what is it? Will transmedia production ultimately be more successful on a smaller scale or a bigger scale? How does the pursuit of profit affect the production of transmedia content, and its acceptance by audiences? How does profit maximization affect fan perception of the content? How will the profit motive (or lack of it) affect a producer's rationale and ability for creating transmedia?

Future research should also consider the development of more accurate measurement standards regarding the effectiveness of transmedia content on the audience. Whether measurement methods rely on simple surveys or on biometric measuring tools that record changes in heart rate or respiration to determine transmedia effectiveness remain to be seen. Some type of standard measurement system should be considered and formed, however, in order to better understand the effectiveness (or lack of) transmedia content on audiences.

Just as important, however, future research efforts must find a way to determine the success of transmedia that does not rely so heavily on profit. The term "valued content," for instance, has been proposed as a primary measure of the success of a website (and by extension transmedia content). Valued content has been defined as "content for which people will pay" (Wilkinson et al., 2009, p. 76). The point of contention is that using only that measure as an indicator of "value" is incongruous and unfair. Historically, part of the problem determining the "success" of any small media production outfit has been the constant financial comparison to production efforts by large-scale organizations with multi-million dollar budgets and high-end facilities. Basically, if it doesn't make a profit it isn't successful, and therefore has no value. The prevalence of small-scale transmedia production efforts that are not concerned with turning a profit requires future researchers to consider developing broader, more holistic definitions of "valued content."

In the end, Norwegian Recycling provides an example of successful transmedia production on an individual scale. Bull shows that it is not necessary to have a multi-million dollar budget, a massive support staff, and cutting-edge production equipment to succeed. Norwegian Recycling shows it is important to consider that transmedia production does not necessarily need to be done on a large scale, and that the profit motive does not have to be the determining factor regarding the success of a production. Bull shows that with minimal financial investment, dedication to his craft, and a relaxed emphasis on profitability, practically anyone can participate successfully in transmedia production.

Notes

1 Available on the album *So Far*, online via Rar or Torrent download at http://norwegianrecycling.net/category/albums/. The video for *How Six Songs Collide* can be seen online at: http://norwegianrecycling.net/2010/09/how-six-songs-collide/.
2 Available on the album *Cutting Edge*, online via Rar or Torrent download at http://www.divshare.com/download/16848299-7b7/. The video for *Don't Stop Believin'* can be seen online at http://norwegianrecycling.net/2012/03/dont-stop-believin/.
3 Although the video has been disabled, the YouTube link is still active and can be seen at http://youtu.be/BcAYro2PCvI. The song is available on the album *So Far*, online via Rar or Torrent download at http://norwegianrecycling.net/category/albums/.

References

Albums–Norwegian Recycling (2012). Retrieved April 24, 2012 from http://norwegianrecycling.net/category/albums/
Bendis, B.M., Reed, B., & Cheung, J. (2008). *The New Avengers: Illuminati*. New York: Marvel Publications.
Burnett, R., & Marshall, P.D. (2003). *Web theory: An introduction*. London: Routledge.
Grant, A.E., & Wilkerson, J.S. (2009). *Understanding media convergence: The state of the field*. New York: Oxford University Press.
Jenkins, H. (2006). *Convergence culture: Where old and new media collide*. New York: New York University Press.
Jenkins, H. (2010). Transmedia storytelling and entertainment: An annotated syllabus. *Continuum*, 24 (6), 943–958.
Morreale, J. (2010). Lost, The Prisoner, and the end of the story. *Journal of Popular Film and Television*, 38 (4), 176–185.
Norwegian Recycling—Don't Stop Believin' (2011). Retrieved April 24, 2012 from http://youtu.be/JUVSLJSWIC4
Norwegian Recycling—How Six Songs Collide (2007). Retrieved August 13, 2011 from http://youtu.be/3JKKl95Ttrc
Quinn, S. (2005). What is convergence and how will it affect my life? In S. Quinn & V.F. Filak (Eds.), *Convergent journalism: An introduction* (pp. 3–19). Boston: Focal Press.
Stark, C. (2011). How six songs collide: Using Norwegian Recycling to demonstrate transmedia convergence. *Journal of Media Education*, 2 (4), 5–10.

Stein, L. (2009). Playing dress-up: Digital fashion and gamic extensions of televisual experience in *Gossip Girl's Second Life*. *Cinema Journal*, 48 (3), 116–122.

Wilkinson, J.S. (2009). Converging communication, colliding cultures: Shifting boundaries and the meaning of "Our Field." In A.E. Grant & J.S. Wilkinson (Eds.), *Understanding media convergence: The state of the field* (pp. 98–116). New York: Oxford University Press.

Wilkinson, J.S., McClung, S.R., & Sherring, V.A. (2009). The converged audience: Receiver senders and content creators. In A.E. Grant & J.S. Wilkinson (Eds.), *Understanding media convergence: The state of the field* (pp. 64–83). New York: Oxford University Press.

INDEX

Note: *italic* page numbers denote references to figures/tables.

4G wireless connections 32
80/20 principle 73

ABC8 178, *181*, *182*, *184*, *187*, *188*, 191
Abrahamson, E. 222
advertising: China 140; Colombia 162, *166*, 167; Latin American TV *166*; Mexico 149, 153, 155, *156*; online 71, 233–4, 236; Spanish language media (US) 205, 207, 210–12; Taiwan 73, *74*
affective economics 246–7
Albarran, A. B. 5–7, *10*, *12*
Alexander, A. *12*
Amazon 72, 95; China 141; PlanetAll acquisition 103, 104
América Móvil 149–50, *151*, 157
American Express *127*
American Society of Magazine Editors (ASME) 128
Anderson, C. 62, 72, 73–5
Antioco, John 60, 62–4
AOL (America Online) 95, 238
Apple 47, 51, *127*
Arango-Forero, G. 167
Argentina, pay TV 165, *166*
AT&T 20–2, 35; organisational culture and breakup 49–50
Attaway-Fink, B. 126
attention economics 13
audience participation, TV 163–4, 168, 237, 238; *see also* viral viewers
audience research: local TV stations 247–58; in news media 121–9

Axtel *151*
Azteca 149–50, *151*, 157
Azteca América 203–4

Badoo *101*, *106*, 110, *112*
Bebo *101*, *106*, *109*, 110, *112*
Beck, J. C. 13
Becker, B. W. 123
Beijing Publishing Industry Creative Park 138
Bellamy, R. V. 242, 245
Berndt, E. R. 95
Blacker, L. 211
Blockbuster 59–65
Boczkowski, P. J. 122–3
book publishing, China 133–42
Bookstacks 95
Brakus, J. J. 126–7
brand experience 126–8
brand identity: social networking sites 110–11; television 37, 242, 245–6
Brazil: pay TV *166*; social networking 110–11
broadband services 19, 20–2, 31, 39
Broadcasting & Cable (B&C) 224
Brynjolfsson, E. 76
Buena Vista International 170
Bui, L. 95
Bull, Frans Peter *see* Norwegian Recycling
Burnett, R. 263
business failure, reasons 47–53

Cable Communications Act (1984) 28, 35

INDEX

cable telecommunications
  industry 19–20; future viability
  and predictions 39–41, *40*;
  opportunities and threats for
  MVPD *21*, 26–38
Cable Television Consumer Protection
  and Competition Act (1992) 27,
  34, 35
Cablevision (US) 35
Caldwell, J. 224, 246
Canal Uno (1) 161, 165
Caracol TV 160-7, 170-2
Carpenter, G. S. 95
Carpenter, S. 76
Carveth, R. 12
Cauley, L. 49
CBS11 178, *181*, *182*, *183*, *184*, *187*, *188*, 191
Chan, A. 26
Chan, J. K. 123
Chan-Olmsted, S. M. *10*, *12*, 246, 248–9, 256
channel repertoire 242, 245
Cheong, H. J. 244
Chile, pay TV 166
China, book publishing 133–43
China Times 72
Cho, D. 95
Christensen, C. 53
Chyi, H. I. 123
Classmates 100, *101*, 102–3, *105*, 112
Claxson Interactive Group 150
Clear Channel 198
collaborative filtering 76
Collins, J. 48, 52, 53, 64
Colombia: advertising *162*, *166*;
  television industry 160–72
Comcast 19, 35, 202
Committee of Concerned Journalists 126
common carrier status 28
competitive advantage: literature
  review 94–9; social networking sites
  99–113
Connor, P. E. 123
convergent media 263–4;
  see also transmedia
Copay, A. 220
copyright issues 27–8, 29, 33, 268
Copyright Revision Act (1976) 28

corporate governance 52
creative destruction 46, 65–6*n*
Croteau, D. 12
culture, organisational 49–50, 50–1, 222–3
Cyworld USA *101*, *106*, *112*

Dangdang 141
Davenport, T. H. 13
DBS (direct broadcast satellites) *19*, *20*, *22*
Deo, N. D. 26, 31
digital convergence, Mexico 147–8, 154–7
digital photography 55–6
digital publishing, China 136, 140–1
digital terrestrial television (DTT), Colombia 171
Dillman, D. A. 250
Dimmick, J. 12
direct broadcast satellites (DBS) *19*, *20*, *22*
DirecTV 20
DISH Network 20, 59
Disney 168, 170, 263
disruptive innovation (technology) 52–3, 56, 221–2
diversification of TV business model 163–4, 167–72
Doamekpor, P. 256–7
Dominick, J. R. 257

Eastman Kodak 53–9, 64–5
Elberse, A. 77
Ennovva 168–9
Estrella TV 204

Facebook *101*, 103, *106*, *109*, 110, *112*, 113; Colombia television 164; US Hispanics use 209
Feick, L. F. 245–6
Fenwick, I. 76
Ferguson, D. A. 176–7
Fiorina, Carly 57
first mover advantage theory 94–5
Fisher, George M. C. 56–7, 58*n*
FOX4 178, *181*, *182*, *184*, *185*, *187*, *188*, *188*, 190, 191–2
Freeman, L. 242
Friendster 100, *101*, *105*, 107, 110, *112*
Fujifilm 55

274

INDEX

Future of Journalism and Newspapers (2009 Senate hearing) 122

Galavisión 201–2
General Administration of Press and Publication (GAPP) 134, 136, 138
GenTV 170
Gentzkow, M. 124
Genzlinger, N. 54
Gershon, R. A. *10*
Giles, D. 255
Giles, R. H. *10*
Goh, J. M. 64
Golder, P. N. 95
González Bernal, M. 167
Google *127*, 238; Buzz *101*; G+ *101*
Greer, C. F. 176–7
Grupo Reforma 153, *153*, 155
Gupta, S. 246, 248–9
Gutiérrez, Sara 167, 169–70

Ha, L. 246, 248–9, 256
Hawley, S. 30, 31, 37–8
Hi5 *101*, 104, *105*, *109*, 110, *112*
Hidding, G. J. 95
Hoerner, J. 243, 248, 249
Hoffman, D. L. 123
Holcomb, J. 176–7
Hollifield, C. A. 10
Horton, D. 247–8
Hoynes, W. *12*
Hu, Y. J. 76
Hughes, M. 245, 249
Huizenga, H. Wayne 59–60, 61
Hulu 237, 238
Hunan Tianzhou Science, Education and Culture Co 138

IBM 48–9
Icahn, Carl 63–4
iHeartRadio 198
ImpreMedia 205
incrementalism 48–9
India, social networking 110
industrial organizational (IO) model 11–12, 96
innovation 47; business process 60–2; defined 52–3, 221–2; fashion and fad perspective to diffusion of 222; success features 47
innovator's dilemma 53

intellectual property rights 29, 33, 95; *see also* copyright issues
Internet: monetization of 73, 122, 235–6; and television industry (US) 219–39; US use 207–9
Internet radio 198
Iusacell *151*, 157

J.D. Power and Associates Power Circle Ratings for Residential Telecommunication Services 36
Jenkins, H. 242–3, 246–7, 263, 264–6
Jingdong Mall 141–2
Jiuge Distribution Company 139
Johnson, T. J. 122

Kanter, R. 64
Katz, E. 245
Kaye, B. K. 122
Keohane, R. O. 95
Kim, D. 95
Kim, H. 246, 248–9
King, T. 220
Kodak 53–9, 64–5
Kolsbeek, W. D. 123
Kotter, J. 51
Kovach, B. 126
Krishnamurthi, L. 95

Lasorsa, D. 123
Lavine, J. M. *10*
Lazarsfeld, P. F. 245
leadership 51–2
Leblebici, H. 220, 223
Leung, L. 123
Levy, M. R. 243, 245, 247
Lieberman, M. B. 95, 111, 113
LinkedIn, US Hispanics use 209
Liu Qiangdong 142
Livingston, G. 208
local TV stations: brand identity 37, 242, 245–6; news personalities 254–5; parasocial interaction (PSI) and viewer research 247–58; transmedia environment 243–5, 246–7; websites 255
long tail economics 66n, 72; online news services 73–7; Taiwan online news market 77–90; US online news market 84–5, *90*
Lopez, M. H. 175
Lucas, H. 64

INDEX

McCombs, M. 12
McLuhan, M. 72
Magazine Publishers of America (MPA) 128
magazines: readership experiences 128, *129*; Spanish language (US) 206–7
management, responsibilities of 8–9
management schools (theoretical) 6
Mantrala, M. 256
Marshall, P. D. 263
Martin, L. A. *10*
Marty, E. 76
media economics: defining 5–8; interdependency with media management 8–9; published books 11, *12*; research propositions 13–16; research theories 11–13
media management: defining 5–8; interdependency with media economics 8–9; published books 9–10, *10*; research propositions 13–16; research theories 10–11
Media Management Center 128
Megacable 150, *151*
MemoryLane 103
Mersey, R. D. 124
Mexico: media industry 147–57; newspapers *153*; pay TV *166*; radio companies *152*; telecommunications alliances *151*
Microsoft: MSN 72, 168; US Hispanics use of Internet sites 209; Windows Live 168, 209; Windows Live Spaces *101*, *107*, *112*; Windows Vista 50, 66*n*; Xbox 35, 198
Mierzjewska, B. I. 10
milestones, media and technology *14*, 226–32
mobile publishing, China 140
Moffett, C. 26, 31
Montgomery, D. B. 95, 111
Morrison, M. A. 244
Mo Zhixu 141
MSN 72, 168
multichannel video program distributors (MVPD) *see* MVPD
multimedia services, social networking sites *105–7*, 108
Multimedios *153*, *155*
Multiply *101*, *105*, 111, *112*

Mun2 203
MundoFox 171
MVPD: industry issues and predictions 26–41; market overview 18–22, *19*
MySpace *101*, *105*, *109*, 110, *112*; US Hispanics use 209
myYearbook *101*, *106*, *112*

Naik, P. 256
NBC5 178, *181*, *182*, *183*, *184*, *187*, *188*
Negroponte, N. 48
Netflix 29, 32, 61–2
network externalities 98–9; social networking sites 112–14
News Corporation 171
news media, audience research 121–9
newspapers: Mexico 152–4; online editions 71, 72–3, 123; Spanish language (US) 204–6
news portals, Taiwan 72–3
niche theory 12–13
Ning *101*, *106*, 111, *112*
Norwegian Recycling 261–2; business model 268–9; as convergent media experience 264; mash-ups 266–8
Novak, T. P. 123
NTN24 168, 171
Nye, J. S. 95

Oberholzer-Gee, F. 77
online bookstores, China 141
online news services 71; economic principles 75–7; Taiwan 77–90
OnSale 95
Orkut *101*, *106*, 110–11, *112*
Over-the-Top (OTT) video 23–6, 39–41; opportunities and threats 25, 27–30, 32–3, 35–8
Owen, B. M. 12
Owers, J. 12

Pandora (Internet radio) 198
parasocial interaction (PSI) 243, 247; local TV news 248–58
Pareto Law 73
patents, social networking sites 104–7
paywall online news services 71
Peer, L. 122–3
The People's Military Medical Press 141

Perse, E. M. 248, 249
Photosynthesis Books 140
Picard, R. G. 5–6, *12*
PlanetAll 100, *101*, 102–3, 104, *105*, *112*
Plurk *101*
Polaroid Corporation 55
Porras, J. 53
Possavino, R. 31
Powell, R. A. 248
Pownce *101*, *107*, *112*
Price, L. L. 245–6
product development times 50
product placement 169
Program Access Rules 34
public, educational, and government (PEG) access channels 34

Quall, W. L. *10*
Quinn, S. 263

Radhakrishna, R. 256–7
radio industry: Mexico 150–2, *152*; Spanish language stations (US) 196–8
RCN Televisión 160–1, 164–72
reality TV shows 161–5, 168–70, 237
Really Simple Syndication (RSS) feeds 191–2
Rebillard, F. 76
RedBox 62, 64
Redstone, Sumner 60, 65
Reily, D. R. 95
Reinsch, J. L. *10*
relative constancy, principle of 12–13
resource-based view (RBV) 12, 96–8
Reunion *101*, *105*, *109*, *112*
Rhee, D. 95
Roberts, Kevin 128
Rogers, E. 52
Rosenstiel, T. 126
RSS feeds 191–2
RTI Colombia 170
Rubin, A. M. 248, 249

Salancik, G. 220
satellite radio 198
Schmitt, B. H. 126
Schumpeter, J. 46, 66, 65–6*n*
Shanda Literature 140
Shankar, V. 95
Shapiro, J. 124

shareholders 52
Sherman, B. *10*
Siapera, E. 220
SiriusXM 198
SixDegrees 100, *101*, 102–3, 104, *105*, *112*
Slim, Carlos 149, 157
smartphones 32, 174, 208
Smith, M. D. 76
SMS text messaging, TV programs 163, 168
Smyrnaios, N. 76
social entertainment sites 111
social networking sites 100; acquisitions 109; first movers advantage 99–113; growth 243; importance for legacy media 192; media industry use in Mexico 155; news dissemination 73, 244; *see also* Facebook; Twitter
Sony: digital camera 55; Walkman 47, 51
Sony Pictures Television International 171
Southwestern Bell Corporation (SBC) 50
Spanish language media: advertising 210–12; Internet 207–9; magazines 206–7; newspapers 204–6; radio 196–8; television 177–92, 199–204
Sridhar, S. 256
Starbucks 127
Starting Point Chinese Network 140–1
Starz 29
Stone, G. 125
Structure–Conduct–Performance (SCP) model 12
subscription revenue models 26, 165, 233–4
Suning Electronics 141–2

tablets 32
Tagged *101*, *106*, 107–8, *109*, *112*
Taiwan online news market 72–3; advertising revenue 74; long tail economy 77–90; traffic 80–*1*
Teece, D. J. 97
Telcel 150
Telecommunications Act (1996) 20
telecommunications industry: Mexico 148–50; as MVPDs *19*, 20–2, *23*

INDEX

Telefónica 171
TeleFutura 200–1
Telemundo network 170, 171, 202–3; Telemundo39 177–9, *181*, *182*, *184*, *187*, 188–9, *188*
telephone services 19, 39
Televisa 149–50, *151*, 155, 157, 169–70, 206–7
television: Colombia 160–72; Internet use (US) 219–39; Spanish language stations (US) 199–204; Twitter use by Dallas-Fort Worth stations 174–92; *see also* local TV stations
Tellis, G. J. 95
TEPUY 170
Thayer, F. *10*
Thorson, E. 256
Time Warner Cable 19, 204
Toussaint Desmoulins, N. *12*
transmedia 246–7, 264–6, 270–1; *see also* Norwegian Recycling
Traudt, P. J. 242, 245
triple play: Mexico 149–50; US cable 19–20
TV Everywhere (TVE) 30, 35, 37, 38, 41
Twitter *101*, *107*, *109*, 110, *112*; Colombia television 164; Dallas-Fort Worth TV stations 174–92; US Hispanics use 209
twitterfeed 188

United Daily News (Taiwan) 72–3, 74, *80*
United Online, Classmates acquisition 103
United States: Hispanic population 177, 196; online news sites and long tail tools 84–5, *90*; smartphone penetration 174–5
Universal, El 152, 153–4, 155
Univision network 167–8, 171, 200; Univision23 177–8, *181*, *182*, *184*, *187*, 188, *188*
Univision Radio 198

Urban, G. L. 95
usage based pricing 27, 31–2, 36, 39

Varian, H. R. 76
Verizon 20–2, 35
versioning 75–6, 86
Viacom 60, 63
video aggregators 234; *see also* Hulu
video distribution: industry issues 36–41; market overview 18–26
viral viewers 244–5, 256
Virb *101*, *107*, *112*
Vogel, H. *12*
VoIP services 19, 39

Wackman, D. B. *10*
Walt Disney 170, 263
Web PSI 248
WeOurFamily *101*
Wertime, K. 76
WFAA *see* ABC8
Wildman, S. S. *12*
Wilkinson, J. S. 263, 269
Williams, J. R. 95
Wimmer, R. D. 257
Windows Live 168; US Hispanics use 209
Windows Live Spaces *101*, *107*, *112*
Wirth, M. O. *10*, 12
Wohl, R. R. 247–8
word-of-mouth (WOM) communication, electronic 244

Xbox 35, 198
Xinhua Bookstore 138, 142

Yahoo!, US Hispanics use 209
Yahoo! Kimo 72–3, 74, *80*
YouthStream Media, SixDegrees acquisition 103, 104
YouTube 234–5, 238, 243–4

Zarantonello, L. 126
Zuker, Jeff 9